TWA 800

ACCIDENT or INCIDENT?

TWA 800

800

ACCIDENT or INCIDENT?

By
Kevin E. Ready and Cap Parlier

SAINT
GAUDENS

SAINT GAUDENS PRESS
Prescott, Arizona & Ventura, California

Other Books Available from Saint Gaudens Press

By Kevin E. Ready

Gaia Weeps
The Big One

By Cap Parlier

The Phoenix Seduction

Saint Gaudens Press
Post Office Box 2646
Ventura, CA 93002-2646

Saint Gaudens, Saint Gaudens Press and
the Winged Liberty colophon
are trademarks of Saint Gaudens Press

ISBN: 0-943039-80-0
Library of Congress Catalog Number: 98-87155

Please visit the following Web sites:
        http://www.saintgaudenspress.com
        http://www.theauthor.com
        http://www.parlier.com

Printed in the United States of America

This book is printed on recycled and/or non-forest product paper.

Text of a letter to the world from relatives of victims of the TWA Flight 800 explosion on the second anniversary of the disaster, July 18, 1998.

"It's been two years since the fateful crash of TWA Flight 800, since the fire, the blackness and the denial. Yet the memory of that night continues still to burn in our minds and hearts.

"Like the waves here on the beach that endlessly roll to embrace the shore, our love for those we lost that night is timeless and will stay with us always. In the same way we will always remember with love and gratitude those whose lives became entwined with ours. All of us were strangers. Families with parents, spouses and children torn from them. And friends whose heroic deeds in those desperate hours forged, in a thousand hearts, bonds a lifetime long.

"The crash of this flight is still being investigated and its true cause may never really be determined. The retrieval and reconstruction of the wreckage will be marked in history as a miracle of modern technology. But we as family members believe the real legacy that will endure is the way people were able to rise above the shocking trauma of this tragedy and sweep aside all their human differences to profoundly help one another. It is this extraordinary outpouring of love and kindness that will remain in our hearts and memories forever. We the families of TWA Flight 800 thank all of you who have joined us in coming here today. We thank you for praying with us and remembering the long dark night of July 17, 1996, that took away our loved ones and changed forever so many lives."

A portion of the proceeds from the sale of this book will be donated to **The Family Assistance Foundation**.

Readers may donate to the families of the victims of this disaster by contacting:

The Family Assistance Foundation
c/o The Families of TWA Flight 800, Inc.
PO Box 1061
Clifton, New York, USA 12065

Web site:
http://members.aol.com/hseaman275/charity.html

This notice has been donated by the publisher and authors of this book. This notice does not imply agreement with the contents of this book or any level of cooperation or consent by The Family Assistance Foundation, The Families of TWA Flight 800, Inc. nor Trans World Airlines, Inc.

FOREWORD

The images of the carnage electrified the nation. Scores of charred bodies floated in the ocean amongst the scattered wreckage of the airliner. Television carried scenes of young sailors pulling the bodies of children out of the water, up onto their patrol craft. Nearly three hundred people, tourists, school children and business leaders, had been on the international flight when the explosion blasted it out of the sky. Families and friends cried, and the nation mourned. The world was shocked. The nation's leaders demanded answers and vowed revenge against the perpetrators of this evil act of mass murder.

The average citizen of the United States or France would recognize the foregoing incident as a recounting of the TWA Flight 800 disaster. However, to the average citizen of Iran and much of the rest of the Islamic world, the scenario recounted above would just as readily bring to mind the Iran Air Flight 655 disaster.

The similarities of these two incidents go farther. The US Navy was conducting maneuvers in the vicinity of both tragedies; in fact, very similar AEGIS-type cruisers were watching both doomed aircraft with their AEGIS SPY-1 radar systems. A P-3 Orion aircraft was in the vicinity of both incidents; one was American and the other Iranian. Both airliners were taking off from busy airports with seasoned flight crews. Both airliners were at about 13,000 feet flying near a long, narrow island just off-shore of their nation's main port city. Both incidents occurred in clear July weather. The victims of both incidents came from a number of countries, but primarily the countries of the flights' origin, the United States or Iran. Both incidents were witnessed to some extent, on radar or visually, by many people.

There is one major difference between these incidents. The cause of the Iran Air Flight 655 disaster off the coast of Bandar Abbas, Iran, in July 1988, was almost immediately known. The captain of the US Navy's modern, AEGIS cruiser, the USS *Vincennes*, had ordered his missile battery to shoot down the aircraft he believed to be hostile, while the true cause of the TWA Flight 800 disaster off the coast of Long Island, New York, in July 1996, has been the subject of much speculation for many months and remains unsolved to the date of this printing. There are theories of terrorist bombs, static electricity in a fuel tank, an arc in the shorted electrical wires of a fuel tank scavenge pump, structural failure, and a chance encounter with a meteorite among others. There has even been a theory brought forth by a respected journalist and former government official, Pierre Salinger, that the US Navy and its nearby AEGIS cruiser, the USS *Normandy*, may have brought down the TWA flight by another missile accident, during a weapons system test (a theory first proposed by an Islamic fundamentalist journalist in the first months after the accident).

In this book, we will explore the possibility that these two horrible air tragedies are linked and not by mere chance coincidences. We will present a reasonable, plausible explanation which examines the possibility that the TWA Flight 800 disaster was the culmination of one of the most elaborate efforts in state sponsored terrorism yet, and that there may be a direct causal link between the Iran Air and TWA disasters — retribution. This is not to say that this explanation of a possible terrorist link is necessarily the entirety of the truth about this horrible event, but it may very well be the best explanation. This rationale answers some questions the official US Government explanation leaves unanswered. Further, the instrumentality of the terrorist act is not necessarily the only method of carrying out the attack on TWA 800, but it is feasible, unrebutted and fits into the facts we do know.

This book is, of necessity, an admixture of facts, assumptions, and conjecture — it is a hypothesis of sorts. The conjecture, in the form of fictionalization of the actions of the possible perpetrators of the TWA 800 shootdown, is kept to a bare minimum and is limited to this one aspect. We believe that the scenario postulated herein is the pre-eminent, although unspoken and necessarily confidential, suspicion of the authorities investigating TWA 800. When these facts are finally proven, we are sure an appropriate response will be forthcoming. It would be highly presumptuous of the authors to present this part of our story as anything other than theory, at this point.

A common technique used by many investigators is the process of elimination. If you list all the possible causes, then eliminate each cause for which no facts can be found to support it, what is left is probably the cause. In this case, there are several remaining possible causal factors.

Given the supposition of a criminal cause, one could

also look at this book as a circumstantial evidence case. Who had the motive, the means, the will, the methods, the professed objective? When you take the dots of fact, place them on the page, and connect the dots, what does the picture look like?

The use of fictional amplification should not degrade the importance of the remainder of the data. The information presented herein makes use of the entirety of the hard public evidence available, both as to the TWA 800 incident, the total picture of state-sponsored terrorism and the growth of Islamic extremism worldwide. The use of fictionalized amplification evidence is nothing more than what a prosecutor does to weave a scenario which explains a crime for presentation to a judge in a 'probable cause' hearing, or the method a defense attorney uses to provide a jury with an explanation which establishes a 'reasonable doubt' that the prosecutor's case is true. These very fundamental methods of American jurisprudence require the creation of a 'story' which links the individual items of evidence into a reasonable explanation. That is all we have done in this book.

The events involving the Iran Air disaster are all true. Our information came from the Navy's Fogarty Report, congressional hearings, news reports and an excellent round of journalism by both ABC News and *Newsweek* magazine, which resulted in an intriguing *Nightline* show and a feature story in *Newsweek* in 1992 exposing the coverup by the US Navy. The identities of all participants in this aspect of the story are true, although the minute details of their actions have been enhanced by the authors' own experience.

A driving force for the authors is the 'stand back away from it' reality that airplanes simply do not explode in flight.

The NTSB has drawn attention to several suspicious accidents involving fuel systems, however the preponderance of commercial aircraft operating time makes these isolated events highly improbable. Aircraft designers build in redundancy where safety is paramount. Maintenance personnel develop meticulous inspection and maintenance procedures to ensure critical components do not fail. As you will see, we agree with the NTSB & FBI, there is no conclusive cause determined for this tragedy, however we suspect there is much more to this incident than the highly remote, multiple levels of associated failures the NTSB offers to explain the cause of such a catastrophic event. Is it possible a simple, electrical short in a most crucial location caused the entire event? Yes, however, we want readers and investigators to take a much larger view. The picture may look fundamentally different.

Likewise, all evidence and activities involving the flight of TWA 800, its crash and the investigation therein are fact, as reported widely in the media and gleaned from the NTSB reports.

The identities, duties, and public statements of all identified Iranian and American government and clerical officials are true. The information concerning Iranian intelligence operations, organization, leadership and its connection with and control of Hizbollah are true, while the actual dialog and other details of their internal meetings and decisions is obviously a fictionalization based upon the result of those meetings, although the content of speeches is based upon Iranian news sources. The direct connection between the Iranian politicians and their operatives is a matter of conjecture, the heart of the theory herein. The identities of

Iranian military personnel and their actions are invented.

The American intelligence analysts are composites and their level of knowledge is created to provide necessary narrative to the events. Likewise, the identities of some US military aircrews are composites, although the true identities of others are known. The actions of other identified American aircrews have been enhanced, as were the *Vincennes'* crew, based upon the authors' experience and the crewmembers' accounts given to the press and Navy JAG investigators. The SOSUS data, satellite and other intelligence data available to American authorities during and immediately after the TWA 800 incident is speculative based upon the authors' experience. The actual data has not yet been disclosed, for obvious reasons.

To assist the reader in determining when we are discussing matters of supposition or speculation about the shootdown and related events, we have chosen to start those portions of our text with a white, outlined 747 icon:

instead of the solid black 747 icon we use elsewhere in this book to denote chapters of fact:

As a point of clarification, we use the Anglicized word, Hizbollah instead of the commonly seen version Hezbollah or the academically correct HizbAllah to describe the Iranian or Shiite organization otherwise know as the Party of God.

The reader should note that there are many different uses of this word, Hizbollah. It is most often seen in the Western press to denote the Lebanese Palestinian terrorist faction responsible for the Beirut Marine barracks bombing and numerous other violent acts. From the Iranian standpoint, it means the political and theocratic movement behind the current regime in the Islamic Republic of Iran. Iranian leaders often call the Iranian populace the Hizbollah nation. From the standpoint of international terrorism, Hizbollah International is the broad coalition of fundamentalist radical groups who are generally under Iranian leadership, finance and control.

Lastly, the authors wish to point out that the inclusion of references to Islam and the Holy Koran are not meant to denigrate the Islamic religion or its believers, the vast majority of whom are peaceful, and in no way involved in the extremism and terror which has been promulgated by some in the name of Islam. Our references are simply meant to explain the rationale, albeit misguided, of those, such as Hizbollah International, who use Islamic law and scripture to justify acts of murder. We need not look far to see where the tenets of other major religions have been, throughout history, twisted to justify war and the death of innocent victims. We apologize in advance if our approach offends anyone. It was not our intent.

O, ye who believe, an equal retaliation for those who are slain is required of you: a free man for a free man, a slave for a slave and a female for a female. But if the brother of the slain grants a remission, then the collection of the blood money shall be done with fairness and the murderer shall pay him the blood money handsomely. This is a pardon from your Lord and a mercy, and for whomever transgresses thereafter there shall be a grievous punishment.

The Holy Koran, Al-Baqarah verse 2:179

[The Islamic Law from the Koran which requires the faithful Muslim to retaliate for the wrongful slaying of the innocent.]

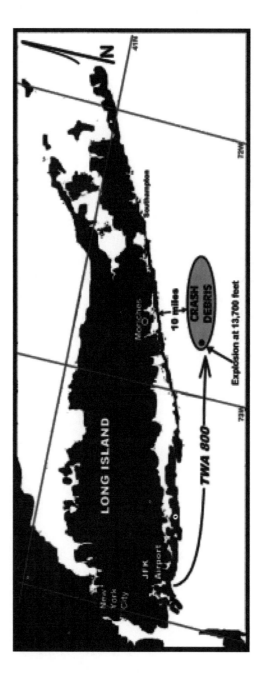

TWA Flight 800 crashed about fifteen minutes into its flight from New York to Paris on July 17, 1996. The crash site was approximately ten miles offshore from Center Moriches, Long Island, New York.

2018 EDT (0018 GMT), July 17, 1996
John F. Kennedy International Airport, NY

"TWA Eight Hundred Heavy, caution wake turbulence from a seven fifty seven, runway two two right, taxi into position and hold," the tower controller broadcast.

"TWA Eight Hundred Heavy, position and hold, two two right," Captain Ralph Kevorkian repeated back to confirm the clearance and restriction. "Alert the cabin, please," he said to his First Officer, to signal everyone on board the large aircraft. They were about to takeoff on their overnight journey to Paris. This was also a check ride flight for Captain Kevorkian, a routine periodic evaluation of his skills in commanding the crew of the Boeing 747 aircraft and managing the cockpit activities.

"Flight attendants, please be seated for takeoff," said Captain Steve Snyder over the aircraft's intercom system. The seasoned evaluation pilot occupied the First Officer's seat and would perform the duties of first officer under the direction of Captain Kevorkian.

The cockpit crew did not need to have one more thought about the preparation of the aircraft, crew and passengers for the moderately long flight. The cabin crew would soon click the locks of their seat harnesses in anticipation of the next step.

The behemoth machine rolled smoothly onto runway 22R, then came to a full stop. The crew stepped through each item of the before takeoff checklist in the typical challenge and reply manner common to crew served cockpit procedures familiar to most pilots. Everything was as it should be. The engines were all running well within normal limits. Kevorkian glanced down at the thin, paper chart clipped to the hub of his control yoke. They would soon takeoff toward the southwest, then promptly turn toward the east, and shortly after that turn northeast to join the well traveled, great circle, air routes across the northern Atlantic Ocean.

"TWA Eight Hundred Heavy, wind is two four zero at eight, runway two two right, cleared for takeoff," the tower controller radioed the 747 airliner.

"TWA Eight Hundred Heavy, cleared for takeoff two two right," Captain Kevorkian responded through his headset microphrone. He pushed the four throttle levers forward. "Trim the throttles," he commanded the second officer, a flight engineer trainee, Oliver Krick, to adjust the throttle levers of each engine to attain the calculated and prescribed takeoff performance values.

The fourth person on the flight deck was a veteran instructor flight engineer, Richard Campbell, sitting in the jump seat to monitor Krick's performance of duties, watched every action on the flight deck. With only 30 hours in the 747-131, Krick was technically not yet fully certified as a 747 flight engineer, thus Campbell's presence.

In-flight evaluations and training are normal, everyday activities for scheduled airline crews. Simulation training accomplished a substantial portion of each crewmembers qualification, but the flight evaluation was the final required step to full certification.

The enormous aircraft with its crew of 18 and 212

passengers accelerated down Runway 22 Right, at New York's John F. Kennedy International Airport. Kevorkian scanned his instruments. Everything looked perfectly normal as he felt the big machine move to his commands.

"Eighty knots," the First Officer announced as the aircraft's pitot-static airspeed indicator needle bounced to life telling the cockpit crew the machine was responding normally.

"El Al 557 Heavy, position and hold two two right," the tower controller broadcast.

"V One," announced Snyder as they passed their rejected takeoff speed.

Everything in the cockpit of the aging Boeing 747-131 airliner remained normal. The routine, to which Captain Kevorkian and his crew had become accustomed, would be no different this night.

"V R," announced the First Officer as the Captain increased the back pressure on his control column. The nose of the jumbo jet rose as it always did. "V Two," coincided with the disappearance of the thumps of the runway falling away beneath them.

"Positive climb."

"Gear up," commanded Kevorkian.

"Gear up," responded Synder as he moved the lever with the wheel on the end, from the down to the up position.

The gush of hydraulic fluid and muffled clunking of the aircraft's landing gear retracting into the fuselage confirmed the action. The activity in the cockpit remained precise and busy as they changed the aircraft configuration to its proper climb settings.

"TWA Eight Hundred Heavy, contact New York Departure, one three five point niner, good evening," the tower controller broadcast when he observed the 747 safely airborne.

"TWA Eight Hundred Heavy, good night."

Within minutes, TWA 800 was established in its proper configuration and climbing well as they began the journey to Paris, France. The crew responded to departure instructions from New York as they received vectors turning them gradually toward the east. The New York area was always busy, and this night was no different. Traffic calls from the ground controllers gave them some clues, but they could not always find the other aircraft the controllers called out.

Captain Kevorkian checked his altitude bug set for 5,000 feet, their first clearance ceiling. He rolled the enormous aircraft slightly to the left to center up the heading cue as directed by the ground controllers. Within seconds, the ground controllers cleared them to 11,000 feet altitude causing the crew to turn the knob on their altitude alert system to indicate the next limit altitude.

"TWA Eight Hundred Heavy, direct Betty, resume own navigation."

"TWA Eight Hundred Heavy, direct Betty, own navigation," answered the First Officer.

The crew set up their navigation systems to their first navigational fix, BETTE intersection, 109° at 35 nautical miles from the Kennedy VORTAC navigation aid. They had flown the BETTE ONE departure so many times, they knew it by memory, but they still cross checked every setting in the navigation systems.

There was no need for conversation in the cockpit this evening. Actions had been scripted and rehearsed a thousand times in simulation qualification sessions and many thousands of flight hours by the crew. Modern methods of crew resource management established the parts played out by every member of the cockpit crew. Plus, the northeast corridor into which they were now climbing was one of busiest chunks of airspace in the world, and tonight was a typical night. They listened to the myriad of radio calls as they monitored their aircraft's performance and progress on the prescribed flight plan.

The lights of urbanized Long Island and New York City began to vanish behind them. Even through the brightness of the cockpit lights, a few of the brighter stars could be seen through the windshield glass.

"TWA Eight Hundred Heavy, contact Boston, one three two point three," radioed the New York controller.

"TWA Eight Hundred Heavy, switching to three two point three, good night," answered Synder, then turned the knobs on the radio controller on the panel in front of them to the prescribed frequency. He listened first to make sure no one was trying to talk to Boston Center. "Boston, TWA Eight Hundred Heavy, with you at eight thousand, two hundred, climbing to one one thousand."

"TWA Eight Hundred Heavy, Boston Center. Roger. Climb and maintain one three thousand."

Captain Synder repeated back the controller's commands and made the appropriate adjustments to the controls of the cockpit systems, and all the appropriate alert alarms were properly set to ensure they followed the directions given to them from the ground. The mark of professional pilots remained the precise execution of directions and commands from the ground controllers.

The radio calls came incessantly. Other aircraft moved all around them, above, ahead, behind and to the left. There were no traffic calls for aircraft to the right. The military warning areas had been reported active during their pre-flight planning. The sky was ink black out the right side windows. The last remnants of the setting sun added just a veil of illumination toward their left rear.

"TWA Eight Hundred, what's your rate of climb?" asked the Boston Center controller.

Synder quickly scanned the altimeter and vertical speed indicator. "TWA Eight Hundred Heavy...ahh...about two thousand feet a minute here, until accelerating out of ten thousand."

"Roger, sir, climb and maintain flight level one niner zero, and expedite through fifteen."

"TWA Eight Hundred Heavy, climb and maintain flight level one niner zero and expedite through one five thousand."

"Climb to one nine zero, expedite through one five thousand," Kevorkian repeated to acknowledge the command from the ground and the radio call of his First Officer. As the altimeter wound up through 10,000 feet, the Captain challenged, "Pressurization?"

"Checked and functional," came the response from the flight engineer.

The crew continued through the routine takeoff procedures listening to the traffic calls to other aircraft on the same frequency, as they correlated their view of the world around them. Snyder switched off the landing lights and checked the exterior light switches in the cruise positions. He rechecked his navigation maps and the next few check points on their departure route.

"TWA Eight Hundred, amend the altitude. Maintain...ahh...one three thousand, thirteen thousand only, for now."

"Thirteen thousand," Kevorkian said to his copilot.

"TWA Eight Hundred Heavy, OK, stop climb at one three thousand," answered Synder to the controller's instruction.

As the altimeter passed 12,000, the normal altitude alert sounded.

"Twelve for thirteen," stated Synder as a standard call to recognize the altitude alert.

The Captain nodded his head and clicked his intercom button, but did not feel the need to verbally answer his first officer's observation of 1,000 feet to reach their altitude clearance limit.

They called the TWA Flight Information Controller to provide their takeoff information including their fuel load of 179,000 pounds of fuel on board. They also provided their estimated arrival time of 0628 local at Charles DeGaulle Airport, Paris.

Kevorkian noticed movement on one of the instruments in front of them, movement that should not be there. "Look at that crazy fuel flow indicator there on number four," he said nodding his head toward the errant instrument. "See that?"

The crew watched the erratic fuel flow indicator. They also instinctively scanned the other engine instruments to cross check them for any confirmatory signs. Everything else including the No.4 engine speeds and temperature remained rock steady.

Satisfied the bouncing indicator was just that, Kevorkian turned his attention to other tasks. "Somewhere in here, I had better trim this thing." The Captain stepped through the normal process of trimming the aircraft's controls to minimize any control forces and prepare the aircraft for the greater speeds of higher altitude, cruise flight.

"TWA Eight Hundred, climb and maintain one five thousand," said the controller.

"Climb thrust," commanded the Captain.

"TWA Eight Hundred Heavy, climb and maintain one five thousand, leaving one three thousand."

"Ollie," said Kevorkian, when the throttles had not been moved to his command.

"Huh?" said Krick, distracted by the erratic fuel flow indication.

"Climb thrust," Kevorkian repeated for his flight engineer.

Oliver Krick pushed the four throttles slowly forward to 1.30 Engine Pressure Ratio — climb thrust. "Power's set."

In less than a minute, at 13,700 feet, a loud bang was heard throughout the aircraft. The jumbo jet shuddered violently as a consequence. The tearing, crunching, snapping sounds came very fast — almost instantly. The speed of the moment precluded any response of any kind by the crew in the cockpit of TWA 800.

The end came in the ink of night over the Atlantic Ocean off eastern Long Island.

2031:12 Eastern Daylight Time, (0031:12 Greenwich Mean Time), 17.July.1998

There were additional radio calls occupying the sky that night.

0031:50 [EASTWIND AIRLINES 507] "We just saw an explosion out here, Stinger Bee Five Oh Seven."

0031:57 [BOSTON ARTCC SARDI SECTOR, RADAR POSITION]

"Stinger Bee Five Oh Seven, I'm sorry I missed it...ah...you're out of eighteen. Did you say something else?"

0032:01 [EASTWIND AIRLINES 507] "Ah, we just saw an explosion up ahead of us here about sixteen thousand feet or something like that. It just went down — in the water."

0032:25 [VIRGIN ATLANTIC 009] "Boston Virgin Zero Zero Nine, I can confirm that out of my nine, ah, three, my nine o'clock position. We just had an explosion. It looked like an explosion out there about five miles away, six miles away."

0032:36 [BOSTON ARTCC SARDI SECTOR, RADAR POSITION] "Virgin Zero Zero Nine, I'm sorry your transmissions broken up."

0032:39 [VIRGIN ATLANTIC 009] "Our nine o'clock position, sir. It looked like an explosion of some sort about maybe six to five miles out from my nine o'clock position."

0033:01 [UNKNOWN] "Investigate that explosion. If you can, get a lat-long."

0033:04 [BOSTON ARTCC SARDI SECTOR, RADAR POSITION] "TWA Eight Hundred, Center."

0033:09 [BOSTON ARTCC SARDI SECTOR, RADAR POSITION] "TWA Eight Hundred, if you hear Center, ident."

0033:17 [BOSTON ARTCC SARDI SECTOR, RADAR POSITION] "Stinger Bee, ah, Five Zero Seven, you reported an explosion. Is that correct, sir?"

0033:21 [EASTWIND AIRLINES 507] "Yes, sir, about...ah...ah...five miles at my eleven o'clock here."

0033:48 [EASTWIND AIRLINES 507] "And Center, for Stinger Bee, ah, Five Oh Seven, we are directly over the site with that airplane or whatever. It just exploded and went into the water."

0033:56 [UNKNOWN] "I have eighteen or nineteen miles on the two thirty six radial off, ah, Hampton."

0034:01 [BOSTON ARTCC SARDI SECTOR, RADAR POSITION] "Roger that. Thank you very much, sir. We're investigating that right now. TWA Eight Hundred, Center." The long pause caused everyone to swallow hard as they waited and prayed for a radio response. "TWA Eight Zero Zero, if you hear Center, ident."

0035:36 [BOSTON ARTCC SARDI SECTOR, RADAR POSITION] "TWA Eight Hundred, Center."

0035:43 [UNKNOWN] "I think that was him."

0035:45 [BOSTON ARTCC SARDI SECTOR, RADAR POSITION] "I think so."

0035:48 [UNKNOWN] "God bless him."

Many other aircraft in the vicinity depended upon directions provided by the air traffic controllers. The professional conduct of operations in the national airspace continued. The controllers maintained their professional demeanor as they directed other aircraft in their sector to climb, descend, change direction and transfer them to adjacent control sectors.

0036:58 [BOSTON ARTCC SARDI SECTOR, RADAR POSITION] "Stinger Bee Five Oh Seven, thanks for that report, ah, New York on one three three point zero five, good day, sir."

0037:05 [EASTWIND AIRLINES 507] "Thirty three oh five, so long. Stinger Five Oh Seven. Anything we can do for ya before we go?"

0037:11 [BOSTON ARTCC SARDI SECTOR, RADAR POSITION] "Well, I just wanna confirm that, ah, that you saw the...ah...splash in the water approximately...ah...twenty southwest of Hampton. Is that right?"

0037:20 [EASTWIND AIRLINES 507] "Ah, yes sir. It just blew up in the air, and then we saw two fireballs go down to the water, and there was a big...ah...smoke...ah...coming up from that also, ah, there seemed to be a light. I thought it was a landing light, and it was coming right at us at about...I don't know...about fifteen thousand feet or something like that, and I pushed on my landing lights...ah...you know so, I saw him, and then it blew."

0038:44 [UNITED AIRLINES 2] "It's...ah...north, forty thirty nine point one, west, zero seven two three eight point zero."

With all the emergency agencies and procedures activated, the business of flight operations continued. The response to the disaster was now in other hands.

2030 EDT (0030 GMT), July 17, 1996
The southern coast of Long Island, New York

"Traffic at 3 o'clock." Ken Wendell pointed out to the pilot next to him.

Sven Faret looked to the right, in the southern sky. He could make out a pinpoint of light. Flying in the busy traffic patterns of suburban New York, Sven was careful to track everything around him. He had excellent visibility at his 8,500 foot altitude, perhaps 50 plus miles. There was a haze below 6,500 feet obscuring vision to less than eight miles. He knew of the usually heavy traffic out of Kennedy International, and he had some idea of the Air Force C-130 flights in the area.

Continuing to head due east, Sven Faret saw that what had first appeared to be a single light to the south actually was two lights close together. Just as his eyes made this out, he saw from below, on the surface of the water what he would later describe as a "pin flash of light." Shortly after the light appeared and arced upward it exploded into a huge red-orange fireball. The fireball started to fall, like a teardrop toward the water below.

The two men watched intently as the fireball crashed into the Atlantic. As they watched, they heard someone else on the air traffic frequency report the fire. Then another person radioed and finally Sven called in himself.

"What was that?" Sven said to Ken as they watched

the debris and fire hit the water, then went on to answer his own question. "It's probably the National Guard guys losing a C-130 or something. Maybe they shot down one of their own planes."

They flew over the smoke cloud that now rose into the evening air, almost up to their altitude, 8,500 feet. They saw several small boats heading for the scene of the crash, now maybe a quarter of the way out.

"I have an eerie feeling about this place, whatever stung this thing could sting us too. Let's bolt out of here," Sven told Ken as he turned north toward his home field, obviously thinking that he had just seen a plane shot out of the air.

As Faret flew toward Islip, Long Island, he reported the events he had seen to both the Flight Service Station on one frequency and to Islip Approach Control on another. When they landed at the airport, Ken Wendell and Sven Faret called their wives in case they heard about an air crash while their husbands were up flying. By the time they got to Ken's house, the news was out that a TWA 747 had gone down. They called FOX News in New York and told their story.

Both the National Transportation Safety Board (NTSB) and Federal Bureau of Investigation (FBI) interviewed both men. Sven told reporters and others later that he did not feel the investigators had acknowledged the full import of his observations, that is, he thought at the time that he had seen the plane being shot down, not simply explode.

Faret and Wendell were not alone in their perception that an arcing light lifted off from the water south of Long Island and struck the 747.

Roland Penny and his family were in a boat off the

coast and saw "a pencil-thin white trail rising up...that hit the plane."

Victor Feyner told the St. Louis Post Dispatch that he thought there was someone shooting flares into the sky until he saw the huge fireball erupt.

Lou Desyron told ABC News, "We saw what appeared to be a flare going straight up. As a matter of fact, we thought it was from a boat. It was a bright reddish-yellow color. And once it went into flames, I knew it wasn't a flare."

The important issue of eyewitnesses and the task of interviewing them developed into the first of several turf battles between the FBI and NTSB with the FBI and Justice Department forbidding the NTSB from interfering with the witness interview process.

On the morning of July 19,1996, NTSB Investigator Bruce Magladry established a 'witness group' to include members from TWA, Airline Pilots Association and the FAA. Immediately after forming this NTSB investigating group, Magladry was informed by FBI Agent Robert Knapp that the FBI was not willing to share any information outside of the NTSB, so the members who usually helped the NTSB were unwelcome. Further, the FBI informed the NTSB that they would not be permitted to conduct any interviews. The NTSB group was discontinued.

On July 21, 1996, the United States Attorney's Office in New York backed up the FBI refusal by reiterating the ban on NTSB interviews of witnesses, but they condescended to allow the NTSB to review certain documents, provided no notes were taken or copies made. Finally, after much complaint through the highest level of government, on July 22, 1996, the FBI agreed to allow the NTSB to interview with the FBI present, but no notes could be taken.

The FBI stonewalling on eyewitness statements has apparently continued throughout the investigation, since, at FBI insistence, the December 1997 NTSB hearings in Baltimore had no eyewitness testimony and the interim NTSB report was likewise devoid of witness statements.

In the aftermath of July 17, 1996, many of the people who saw the explosion made statements to the local police on Long Island, New York. These statements were turned over to the FBI, and the FBI followed up with their own interviews which have still not been disclosed. However, some of the initial statements to the local police have been made public.

For example, on July 20, 1996, Suffolk County Police detectives S. Jensen and C. Awell interviewed Joseph McBride and Vincent Bilodeau. The police report for this interview states, ". . .that on 7/17/96 at about 2045 hours they were at the Moriches Inlet, south shore of Long Island, facing south to southeast. Bilodeau and McBride observed a reddish, glowing flare arch skyward from due east, but could not tell if from land or water. Flare was tight, corkscrew shaped with an even but fast speed."

Other Police reports to the Suffolk County Police Department included:

- Edwin Evans was fishing in a boat off Shamrock Inlet. He saw what he thought was a flare straight behind the boat, out to sea. He described the flare as going straight up from his vantage point. He pointed it out to other people on the boat. After five seconds of flight the flare turned into an orange burst.
- Anthony Curreri saw a red streak rise from the horizon. He saw it from approximately 200 feet high rise straight

up then arch and level out before hitting the airplane. He thought it was fireworks fired from Smith Point out over the ocean.

• Carlo Verrardi was driving his van along Center Moriches shore. He saw a gray smoke trail rising straight up, not in a zig-zag. The smoke trail rising to the explosion location was visible for several minutes after the explosion.

• Derek Miron observed a white streak moving skyward from east of him moving southerly. He could not see if the streak started from land or out to sea. The original white streak burst into yellow sparks, after a puff of smoke and then a burst of orange flames.

• Margaret Greig was sitting on the sand at Smith Point Beach. She was facing southeast when she saw a flare shoot <u>from the water</u>. The flare went upward in a concave arc. She watched the flare turn from pink flame to orange a quarter of the way up. After five seconds she saw it burst into a large ball of fire. She estimated the distance from where she was sitting on the beach to where the flare took off out on the sea to be about one mile.

In all, there were over one hundred reports of witnesses seeing this flare-like, arcing trail of something rising from the sea and hitting the airliner. The *New York Post* reported this number of witnesses as 154 and quoted a federal official as verifying that the witnesses were extremely credible. The *Post* also reported that FBI technicians mapped the flare trail sightings and triangulated them at the precise site of the 747 crash. The FBI would ultimately disclose, in November 1997, that 244 people had witnessed an event relevant to a possible missile firing.

The credible witnesses included the crew of an Air

National Guard helicopter from the 102nd Rescue Squadron, 106th Rescue Wing at Gabreski Airport, Westhampton Beach, New York. Major Fred Meyer, Captain Chris Baur and Sgt. Dennis Richardson, who are reported to have seen the arcing streak and wondered aloud whether they had seen "pyrotechnics."

Major Meyer later explained what he saw, "I was looking right straight down the runway at this streak of light. It was right in front of me. It was at a good distance, somewhere between 10 and 15 miles, and I estimated it at somewhere around 10,000 feet. The streak of light lasted for 3 to 5 seconds. Then, it stopped. Then, just about a second later, further to the left and approximately on the same line I saw an explosion. A high velocity explosion. It looked all the world to me like ordnance, a warhead.

"About a second to two seconds after that ordnance explosion, there was a second high velocity explosion of brilliant white light like nothing I've seen before or since. And then about 2 or 3 seconds after that there came a petrochemical explosion, which was the fuel burning bright orange, mottled color, and a lot of black."

The National Guard pilot was not alone in what he saw. Many others — a cop, a housewife, a meteorologist, an FBI agent, dozens of people — saw what they earnestly believed was a missile rising and shooting the airliner from the sky. Some just saw the explosion. Others saw the arcing streak of what they called "fireworks" or "pyrotechnics" come from sea level and in a time period of several seconds strike the aircraft, which then exploded in an orange ball of fire. A few thought they saw the source, a boat or ship on the horizon. The FBI methodically took down the eyewitnesses' statements, but, strangely, they have never released those statements, even after they subsequently suspended the investigation due to lack of evidence of 'criminality.'

While the senior FBI and NTSB officials and many other US authorities have been unanimous in denying that published reports of an explosion caused by an errant US Navy missile, none has ever fully disproved the possibility of a terrorist missile attack. In fact, although FBI Deputy Director James Kallstrom (now retired) has since discounted the terrorist incident possibility, he acknowledged as recently as March 24, 1997, that this possibility is still under consideration. At that time, there were published reports of federal investigators passing out pictures of a missile launcher to fishermen, in case any such debris was found in the ocean.

On September 5, 1996, John Deutch, the Director of Central Intelligence, chief of the Central Intelligence Agency, gave a speech at Georgetown University concerning the fight against foreign terrorism, stating, in part (underline added for emphasis):

"...foreign terrorism is a major and growing national security concern.

"Events in the past year have driven this home to all of us:

- The suicide bombings in Israel this spring that led to the international terrorism summit at Sharm el Sheik.
- The OPM/SANG Military Training Center bombing that killed five US citizens at Riyadh, Saudi Arabia last November.
- The truck bomb that killed 19 US service personnel at the Al Khobar Towers in Dhahran, Saudi Arabia in June.
  <u>"There also remains a possibility that a terrorist act brought down TWA Flight 800 in July with a loss of more than 200 lives</u>."

The Central Intelligence Agency's concern over the terrorist threat and Iran was further outlined on February 5, 1997 when the new Acting Director of Central Intelligence, George L. Tenet, gave his report to the US Senate, which included the following (underline added for emphasis):

"[In] Iran, conservatives secured a plurality in last March's Majlis, or parliamentary, elections and are positioning themselves to capture the presidency in June. This political feat will not blot out the reality of Iran today: economic stagnation, rising numbers of disaffected youth, and questions about the clerics' day-to-day role in governance.

"Despite growing discontent among many Iranians, opposition to clerical rule lacks a charismatic leader or an institutional power base. Moreover, the clerics are adept at burying their differences in the interests of retaining their control.

"Iran's leaders know they face twin challenges of ebbing public support for the revolution at home and superior American military power abroad as witnessed in Desert Storm. But, they have no intention of abandoning their anti-Western stance or their goals in the region. Rather, they will seek other ways to undermine the US position — for example, by improving their military capabilities relative to their neighbors and by using what we call asymmetric means — ranging from the increased use of terrorism to developing weapons of mass destruction — in order to subvert or intimidate our allies, undermine the confidence of our friends and allies in our military presence, and eventually expel us from the region. Moreover, the Iranians are attempting to improve their foreign ties by reaching out to the Turks and Kazaks, and by solidifying their oil supplier relationship with Japan and

Germany.

"Iran is improving its ability to potentially interdict the flow of oil through the Strait of Hormuz. For example, it has acquired Kilo-class submarines from Russia and is upgrading its antiship missile capabilities. It is building its capabilities to produce and deliver weapons of mass destruction — chemical, biological, and nuclear — and in less than 10 years probably will have longer range missiles that will enable it to target most of Saudi Arabia and Israel.

"Iran sees terrorism as a useful tool. In addition to carrying out its own acts, Iran continues to sponsor training in the region and millions of dollars to a variety of militant Islamic groups such as Hizbollah and Palestinian groups opposed to the peace process."

Later in his speech, Tenet continued, "Although recorded incidents of terrorism in 1996 were fewer than at any time since 1971, total deaths and injuries from terrorist attacks have increased during the period 1992-1996. Indeed, even as our counterterrorism efforts are improving, international groups are expanding their networks, improving their skills and sophistication, and working to stage more spectacular attacks.

"International terrorist groups have developed large transnational infrastructures, which in some cases literally circle the globe. These networks may involve more than one like-minded group, with each group assisting the others. The terrorists use these infrastructures for a variety of purposes, including finance, recruitment, the shipment of arms and materiel, and the movement of operatives.

"With regard to finance, we have seen increasingly complicated channels for soliciting and moving funds, including the use of seemingly legitimate charitable or other nongovernmental organizations as conduits for the money.

"These globe-circling infrastructures can also be used by the terrorists to attack at times and places of their own choosing — as demonstrated by the two bombings by Lebanese Hizbollah against Israeli or Jewish targets in Buenos Aires in 1992 and 1994.

"Modern international terrorists also exhibit a high degree of sophistication and expertise. We see this whenever a successful counterterrorist operation provides a glimpse into their operations, including how they communicate, conduct surveillance, and maintain operational security. We see the same level of sophistication in actual or attempted terrorist attacks."

The CIA Director concluded, "State sponsorship of terrorism continues. I noted Iran's significant involvement earlier. Sudan also is continuing to support terrorism by providing a safe haven for a variety of Islamic extremist and opposition forces. We cannot rule out that Iraq, or surrogate groups, will aim for US or UN targets."

The question is; would the Iranian Government do such a thing as shoot down an American airliner? Why? How?

0954 Local (0554 GMT), July 3, 1988
Straight of Hormuz, Persian Gulf

"Birds free!"

These two simple, seemingly innocuous, words spoken by a US Navy officer signaled the immediate death of some 290 innocent victims of circumstance and, in the tangled webs of destiny and international intrigue that these words set in motion, they may be the cause of death for another 230 innocent victims on another July day some eight years later.

These two words, "Birds free!" were spoken by Captain Will Rogers III as he switched the command override switch for the USS *Vincennes'* missile circuits to allow the battery to launch two missiles against an unidentified, presumed hostile target that was actually an unarmed passenger airliner, Iran Air 655, on a scheduled flight to nearby Dubai. What led up to that decision for the world's most advanced surface warship to open fire on a civilian airliner has been the subject of much speculation, and much soul searching.

The exact results of that action are likewise the subject of much speculation. It has been explained as the cause of the Pan Am 103 bombing, numerous other acts of terror or revenge, depending on the perspective of the pundit. The question remains as to whether and why these words may have led to the downing of TWA Flight 800.

The situation Captain Rogers found himself in that morning in the Persian Gulf was, in every sense of the word, complex. He was a military commander, in the heat of battle, who faced a set of choices that had little chance of a positive outcome. The fact that his being 'in the heat of battle' in the first place was of his own doing is another aspect of the complexity. On a strategic level of complexity, the entire Iran-Iraq War, which his action was a small part of, was a confusing mix of national agendas. On a tactical level of confusion, there may have been intent by some persons within the US Navy to draw the Iranians into a more direct confrontation with the US. It is entirely possible that Captain Rogers, unknowingly, took the bait intended for Iranian gunboat captains and blundered into a confrontation that was not the sort intended by the US Navy tacticians. On the other hand, if Captain Rogers was complicit in the baiting of the Iranian gunboats, he would have acted and, later, responded to criticism of his actions no differently than he did. His continued service until retirement upon which he was awarded a Legion of Merit medal for his career of service shows that Captain Rogers's actions were not viewed as entirely untoward by the US Navy establishment.

That morning started out for Captain Rogers with a report, as he shaved, of trouble brewing to the north in the Gulf. A sister ship, the USS *Montgomery*, was reported to be encountering Iranian gunboats. The *Montgomery*, like the *Vincennes*, was part of a task force sent to ensure 'safe passage' for Kuwaiti tankers and other ships through the Gulf at the height of the Iran-Iraq conflict.

Captain Rogers received the call in his sea cabin from

the Combat Information Center (CIC) Watch Officer, "Captain, you better come down. It sounds like the *Montgomery* got her nose in a beehive."

CIC is the tactical operations center of the cruiser, a large room two decks below the captain's sea cabin and the ship's bridge. It had rows of tactical data systems consoles which combined the power of digital processing with the data input from the several radar, electronic intelligence and sonar systems on the ship. It has a section nicknamed 'air alley' for tracking hundreds of air targets, 'surface plot' for plotting the positions of all surface ships, an Anti-Submarine Warfare center and a central group of consoles where the ship commander and his senior combat advisor, the Tactical Action Officer, were stationed to direct the ship in battle.

On his way from his sea cabin to CIC, Captain Rogers poked his head out onto the ship's bridge to see that the day was typical for the Persian Gulf. Already muggy, the oppressive heat of the day was just beginning and the ever present dusting of red sand from the Saudi desert to the west obscuring the horizon.

Reaching surface plot in CIC, Rogers learned that the *Montgomery* had spotted six suspected Iranian gunboats. At 0633, Captain Rogers ordered the *Vincennes* to proceed north toward the *Montgomery* at top speed, "All ahead flank!"

The USS *Montgomery* was an older frigate, not a high-tech wonder like the *Vincennes*, but nevertheless a capable warship especially against lightly armed patrol boats. In fact, in a battle against the gunboats, the *Montgomery* was essentially as capable as the *Vincennes*, which was primarily designed to confront an airborne assault of Soviet jet aircraft and missiles of the type the US Navy might have expected in

Cold War days on the high seas. The *Vincennes'* main gun's capability against high-speed, close-in, patrol craft was severely lacking and the machine gun pedestals on its bridge wings and gunwales were strictly an afterthought. The *Vincennes'* main and unique capability, its AEGIS computer system and powerful SPY-1 radar to track and engage hundreds of enemy aircraft at once and automatically coordinate and fire its Standard missile battery, was of absolutely no use against the threat mentioned in the Straits by the *Montgomery*.

Later, official reports of the incident indicated that at 0650 the *Montgomery* reported thirteen gunboats harassing a Liberian tanker called the Stovall. (The fact that no ship of such name was present that morning or even exists in any ship registry is given by some as evidence the Navy was baiting the Iranians to come out into the shipping lanes.) The *Montgomery* was near the main choke point of the Persian Gulf, the Straits of Hormuz, a narrow, 35 mile wide, channel between Iran and the Arabian Peninsula which links the Persian Gulf with the Indian Ocean. The Straits were the focus of much of the US Navy's attention on their mission to ensure safe passage for the merchant shipping heading to and from Kuwait and the Gulf states since the Straits were flanked in Iranian waters and adjacent to the major Iranian port of Bandar Abbas. In previous months, there had been several confrontations between Iranian and US vessels, including a mine hit on a US frigate, USS *Samuel B. Roberts*, and the sinking of several small Iranian ships. The US had countered the Iranian actions with strikes at a couple Iranian oil platforms in the Gulf north and west of the Straits.

The *Vincennes'* station, farther to the south from

Montgomery's position, covered the southern approaches to the Straits. By turning to the north at flank speed without either the request for help from the *Montgomery* nor orders from Rear Admiral Anthony Less, the commander of the Joint Task Force - Middle East, Captain Rogers was assuming, on his own, responsibility for the consequences of sailing into harm's way. This was not the first time Rogers had displayed a 'gung ho' attitude in approaching the possibility of direct confrontation with the Iranians. He had angered a fellow skipper, Capt. Robert Hattan of the frigate USS *Sides*, by ordering him to approach an Iranian warship in a manner Hattan considered provocative. Hattan had refused Rogers' direction, and it was Hattan who had been supported by the flag officers in Bahrain after that incident. By July, the *Vincennes* was referred to as 'Robocruiser' and fellow commanders regarded Captain Rogers as 'trigger happy.'

The Straits are peppered with small islands that are Iranian territory; Abu Musa, Hengam, Tunb and others. Iran's Revolutionary Guard forces manned the small gunboats patrolling these waters and fortified the islands.

At 0711 local time, the *Montgomery* reported several explosions from the vicinity of the tanker they had earlier reported, the Stovall. At this report, the Joint Task Force command in Bahrain ordered Rogers to send his on-board helicopter north to support *Montgomery* and reconnoiter, but for the *Vincennes* itself to remain to the south in case any further gunboats emerged from Abu Musa Island. Captain Richard McKenna, the admiral's surface warfare chief, later reflected that he thought these orders were sufficient and clear, that *Vincennes* should stay to the south.

Eleven minutes later the *Vincennes*' helicopter lifted

off with Lt. Mark Collier piloting and Lt. Roger Huff in command in the copilot's seat. Within minutes, the SH-60B Seahawk was over the critical area. Collier located not the Stovall, but a German-flagged cargo freighter, the *Dhaulgiri*, as being surrounded by Iranian patrol craft. However, he reported no firing nor hostilities, just the usual pestering harassment by the gunboats.

Two of the US Navy captains hearing this report by Collier, had totally different responses to this news. Hearing that there were no hostilities in progress, Captain Richard Watkins, the admiral's chief of staff in Bahrain, decided things were winding down and went off to do some paperwork. On the other hand, hearing that the Iranians were surrounding a innocent merchant vessel, Captain Rogers had his Boatswain Mate sound the General Quarters klaxon and announced, "Battle stations, repel small craft." *Vincennes* went on a battle footing.

The *Vincennes* hurried north, past the German vessel whose crew signaled that all was well with them. *Vincennes* finally stopped its charge as it pulled abreast of *Montgomery*. The Omani coast guard, who were monitoring this part of the Gulf that bordered their territorial waters, ordered the Iranians away and rebuked Rogers by telling him that his high speed run was not consistent with support of the right of innocent passage. Neither the Iranians nor the Americans responded to the good advice from the Omani.

When the admiral's surface warfare chief returned to the command center at 0840, he found the *Vincennes* forty miles north of where he expected her. After a heated exchange with Rogers, Captain McKenna ordered both the *Vincennes* and the *Montgomery* out of the area toward the south.

McKenna was furious when he heard laughter on the radio from the *Vincennes'* CIC when he first ordered them south. Finally, Captain Rogers reluctantly obeyed the order, but, unfortunately, he left his helicopter in the air over the Iranians.

The Iranians were turning north toward their bases on Hengam and Qeshm Islands. When Lt. Collier circled lower to check on the gunboats, the Seahawk encountered anti-aircraft fire from the gunboats. Collier dove the chopper toward the ocean to gain speed and lessen the effectiveness of the anti-aircraft fire from the surface craft, and Lt. Huff radioed to Captain Rogers (Codenamed Trinity Sword), "Trinity Sword, this is Ocean Lord 25. We're taking fire, taking evasive action."

At this news, Rogers again ordered General Quarters and flank speed to the north toward Hengam Island. With the hostile fire on US forces, the Iranians had set in motion the portion of the American's Rules of Engagement which allowed Rogers to pursue and engage the Iranians. Two hundred miles to the southeast in the open seas of the Gulf of Oman, the Commander of Carrier Battle Group 6, two-star, Rear Admiral Leighton Smith, ordered two F-14 fighters and two A-7 attack bombers from the carrier *Forrestal* into covering patterns where they could support the *Vincennes* in minutes, if necessary. At 0828 local time, the four planes launched and assumed station at Point Alpha some eighty miles from *Vincennes*.

Racing north towards Iranian waters, Captain Rogers sat in the windowless CIC urgently seeking information on his chosen opposition. The vaunted radar systems of the *Vincennes* were of marginal use against the small motor launches whose radar silhouette bounced in and out of radar view with the rise and fall of ocean swells. The automatic tracking provisions of the tactical data system merely lumped the numerous small contacts into a single computer symbol, a small red diamond. Lookouts on the bridge wings with high-powered binoculars could barely make out the small boats, when they were visible at all, through the dusty haze of the Gulf.

At 0939 local time, with the enemy boats occasionally in visual range, Captain Rogers radioed Task Force Command in Bahrain that he intended to open fire. The admiral's chief of staff requested more information on the status of the Iranian boats, "Were they clearing away?"

By now, the gunboats were all within the territorial waters near the Iranian islands and without the towering bridge wing vantage point of Captain Rogers' lookouts and the Americans' high-powered optics, the Iranians were possibly unable to see the American vessel. The gunboats were meandering about in Iranian territorial waters. Finally, in reporting that the Iranians were turning and traveling in varying directions, a lookout reported that it seemed that two gunboats were pointed toward the *Vincennes.*

Captain Rogers reformatted this lookout's report into a tactical signal to Bahrain that the gunboats were gathering speed and showing hostile intent. He again announced intent to fire. Finally, the flag officer's staff concurred, based on Rogers' rather robust description of the Iranian activities.

At that same moment, at the navigation station on the bridge, the quartermaster of the watch determined that the *Vincennes* had entered Iranian territorial waters, and he announced the same to the *Vincennes'* Executive Officer (XO) at his station on the bridge. The XO relayed this critical information to his skipper. Captain Rogers, although in tacit compliance with the US Navy's Rules of Engagement for facing a hostile threat, had now slipped outside of the bounds of international law. He had entered Iranian territory.

At 0943 local time, at the orders of Rogers' Tactical Action Officer, Commander Victor Guillory, the USS *Vincennes* opened fire on the closest Iranian, a motor launch some 8,000 yards away.

0943 Local (0543 GMT), July 3, 1988
Hengam Island, Persian Gulf

Lieutenant Ali Hassan Mohaddessin shook his head at his sergeant, "No, I don't think we hit him. I saw the air bursts. Off the mark."

"No, maybe not, but that American pilot will not be nosing around the Revolutionary Guards without paying proper respects."

Affirmative chuckles came from several of Mohaddessin's men. The men relaxed on the aft deck of the small tan gunboat. The Guards' Regional headquarters at Qeshm had told all six gunboats to stand down until they could get a good picture of what the American naval vessels were doing. They waited for further orders in the waters near Hengam Island where they had come after the high speed run north following their brush with the Americans and their helicopter.

Mohaddessin went down the steps into the chart room of the gunboat. There, his radioman was listening in on the Guards' command circuit. He reported to Mohaddessin, "They have asked the patrol plane to come down and check the positions of the American cruisers and destroyers. They are not sure where they are."

Mohaddessin nodded. He took some water from the canteen that hung on a coat hook over the radio.

The American Navy's standard 5-inch HiCap round has a proximity fuze, which when armed by the spin the cannon's rifling gives it after firing, will set off the high explosive charge whenever it comes within about twenty feet of any object on its flight. This makes it usable against aircraft as it does not have to actually hit the speeding aircraft to destroy it, it can just come close. A modern five-inch naval gun, as used on the USS *Vincennes*, is radar directed and highly accurate.

Whether it was luck or accuracy, the first five-inch round out of the *Vincennes'* guns came within 20 feet of the aft deck of the tan gunboat. The high explosive charge crushed the small boat, breaking its keel downward. The shrapnel and blast killed all the men on deck. The superstructure and bow of the gunboat tumbled forward with the blast. Lieutenant Mohaddessin and his radioman were thrown clear of the tumbling, splintered wreckage.

Mohaddessin was stunned and barely conscious as he finally broke the surface and gulped air. Struggling to stay afloat in the gasoline-streaked waters, the Guards officer spun around in the water, looking to find his men and see what was left of the boat.

The boat was on two sides of him. The upended bow slowly sinking on one side and the burning stern on another. He only saw one other survivor, the radioman, who was swimming away from the wreck. Seeing the wisdom of this, Mohaddessin followed, trying to get away from spreading flames of burning gasoline.

0945 Local (0545 GMT), July 3, 1988
Bandar Abbas, Iran

In spite of the Iran-Iraq War that was raging on the Iraqi border far to the north and the sporadic overflow of hostilities farther south in the Gulf, life continued on throughout the Persian Gulf area in 1988. This lifestyle included a fairly regular flow of Iranians heading overseas, foreign oil workers, contractors and other business persons traveling from and to southern Iran. The Emirate of Dubai, rich with its oil money, has a modern airport and excellent international connections. It was the airport of choice for Iranians and foreigners traveling in or out of southern Iran since it was ten times closer to the main southern Iranian city of Bandar Abbas than the Iranian capital of Tehran far to the north. Therefore, Iran Air served this link to the outside world with a twice-weekly roundtrip from Bandar Abbas to Dubai. Iran Air Flight 655 was one leg of this routine roundtrip. It was scheduled and identified in airline flight schedules worldwide, including the copy used by Captain Will Rogers' CIC staff.

Flight Captain Mohsan Rezaian was a seasoned airline pilot for Iran Air. The French-built Airbus A300-B2 was in top condition. The two turbofan engines he cycled up to takeoff thrust that morning on the tarmac at Bandar Abbas airport were virtually the same as the four, main, propulsion turbofans Captain Rogers was revving on the *Vincennes* in his efforts to engage the Iranian gunboats. Captain Rezaian's airliner was nearly full, a good revenue producing run. The only problem was that if one draws a straight line from the city of Bandar Abbas to the emirate of Dubai it runs directly over the island called Hengam, whose waters Captain Rogers had now entered in search of gunboats.

The airfield at Bandar Abbas has two sides. One side includes the terminal, the air cargo facility with its mainstay traffic of spare parts for oilfield equipment and hangars for the civilian aircraft. The other, and larger, side of the airport includes the reinforced hangars that house many of Iran's F-14 fighter aircraft and P-3 patrol aircraft which the US sold to Iran during friendlier times under the Shah.

When Captain Rezaian's Airbus cleared the runway at Bandar Abbas, it was immediately picked up on radar by the USS *Sides* sitting offshore of Bandar Abbas. The *Sides'* track symbol for the airliner was immediately conveyed through the interlinked tactical data system to both the *Vincennes* and the carrier battle group with its E-2 Hawkeye tracking aircraft. At 0947, *Vincennes'* sophisticated AEGIS system took over its own track of the airliner, labeling it, as was custom in the Gulf, as 'assumed hostile' particularly when it lifted into the sky from a known source of hostile military aircraft, Bandar Abbas.

Onboard the *Vincennes*, the assumed hostile symbol for the Airbus, a red triangle open at the bottom, popped onto the 'air alley' console screen of Petty Officer Andrew Anderson, whose job it was to run an IFF (Identify, Friend or Foe) transponder check on all new tracks. All aircraft worldwide carry IFF transponders which, when 'interrogated' by a radio signal sent out in conjunction with a radar beam, will 'squawk' a response which tells the radar operator the identity of the aircraft. A Mode 1 or 2 squawk indicates a military flight and a Mode 3 indicates a civilian flight, however most military planes can also squawk Mode 3 in order to make life simpler for air traffic controllers at civilian locations. Petty Officer Anderson's first interrogation indicated a civilian aircraft Mode 3 for the airborne contact.

Anderson's next job was to crosscheck this contact with the long list of known civilian flights. In the darkened CIC space in the midst of the repetitive rounds of gunfire Captain Rogers was now firing toward the Iranian boats, Anderson missed the schedule listing for Iran Air Flight 655.

Along with Anderson in the 'air alley' section of *Vincennes'* CIC was another petty officer and the air-tracking officer, Lt. Clay Zocher. Lt. Zocher was watching a tactical data system track for a Iranian P-3 aircraft coming south along the coast toward Hengam. When he heard Anderson wonder aloud if the new track which squawked as civilian but did not show in the air traffic schedules might be an Iranian ploy, Zocher fit this together with the P-3 that was approaching and might be coordinating an air attack on *Vincennes*, one of the possible uses for the type of P-3 used by Iran. Zocher passed this possibility up the chain of command to LCdr Scott Lustig, the senior tactical officer for air warfare, who sat at Captain Rogers's side. Lustig immediately ordered Zocher to challenge the aircraft on the international emergency frequencies monitored by all aircraft. There was no response and the track continued, inbound toward *Vincennes*.

Captain Rogers was still fully engaged in his attack on the gunboats. Over the phone circuit used by the command team on the *Vincennes*, Captain Rogers was relaying rudder and engine commands to the XO on the bridge, surface ship trackers and lookouts were sounding out contacts and shipboard systems were reported on. To this mix was now added the information that a presumed hostile air track was inbound, "Constant bearing! Closing at 300 knots."

Then, someone on the command phone circuit reported that this track number was 'possible Astro,' the codeword for an Iranian F-14. No one ever found out who sounded this alarm. Anderson and Zocher assumed it was the electronic intelligence (EW) suite that had the capability of identifying an F-14 by its electronic emissions. The Tactical Action Officer and Captain Rogers naturally assumed that such critical information on an incoming 'bogey' would come from Anderson and Zocher in air alley.

Anderson immediately re-interrogated the bogey's IFF. This time it came back as clearly Mode 2, military, but not American. During the ensuing investigation, it would be discovered that Anderson in the interim had left his IFF system on a long range scale after interrogating a farther aircraft, possibly the P-3. Now, the Airbus was directly between them and Bandar Abbas and when he interrogated on long range Mode 2, he got an immediate Mode 2 military squawk on that bearing, but from one of the real Iranian military aircraft, on the ground at Bandar Abbas, not the Airbus. He had no way of telling the difference.

"Possible Astro!" Anderson now resounded the alarm of an incoming Iranian fighter.

There was a temporary cessation of the firing on the gunboats while the *Vincennes*' gunner's mates cleared the jammed main gun. During the pause, LCdr Lustig apprised Captain Rogers of the air 'threat.' The track had now been identified by Anderson as an F-14.

Despite one other CIC officer's continued concern that it was a commercial flight, there were three more frenzied warnings radioed out. "Iranian fighter...you are steering into danger and are subject to United States Naval defensive measures."

Even if Captain Rezaian had heard the warning, there is no reason he would have responded. His plane was not an Iranian fighter, and there was no way of knowing whom in the entire Persian Gulf the Americans were warning away.

To this flow of chaotic information is added one more bit of unexplained error. The two petty officers in air alley now called out that the track was increasing speed and descending, an attack profile. In reality, later evidence would show the opposite, the Airbus was ascending and still at a modest speed for commercial traffic, 380 knots.

It was a critical decision time for Captain Rogers. The type of F-14 sold to Iran was not known to be a platform for anti-ship missiles, like the one launched from an Iraqi F-1 that had nearly sunk another US Navy warship, the USS *Stark*, in the Gulf a year earlier. However, F-14's did carry heat-seeking Sidewinder missiles which could track into the hot exhaust of the *Vincennes* jet turbine engines just as they would into a plane's engine pod. While such a strike could probably not sink his ship, it could cause serious damage and injury.

The track proceeded onward, directly at the *Vincennes*. There was no reason for Rogers to believe that the Iranian Air Force had not sent an aircraft to assist their comrades on board the gunboats that Rogers had stopped shooting at only seconds earlier. The adrenaline of battle was still running full strength. Rogers had to fire before the aircraft reached ten miles from his ship. He had no reason to believe that the information he had been given by his crew was incorrect. At 0954, Captain Will Rogers III turned the key for the command firing link and announced, "Birds Free!"

At the same time, Captain Mohsan Rezaian radioed Bandar Abbas Departure Control that he had reached his first checkpoint on the commercial traffic route. He did not indicate, nor did Bandar Abbas flight control, that he knew anything was amiss in the waters of the Gulf below him.

At 0954:30, the first SM-2 missile from *Vincennes* took the left wing off the Airbus and seconds later a second missile impacted the falling fuselage. All 290 bodies fell into the Gulf from about 13,000 feet up.

Captain Rogers ordered the *Vincennes* south out of Iranian waters. The surviving Iranian gunboats rushed to search for survivors.

1020 Local (0620 GMT), July 3, 1988
Strait of Hormuz, Off of Hengam Island

The radioman had been the only one of Lieutenant
Mohaddessin's crew to be rescued by the nearest Iranian gunboat. The search for other survivors had been cut short by
the frantic calls from Qeshm about the Iran Air disaster. The
boat that had come to Mohaddessin's aid now raced east.

Mohaddessin stood next to his fellow officer on the
short, speed run to the crash site. The radio was abuzz with
misinformation and warnings of the next move by the
Americans. Had the Americans really shot down an airliner?

The site of the wreckage was like a view from Hell
itself. Hundreds of bodies floated in the warm Gulf waters.
The first Guards boats on the scene were joined by an Iranian
Navy cutter and helicopters. The Omanis and even the
Americans called to see if they could help. The Guards
commander on Qeshm refused all help.

The bodies were so numeorus they would not fit on
the decks of the boats. Many bodies were nude, their clothing
stripped by either the force of the blast or the fall through the
thousands of feet to the ocean.

The Guardsmen and the sailors were in shock. Even
though many were veterans of the horrible atrocities in the
war with Iraq, they were stunned by the carnage they found
in the Gulf that morning. The partially clothed, partially burnt
bodies of women, children and men littered the sea in all

directions.

As they labored in the hot sun to gather the corpses and personnel effects, muttering somber prayers as they did, it was certain that no man who saw the sight would ever forget it. Lieutenant Ali Hassan Mohaddessin would not, he vowed that to Allah.

July 3, 1988
Washington, DC

The incident in the Strait of Hormuz had occurred in the middle of the night, Washington time. The Pentagon compiled the information from Captain Rogers's report, relayed through the Joint Task Force headquarters in Bahrain.

The first statement by the Pentagon read, "At 0210 EDT (0610 GMT), July 3, a US Navy helicopter from the AEGIS cruiser USS _Vincennes_ was fired upon by Iranian small craft in the Strait of Hormuz. The _Vincennes_ and the frigate _Montgomery_ returned fire with five-inch guns. Our reports indicate two small Iranian boats were sunk and one damaged. The _Vincennes_ also reported it downed an Iranian F-14 that was approaching at a high rate of speed and in a manner that could have permitted the plane to attack the _Vincennes_, and he was warned before the F-14 was shot down with a Standard Missile. It is not known if the pilot was able to eject, but an Iranian rescue helicopter was searching the area without interference from US forces."

As reports of the airliner downing came in over the wire services, the Pentagon added the following to their statement, "We have no information about the loss of the commercial aircraft. We are aware of the news reports and are now trying to determine the facts. We cannot confirm that an Airbus went down."

As the first television pictures came in of the bodies

floating in the Persian Gulf, both the Pentagon and the White House denied any US involvement, based upon reports from the scene. Eventually, as reports from the USS *Montgomery* (a crewmember saw the huge Airbus wing fall from the sky), the USS *Sides* (they had classified the aircraft correctly as civilian) and other ships in the area came in, the Navy got a clearer picture of the *Vincennes* actions.

Eleven hours after the incident, the Chairman of the US Joint Chiefs of Staff, Admiral William Crowe, finally announced that the *Vincennes* had shot down the passenger plane. But, he still maintained that the airliner was descending, picking up speed and that it was outside of civil air corridors, all untrue unbeknownst to Crowe. He showed a chart that located the *Vincennes* in international waters, also untrue.

What followed thereafter was an involved and unsuccessful coverup by the top brass at the Pentagon. Vice President George Bush was given incorrect information in preparation for a speech to the United Nations in defense of the Navy's actions. An official report by Rear Admiral William Fogarty, senior naval staff officer for the US Central Command, was presented to the public and to the Senate Armed Services Committee. This official report had glaring holes and misstatements of fact. The full scope of the coverup and the disaster was finally reported in depth by ABC News' *Nightline* program on the fourth anniversary of the disaster and in an extensive exposé feature article in *Newsweek* magazine on July 13, 1992.

Captain Rogers left the command of the USS *Vincennes* and went to a teaching position with the Navy in San Diego. In 1991, he retired and, as previously mentioned, he was awarded the Legion of Merit for service to his country.

Such an honor is not unexpected for a retiring senior officer, but it proved extremely galling to victims' families and was widely reported, in the most derogatory terms, in the news media of Islamic countries, particularly Iran.

The Islamic Republic of Iran lodged a formal protest with the United Nations Security Council. When the Security Council route proved unfruitful, Iran filed a legal action against the United States in the International Court of Justice in The Hague, Netherlands.

1040 GMT, June 4, 1993
Gulf of Finland

Captain Abdi Morteza pulled the collar of his wind-breaker higher. He had been in St. Petersburg for nearly two months, he should be accustomed to the cold northwest wind by now. But, he was not. The Russians could keep this weather. He yearned for the warmth of home and the warm Gulf waters.

He shared the cramped standing room on the submarine's conning tower with three other men; the old Russian, Captain Vasili Voroshilov, a Russian warrant officer who barked orders to the teams of line handlers, both Iranian and Russian, assembled on the deck below and the swarthy looking Azerbaijani youth whom the Russians had assigned as an interpreter. Together, they directed the underway refueling taking place between their ship and the Russian fleet oiler that churned alongside.

The interpreter really was not needed except for uncommon cases, which usually taxed his Farsi vocabulary anyway. Morteza and Voroshilov had, in the weeks past, settled into a working blend of some basic Russian and their language in common, English. Voroshilov had a rudimentary command of English, and Morteza spoke it fluently. Morteza had first learned it as a young ensign in the Shah's navy training in Norfolk, Virginia, to eventually serve on one of the new *Spruance*-class destroyers the Shah had intended to buy from the US. Voroshilov had learned what English he knew in the years that he had spent indoctrinating the Indian Navy into the use of the *Granata*-class submarines the Russians had sold them; a task he was now doing for the Iranians. The western countries knew the *Granata* submarine type as the Kilo-class, its NATO designation.

Fate and Khomeini's revolution had interrupted that *Spruance* purchase, but it had not stopped Morteza's naval career. Morteza proved himself worthy to the Islamic revolution in the early gunboat skirmishes in the Abadan Delta before the full scale Iran-Iraq War. He had moved up quickly in an Iranian Navy that had its entire leadership replaced with the defections and political repercussions that came with the fundamentalist Islamic revolution in Iran in 1979. Like the Iranian Army and Air Force, the Navy was completely reconstituted in the decade after Khomeini's revolution. The mullahs of the Islamic Republic did not trust anyone who had been in a high position under the Shah and the many Western-educated military leaders wanted nothing to do with this new and frighteningly radical Iran. However, Abdi Morteza had no problem adapting to the new regime. He was the son of a Moslem cleric, and his strict upbringing fit in well in the new Iran. A devout Moslem with the best naval training the Shah and the United States could give him was a true asset to the Islamic Republic of Iran.

"Pol gradusa na leva!" Voroshilov shouted to make himself heard to Morteza in his sound-powered phone headset.

Morteza nodded and shouted into the microphone in Farsi, "One half degree left."

As they watched, the stout bodied submarine responded by edging minutely closer to the oiler. When the fuel hose strung between the submarine's conning tower and the oiler's rigging had dipped to its normal loop, Voroshilov signaled Morteza with his hand.

"One half degree right, resume standard course, 270 degrees," Morteza ordered the helmsman by phone. Below him in the submarine's main control room, his helmsman was steering with a Russian warrant officer behind his shoulder. Throughout the ship, the Iranians had their Russian mentors beside them. Morteza watched one of his men on deck raise the yellow flag signaling fueling was nearly complete.

This was the last shake-down cruise in Russian waters, but the Russians were scheduled, under the purchase contract between Russia and Iran, to come with the Iranians on the maiden international voyage; down from St. Petersburg, through the North Sea, the Mediterranean and the Suez Canal, ending at the submarine's new home port of Bandar Abbas, where the Russians would leave the Iranians to commission their new ship and fly back to Russia.

The thought of flying out of Bandar Abbas brought painful memories to Abdi Morteza. He had lost his beloved Maryam as she flew out of Bandar Abbas that tragic day in 1988. Morteza had been in Toulon, France, finishing the acquisition of new patrol boats from the French, and Maryam had been coming to him for a summer vacation. Captain Morteza had seen the first television pictures of the tragedy in the break room at the French shipyard.

Morteza's somber thoughts were broken as the crew chief raised the red flag and signaled the deck crew to unhook the fuel line. The crew on the oiler retracted the fuel hose that rolled on pulley wheels along the taut metal cable between the two ships. As the hose retracted, the submarine's deck crew sealed the inner spigot and the outer hatch at the refueling station. When they were done, all the deck crew except two scurried down the hatch into the submarine. The remaining two, a Russian petty officer and his Iranian student, walked to the side of the conning tower below Morteza and Voroshilov. Morteza craned his head over the gunwale of the conning tower to watch them.

The fuel line was back aboard the oiler. Morteza felt the conning tower tilt farther right as the oiler let the tension out of the cable that connected the two ships. When the cable had slackened sufficiently, the Iranian petty officer yanked on a rope connected to the quick release fitting on the conning tower, and the whole guy wire assembly fell into the sea and was rapidly wound in by the oiler's crew. The two petty officers ran back and climbed down the hatch, sealing it behind them.

Captain Abdi Morteza reached down to a lever at his elbow and sounded the submarine's air horn twice. The oiler's skipper responded with two blasts of the oiler's far deeper whistle.

Morteza spoke into the phone's mouthpiece, "Right standard rudder, set new course 280."

"Very good." Voroshilov was nodding. "You see," he pointed to the bow of the submarine, "She's still riding very high in the water, we only filled half full. When you are totally fueled, it will ride another full meter lower in the water, even with full air in ballast. And if you do fuel ballast, it will be another meter lower. You will almost have no deck above water."

Morteza thought for a moment trying to comprehend the Russian's bad English. He pulled one earphone clear so he could hear better, keeping the other on. "Tell me more about fuel ballast. I read about it in the manuals, but...."

"Well, it was a simple process. We modified the basic design after we tested it on one of our early boats. The number 3 and 4 ballast tanks, the ones closest amidships, can be cross-connected with the fuel pumps. So, you pump them full of diesel fuel, instead of sea water. It restricts your attitude control, and you'd better not do an emergency ballast blow and forget you did fuel ballast," said Voroshilov smiling at the thought. "You'd make quite an oil slick. No? But, the loss of attitude control is made up for by the extra range, another 2,000 miles."

Morteza did a mental calculation of the 2,000 miles to kilometers. He asked the Russian, "Will we be doing fuel ballast on the trip to Iran?"

Voroshilov huffed. "*Nyet, ni nada.* We can get to Iran with just one refueling in the *Mediteranskii* without fuel ballast. No, you need to prepare to do fuel ballast, is not normal thing. You need to check the piping and make sure the ballast tanks are clean. *Dostatochno.* Diesel engines don't run if you feed them barnacles," the old Russian captain laughed.

Captain Abdi Morteza considered the concept he had just learned. With this fuel ballast trick, Iran's new submarine, *Noor*, had a range of over 12,000 kilometers. With one refueling he could take the *Noor* almost anywhere on earth.

The Russian warrant officer motioned for the Azerbaijani, unneeded as he had proven to be, to follow him down the conning tower's scuttle into the submarine. Voroshilov said, "*Nu, eto vsyo.* Prepare to dive."

Morteza repeated the last words in Farsi into the phone and pulled the phone from the connection box. He hoped he appeared nonchalant in his actions. He was not yet used to the thought of submerging. He made a last check of the horizon and followed Voroshilov down into the soon to be christened *Noor*.

May 6, 1995
The White House, Washington, DC

President Bill Clinton signed Executive Order 12959 imposing a virtually total US economic embargo on Iran. In so doing, the President stated, "Responding to the country's sponsorship of international terrorism and its active pursuit of weapons of mass destruction, the new sanctions prohibit trade with Iran, as well as trade financing.... New investment in Iran is also prohibited."

At the time of the US embargo, Iran was still struggling to fully recover from a long term economic slowdown. The lingering effects of the eight year Iran-Iraq War, the increased market competition to sell oil production from other Gulf States, particularly Kuwait, following the Gulf War between the West and Iraq, and what is viewed by many observers as a natural block to normal trade which is created by Iran's own myopic political and social values had all combined to strap Iran financially. They were slowly pulling out of the slump, but the US embargo could not have come at a worse time.

The embargo was effective. It further strapped Iran for hard cash. Five months later, the Iranians had still not found a market for 200,000 of the 600,000 barrels a day of crude oil the Americans had been buying. Between this and other impacts, the Americans had stopped almost $1 billion a year of hard cash from flowing into Iran.

One European Union (EU) minister likened the Clinton trade embargo against Iran to "an economic declaration of war" and compared it to the US economic sanctions against Japan that had preceded World War II.

February 23, 1996
Foreign Ministry, Tehran, Iran

Eftekhar Jahromi was at the zenith of his profession. He was walking to the podium, going before the press of his nation, to announce the greatest victory his mind could conceive. As chief of the Office of International Legal Affairs for the Islamic Republic of Iran, he was going to announce that he had reached a settlement with the United States in the Iran Air massacre. As a specialist in international law and as an Iranian, there could be no higher achievement than announcing that you had been successful in forcing the most powerful country on Earth to admit its wrongdoing and pay an enormous amount in reparations.

"In the name of God, the merciful, the compassionate.... On July 3, 1988, the naval forces of the United States of America committed an unspeakable atrocity, the murder of 290 innocent people, when they shot down a civilian airliner at Bandar Abbas. Today, on behalf of the Islamic Republic and in the name of the honored martyrs and their bereaved families, I announce that the government of the United States of America has agreed to pay the Islamic Republic of Iran the total of $131,800,000 in reparations for this atrocity.

"The payment of $131,800,000 includes at least $61,800,000 for compensation to the victims' families. Surviving family members are to get either $150,000 or

$300,000, depending on whether the victim was a wage earner or not.

"Additionally, there will be a payment of $40 million for the Airbus A300 aircraft which was lost to the American missile. The remainder is compensation to the Islamic Republic for earlier claims before the Iran-US Claims Tribunal arising from the illegal seizure of Iranian funds by the American government in 1979."

Eftekhar Jahromi struggled during the statement to remain stolid and serious; to smile would be undignified.

A few hours later, in Washington, a spokesman for the United States Department of State, Nicholas Burns, was exercising a good degree of spin control on the same announcement. While the total figure he announced was the same, he vehemently emphasized that nothing would be paid directly to the government of Iran. He pointed out that the $61,800,000 would be deposited into a trust account that would be paid as death benefits to the families through the Swiss Embassy in Tehran, the Iranian Government would not distribute the money.

As to the remaining $70 million, he declared that it would be put into another bank account to pay off private US claims against Iran for the Iran-US Claims Tribunal. Put another way, the United States would be paying off $70 million in Iranian Government debt.

At the end of his spin doctoring, Burns added the following; "I want to make it clear that this statement does not signal any change in our relations with Iran."

The following Friday in Tehran, the Islamic Republic made it clear that they felt exactly the same about the United

States. Ayatollah Ahmad Jannati, a senior mullah in the hierarchy of the Islamic Republic, and a close confidant and friend of the supreme leader of Iran, Ayatollah Ali Khamenei, spoke at the weekly Friday prayer service, referencing the settlement and the official Iranian view of the United States in a well-known speech.

"The United States is the modern incarnation of Satan. The 'Great Satan' befits the United States better than any other attributive phrase. In the Holy Koran, the Almighty offered a description of the attributes of Satan. Every part of this description is inherent in the government system and society of the United States."

He continued, "Much of the misfortunes being suffered by Muslim nations are the results of plots by the United States. Like Satan, the United States, too, is pushing the world's people here and there to corruption and to prostitution by her schemes, attacks, ploys and intimidations. The Islamic people must be ever vigilant to repel and confront this Great Satan, with martyrdom if necessary."

At the time he spoke these epithets against the Untied States, Ayatollah Jannati was probably aware of the new duties he would be assuming for the Islamic Republic of Iran. In a reformation of the Iranian Government's intelligence system, there would be renewed effort to encourage fundamentalist Islamic revolutionaries in many countries and to foster international actions to destabilize the position of the United States and its allies. An Office of Revolutionary Movements would reinvigorate this radical fundamentalist process under the name of Hizbollah International. Ayatollah Jannati would emerge as the spokesman for Hizbollah International. And, in the theocratic structure of Iranian Government Ayatollah Ahmad Jannati and his virulent anti-Americanism would become a senior policymaker for international terrorist actions against the United States by both Iran and the terrorist cells of a dozen foreign fundamentalist front groups.

In the weeks after the announcement of the American reparations for the Iran Air disaster, there was an interesting colloquy that sprang up in Tehran regarding the payments. The question was whether the payment of the reparations constituted an acceptance of blood money from a murderer by the victim's family, such that the United States must be considered pardoned, both by the family and in the eyes of Allah.

Under the Iranian system of law, Islamic Law derived from the Holy Koran, this was a question for the mullahs to interpret and rule on. Under this system, entitled *vilayat-e-mutlaqa-yi-faqih*, the religious leaders have the total authority to rule on legal issues arising from the Koranic Law. After much discussion, there was an authoritative ruling given.

The senior clerics, the mullahs, speaking with the authorization from the highest levels, ruled that the offer to pay blood money to the victim's family instead of blood for blood, person for person, retaliation is a voluntary matter for the brother (family) of the slain. The offer of payment or even the actual payment of money does not wipe out the need for retaliation unless the payment is accepted as such by the family. Further, even if offered, the murderer must pay the blood money with a contrite, humble spirit, acknowledging the magnanimous pardon he has received from the family and Allah.

The mullahs ruled that the families could accept the payment of the $150,000 or $300,000 per person as full reparation or blood money if they so chose, but they need not. They could even accept the payment, but not acknowledge it as full recompense. The United States had not humbly sought the pardon of the families or Iran itself. The US had refused to pay anything for years and had now refused, in its own words, to pay the Government of Iran anything for its losses. Specifically, the United States had not paid all of what Iran had asked for. It had negotiated the final payment amount. A negotiated partial settlement was not what the Koranic Law required to erase the wrong. In Iranian eyes, the United States was not off the hook for Iran Air 655.

This ruling by the mullahs was not just applicable to families of the victims. As the embodiment of the 'Islamic community,' the Islamic Republic of Iran was required to continue to carry out the Koranic necessity of retaliation. The Islamic Republic stood in the place of those who died without family or the orphans. Taken another way, the government itself, as well as the individual family members, had a duty to avenge the deaths of the 290 passengers of Iran Air 655. The mullahs had spoken.

April 1, 1996
Tehran, Iran

In its efforts to confront the United States, Israel and the Western powers, the Islamic Republic of Iran has always made use of foreign hit squads, operatives and fundamentalist Islamic radicals to carry out its objectives. Such notable actions as the assassination of former Iranian prime minister Shapur Bakhtiar and the bombing of the Beirut US Marine barracks are but two instances of many dozens. The World Trade Center bombing was also carried out by a group supported and financed by Iran and Iran's allies. (See Appendix A).

In the spring of 1996, in order to more effectively manage this network of international terrorists and political operatives, Iran reorganized its intelligence structure with control emanating from President Rafsanjani himself. A Supreme Council for Intelligence Affairs was organized directly under Rafsnajani's control. A close associate of Rafsanjani, but also close to the more conservative mullahs, Mahdi Chamran, was appointed to head the foreign intelligence wing of this new Iranian 'CIA' with the title Chief of External Intelligence. His second in command for international terrorism was the new head of the Office of Revolutionary Movements, Muwahidli Karamani. The function of Karamani's Office was to coordinate, recruit, fund, inspire and supply Islamic activist groups willing to take Iran's confrontation with the United States and its allies as their own cause. Further, it was this office that had authority to take action in foreign jurisdictions to carry out the policy of the Islamic Republic in covert acts, including assassinations and terrorist acts.

Mahdi Chamran and Muwahidli Karamani immediately set about to carry out their mandate. Existing ties with Hizbollah front groups were renewed.

The burgeoning Shiite fundamentalists in Bahrain (America's oldest and firmest ally in the region) were sent funds and their leaders were brought to Tehran for 'consultations.' The Mujahediin guerillas in Afghanistan were invited over the Iranian border to meet, and when mutual agreements were reached with Tehran's representatives, the Iranian Revolutionary Guards started funneling more supplies and equipment eastward. To the north, the ex-Soviet republics of Central Asia and the Caucasus region were ripe for the pan-Islamic rhetoric from Tehran and Hizbollah. All across the Islamic world, Tehran's functionaries were given the green light to encourage the most radical of groups to confront traditional governments and the West, as represented by the United States.

Iran would confront America's efforts to put economic pressure on Iran with its own form of pressure. From the opening days of the Islamic Republic and the Hostage Crisis that followed, Iran had become particularly adept at applying pressure, be it hostage taking, assassination or other forms of violence. (See Appendix A).

0830 Local (0430 GMT), April 20, 1996
Iranian Navy HQ Building, Bandar Beheshti, Iran

Captain Morteza negotiated his way through the overlapping pattern of heavy reinforced concrete panels that served as the entrance to the Navy command building. Newly built, the building and its double walls and roof of reinforced concrete were designed to prevent the wholesale destruction from American 'Smart' bombs everyone had seen in the television pictures of the American air attack on Baghdad in 1991. The graving docks that housed the *Noor* and her sister vessels down the hill were of identical style and structural design. Everything about the new naval facility on the Arabian Sea was meant for survival of a pre-emptive strike by American airpower and still allow the submarines and surface vessels that had been moved here from Bandar Abbas and further north to get to sea and retaliate against American forces at sea.

If the years of hostile opposition between Iran and the US ever turned into open warfare, Iran was determined that the huge investment in submarines, aircraft and surface ships would not be destroyed in the quick strike tactics the Americans had previously shown to their Islamic brethren in Libya and Iraq. The move south to Bandar Behesti and its broad bay on the open ocean had been necessary to prevent the possibility of the submarines from being contained by American anti-submarine warfare units in the confines of the

Persian Gulf and the chokepoint at Bandar Abbas.

Morteza crossed the spartan lobby of the headquarters and passed the trophy display that reminded everyone of the ever present danger from the 'Great Satan.' In the middle of the lobby, on a cement base, stood a blue cylinder that was labeled in English:

This is not an explosive device.
This hydrographic sensing mechanism is
the property of the United States Navy
DO NOT TAMPER WITH THIS DEVICE.

The torpedo-like device had been launched from an American submarine offshore the new Iranian naval base, and it had traveled into the Chah Bahr Bay. It had planted itself on the floor of the harbor where it would pick up acoustic intelligence information and transmit it to American ships and satellites, telling the Americans the details of comings and goings from the base by the Iranian vessels' sound patterns. The Iranians had found the espionage device and deactivated it. It was then put on display to remind everyone of the focus of their work.

As the telephone instructions that morning had said, Morteza went directly to the Fleet Commander's office. Waived by the adjutant into the open door, Morteza went in. The Commander was not alone; he sat behind his desk and two other men sat in side chairs, leaving one chair open. One of the men was in a suit and tie, an unusual sight in southern Iran, and the other wore the uniform of a Revolutionary Guards general. Morteza knew neither man.

The Commander nodded and said, "Captain, please close the door and take a seat."

Before Morteza could be seated, the Commander said, "Perhaps introductions would be in order before we sit. Captain Morteza, this is Reza Salaf Alafi, Chief of Preparations Bureau, Office of External Intelligence, and General Mohsan Reza'i of the Revolutionary Guards." Morteza shook each man's hand. "They would like to discuss something with you."

"Captain," said the civilian, Alafi, nodding his head to the naval officer. "We have a very important mission for you and the *Noor*. You come very well recommended. Combat action in the Delta. Good history of performance in your new submarine command. Fine record in both the French patrol boats and Russian submarine procurement assignments. But, we have a few questions, which may sound a bit strange at first, but, I assure you, they have a high purpose."

Morteza indicated his assent to be questioned.

"Tell me. You are one of the persons entitled to claim reparations from the American fund for families of the Bandar Abbas incident victims. Your wife, *may she be with Allah*, she was a victim, was she not?"

"That is correct," Morteza said, his brow now furrowed.

"Do you intend to apply for the reparations payments?"

Morteza thought, showing his concern at the question. "Well, no. I was not going to apply. I have already signed the form allowing my wife's family to claim it. Her parents are elderly, and they need the money. I do not need it nor want it. I would not touch the filthy cash from America. It could never repay me for my loss."

Both of the two men nodded, almost knowingly. Alafi continued, "We are glad to hear that. It really makes no difference in the assignment. But, your feelings make everything a lot simpler."

Morteza was curious now. What assignment for his submarine could have anything to do with reparations payments for his wife from the air disaster?

Now, the General spoke. "Captain, you are the son of a respected cleric, a fine teacher in Meshad I am told."

"Yes."

"Then, you are well schooled in the Holy Koran. Are you familiar with the duty to perform retribution for the slain innocent?"

"I am."

"Good. Then you should know that the Islamic Republic, at the highest levels, has directed that the edicts of Allah be carried out in regard to the murder of your wife and the other 289 innocent souls. You, Captain, are to be the agent of retribution on behalf of the families of the dead, on behalf of your nation, on behalf of Allah."

They discussed the essence of the mission. They also discussed the capabilities of the country's small submarine squadron versus the known and projected capabilities of their potential adversary in the target area. They all recognized the risks. Morteza thought of several other questions he chose not to ask.

"Is there an expected action date? How soon is this to happen?"

Again, the senior officers looked knowingly at each other. Alafi answered for the group. "We think the first day of Rabia Awal."

Morteza considered time. The proposed date would

not leave him much time to prepare for and execute an operations plan. "Why is that date significant?"

"Perhaps you have forgotten your history," Alafi said. He paused staring at the Navy captain. Morteza racked his brain without the slightest reaction to the retort. Alafi continued. "The first day of Rabia Awal in the year of the Prophet 1417 is the tragic day the Israeli invaders occupied the holy city of Jerusalem. Thus, the proposed date is the 30th anniversary of that insult. We think that is an appropriate date."

Silence filled the room as Morteza searched the eyes of the senior officers. He did his own calculations within the Islamic lunar calendar. On the Gregorian calendar used by decadent Western countries, the date was 17th of July. An appropriate date for the retribution sanctioned by the Holy Koran and reinforced by the Leader of the Revolution. He also did some more crude operational calculations.

"That is less than 3 months from now. There is not much time to prepare."

"Yes," responded the admiral, "but, can you do it?"

"Yes. We will need to move quickly."

"You have the full authority to do whatever is required."

Morteza nodded his head in agreement, stood, acknowledged the respect for the senior officers, then took his leave.

1412 Local (1012 GMT), May 4, 1996
Gaish al Mahdi Training Camp, Qom, Iran

Major Ali Hassan Mohaddessin liked what he saw. He had known that he would. The two Revoltuionary Guards sergeants he watched had been recommended to him by a man he trusted his life to, a man who had said he could entrust that life to either of these men. More importantly, that friend had assured him that either man would put their own lives in jeopardy if such was their mission. They were well-trained, devout Shiites and loyal to the Guards. What more was needed?

The two sergeants were drilling a group of Hizbollah trainees in weapons usage. A long wooden plank table was covered with a variety of small arms and crew served weapons. The trainees watched as the weapons, their ammunition and use were explained in detail. Mohaddessin waited nearby, under a pistachio tree, until the two teachers came to the olive drab tube shape in the middle of the table. When they reached the tube, he stepped forward.

"Attention!" someone shouted as the major was recognized. The rudiments of military demeanor were being drilled into the new trainees.

"As you were," Mohaddessin said. "Please continue. I want to listen," he said to the two sergeants.

The shorter sergeant proceeded to show how the blast shield was installed on the side of the tube, and how it doubled as a sight for the weapon. The other teacher then recited the parameters and capabilities of the weapon.

Mohaddessin cleared his throat and then spoke, "Tell me, Sergeant, what aircraft is this effective against?"

The sergeant curled his eyebrow slightly at the interruption, but answered. "It is a heat seeker device. It works best against high temperature sources like jet engines."

"Will it work against other aircraft, besides jets?"

"Yes, but not as effectively. Of course, many aircraft that are turbo-prop or turbine engines are nearly as hot as jets. It has been successful against an Iraqi Hind helicopter, that's a turbine-powered, rotary wing aircraft."

"Then, you've fired this in battle?"

The sergeant shook his head, "No, not this particular one. I used the Russian Strela. It is a heat seeker also, very similar."

"And you, Sergeant," Mohaddessin turned to the other man. "Have you fired one of these type weapons in battle?"

"Fired in battle? No. I set it up, and let him fire it after I trained him how," he smiled, indicating the other sergeant.

Mohaddessin also smiled. This was perfect. He spoke to both Guards, "If you could, I would like to see you in your Camp Commander's office after this session. I have something to discuss with you. Carry on."

Major Ali Hassan Mohaddessin had his team.

May 23, 1996
Washington Institute for Near East Policy
Washington DC

In a speech to the Institute, American Secretary of State Warren Christopher estimated that the amount of funding going to Hizbollah in Lebanon to be upwards of $100 million. He mentioned several other terrorist groups receiving several million dollars a year plus arms, training and 'operational guidance' from Iran.

Secretary of State Christopher also repeated the US call for its European allies to join in restrictions on trade with Iran. This call was the top priority of US diplomatic efforts throughout 1996. Christopher said that no amount of dialogue would bring about a change in Iranian actions, only firm economic pressure would do so.

State Department spokesperson Nicholas Burns later said that the Secretary of State had made these statements based upon "dramatic and additional evidence that Iran is behind a variety of terrorist groups and terrorist operations throughout the Middle East."

In a March 1997 interview with Mike Wallace of CBS's _Sixty Minutes_, President Rafsanjani was asked about this $100 million dollar figure mentioned by Secretary Christopher. Rafsanjani said that it was not nearly that high, and it was "humanitarian aid." When asked about the lists of hundreds killed by Iranian operatives, Rafsanjani said that "not <u>all</u> of those are true," and he compared those that had been killed in overseas assassinations and bombings to the 'Waco killings' by US federal agents.

2130 Local (1730 GMT), May 30, 1996
Bandar Behesti Naval Base, Iran

Captain Abdi Morteza and Revolutionary Guards Major Ali Hassan Mohaddessin were the only ones watching as the two Guards sergeants carried their gear across the gang plank from the side of the graving dock to the *Noor*. No unnecessary personnel were around to witness the ordnance canisters loaded into the submarine's rear cargo hatch. Except for two line handlers, all of Morteza's crew were below decks, preparing for sea. The arc lights of the graving dock had been switched off and only the red lights remained on, allowing Morteza to adjust his eyes to the dark and also, to lessen the possibility they would be seen by anyone outside when the big dry dock doors opened. They had already begun flooding the dock. Everything was exactly as planned. They would have the water levels equalized in 20 minutes. The doors would open to free the *Noor* at precisely 2200 local time.

The graving dock was minimally staffed tonight and even those who worked were ordered outside while the *Noor* made final preparations. *Noor's* sister ship, *Tareq*, and several surface vessels had left port at staggered intervals throughout the day. An announcement of a huge naval exercise had explained the mass deployment and possibly taken attention away from *Noor*. Hopefully, the *Tareq* putting to sea a few hours before would draw any watching American submarine away from Bandar Behesti to follow *Tareq*, leaving the door open for *Noor* to sneak out into the Arabian Sea unnoticed. The notice of live-fire torpedo exercises would complete the getaway scheme. That should get the Americans out of the way, Morteza thought.

The schedule of American satellite reconnaissance passes, Iranian intelligence had provided, showed a window of opportunity for *Noor* to depart opened at about 2200 local time and lasted between 45 and 90 minutes. It was not guaranteed that there would be no American satellites watching, but it was the best chance Morteza had.

The conning tower took a sudden tilt, causing both Morteza and Mohaddessin to hold onto the rail.

"We're afloat now. The graving dock has filled enough to lift the boat off the support blocks on the bottom," Morteza explained to the non-submariner.

The graving dock had been emptied to allow the central ballast tanks to be cleaned in preparation for the 'fuel ballast' the submarine would use to increase range for this mission. While the fuel ballast technique significantly increased the submarine's range, they would still have to refuel twice for the complete mission. Without the fuel ballast, they would have to refuel four times, thus increasing the vulnerability of the submarine and the possibilities of detection. They had also replaced all battery banks with the new, more efficiently cooled batteries developed jointly between Iran and India.

Looking over the gunwale of the conning tower, Morteza could see the decreased buoyancy with the extra fuel. The water lapped on the very edges of the deck itself, covering the entire rounded shape of the submarine's hull.

The Guards completed their loading task and went

below, the hatch closing behind them. The whir of the huge seawater pumps on the dock stopped. A lone man ran over and swung the gangplank away. The dock's doors swung inward, opening *Noor's* path to open water.

When the doors had finished opening, Morteza shouted to his line handlers, "Cast off!"

The *Noor* had been intentionally backed into the graving dock. They did not want to spend any extra time turning about — time that would allow spies in Bandar Behesti or in orbit above them to see *Noor* go to sea.

"Rudder amidships. Ahead, four turns," Captain Morteza ordered into the microphone. He did not want to waste time leaving the dock.

The *Noor* pulled forward slowly. Outside of the graving dock, Morteza could see the lights of Bandar Behesti reflected on the low-lying cloud cover. Allah had smiled on them with that, too.

Clear of the dock, Morteza ordered, "Right full rudder, course 180. Engines ahead full."

Turning to Major Mohaddessin, Morteza said, "Well, brother, we are off. Forty-six days to New York. We will be able to submerge a few miles out of the harbor. Allah be with us, no one will even know we are gone."

The Major simply nodded. He had never been down in a submarine. Morteza recognized the look. Morteza remembered having the same feelings in St. Petersburg three years earlier.

June 7, 1996
Tehran, Iran

The supreme leader of the Islamic Republic of Iran is titled the Leader of the Revolution, in honor of the position held by Imam Khomeini when his revolution brought down the Shah of Iran in 1979. This 'Leader of the Revolution' must, under the Iranian Constitution, be a Moslem holy man, a mullah or Imam. The position is senior to the President of the country, Ali Akhbar Hashemi Rafsanjani in 1996 (and after August 1997 Mohammad Khatami), and, in any matter this religious Leader deems to be important to the further-ance of Islam, the Leader of the Revolution had virtually un-limited power to act.

The current Leader of the Revolution is Ayatollah Ali Hoseini-Khamenei. (Ayatollah is an honored title given to highly respected mullahs.) Ayatollah Khamenei is not to be confused with Grand Ayatollah Khomeini, the founder of the country.

The Constitution of Iran, in addition to setting up a government structure, also outlines the framework for and devotion of the country to the cause of the Islamic Revolution started by Imam Khomeini. In rather unique provisions, the Preamble of the Constitution of Iran actually denounces the "American Conspiracy" and calls for a jihad, a holy war, for the spread of the sovereignty of Islam throughout the world. In fairness, the Constitution of Iran was written in the heady days of 1979 when the United States had no less than three full carrier battle groups off the southern coast of Iran, and Iran held the American hostages in Tehran. However, when it was amended in recent years, the anti-American provisions of the Iranian Constitution were left untouched. There is no other instance in the world where the basic constitutional laws of one nation vow continued hostility with another nation. By law, the leaders and citizens of Iran are required to confront non-Islamic nations, and specifically naming America, and take whatever action is necessary, including martyrdom, to achieve in the world "the establishment of a universal holy government and the downfall of all others."

The Iranian Constitution, in its substantive articles, goes on to require the government to achieve the "expansion and strengthening of Islamic brotherhood and public cooperation among all the Islamic people and framing the foreign policy of the country on the basis of Islamic criteria, fraternal commitment to all Muslims, and unsparing support to the freedom fighters of the world."

On June 7, 1996, Leader of the Revolution Ali Khamenei during a broadcast sermon in Tehran spelled out an Iranian plan of action for the spread of radical fundamentalist Islam. He vowed Iranian support for an organization called Hizbollah International to allow those operatives "taking action in the name of Islam" to reach "all continents and countries." He called on Iran to finance and otherwise support the operations of Hizbollah International and its activities. Hizbollah is the name used to reference the faction of Shiite Moslem leaders which Khamenei leads. Literally, Hizbollah means the party or faction of God. This was the same Hizbollah that had been the source of innumerable acts of terror throughout the Middle East and the world in opposing the Western powers and Israel, including the bombing of the Marine barracks in Beirut. But now, Iran would openly sponsor the creation of the Hizbollah in non-fundamentalist Islamic countries such as the Arab Gulf States, particularly Saudi Arabia. The Saudi Arabian Hizbollah front group, Hizbollah of the Hejaz, was already one of the most outspoken and vehemently anti-American, lambasting the "American invasion and occupation of Saudi Arabia," their description of America's defense of Saudi Arabia and Kuwait during the Gulf War.

With the restructuring of the Iranian Supreme Council for Intelligence Affairs to focus resources on foreign insurgency operations, this statement by Ayatollah Khamenei was the public announcement of the linkage of Hizbollah International's cells with Iranian foreign policy. It put Iran in the position of having to prove itself and its commitment to this new initiative for international confrontation.

0830 EDT (1230 GMT), June 12, 1996
National Maritime Intelligence Center, Suitland, MD

Captain Judy Weston sipped her coffee as the room filled. She sat in her summer white uniform at the front of the room by the lectern. The gold surface warfare officer insignia and two rows of ribbons on the uniform proudly showed that this female officer's career had been in the operational Navy, not just staff. A trim and attractive woman in her early forties, Captain Weston had a stern gaze, but a quick smile. She was well assigned as Deputy Director at Suitland. The projection screen next to her already displayed the title screen for "Weekly Current Threat and World Maritime Briefing."

Every Wednesday, the senior analysts and department heads of this nerve center for Naval Intelligence met to discuss, analyze, and generally 'bat around' the information garnered from various sources over the past week. The US Navy's intelligence operation had learned the lesson of other agencies, that bits and pieces of intelligence might have little or no meaning in their separate form, but might blossom into full-fledged clarity when viewed by a broad cross section of knowledgeable people in an open forum, a 'fusion cell.' The best way to develop this broad picture was in 'brain storming' sessions like this. The process had proved so effective that it had even served to break down some of the compartmentalization of information the Cold War had fostered. Even the National Reconnaissance Office's (NRO) super-secret satellite imagery and the National Security Agency's (NSA) hush-hush communications intercepts were more openly reviewed than ever before.

There were still exceptions to this openness though. CIA would still not reveal information to other agencies if the information itself might reveal a covert source. NSA would not clarify the communications channels they used for their intercepts, even if it was needed to fully understand the intelligence. And, Judy Weston knew full well that her own fellow officers in the Navy regularly concealed information that had to do with submarine operations, especially for the 'boomers.'

There were some stragglers still being seated when Captain Weston took the podium and signaled the petty officer at the computer next to her to dim the lights and start. She had sent memoranda asking everyone to be seated at 0830 sharp, and she was going to make her point.

"Ladies and gentlemen, we're ready to start." As she spoke, the petty officer clicked the image of a map of the Middle East on the screen. "The past week and a half have shown a marked increase in the traditional level and complexity of naval exercise operations by the Iranian Navy and supporting units. We are going to start off today with that, to be followed with our usual priority list and our old business discussions and pet projects. Lieutenant Commander Winchell has prepared an overview for us, and, as always, jump in if you have something to add to the picture."

Dave Winchell, with a tendency toward paunchiness, his premature baldness and rumpled uniform, contrasted distinctly from Captain Weston in almost every aspect. But, while everyone knew Weston was here in Suitland only as a way station to higher things, it was equally clear that Winchell had found his place in life. He loved intelligence work, pouring over reports, collecting stray facts, digging in other agency's reports for tidbits of information, whatever it took to come up with a good report. He was not an excellent spokesman, but he made up in content what he lacked in charisma.

A computer generated map of the Arabian Sea area flashed onto the screen. Winchell used a small laser pointer to indicate a location and said, "The first indication of the large scale Iranian exercise came with the filing, by the Iranian naval attaché in London, of a Notice to Mariners indicating an exercise would commence at 0001 GMT in the area indicated. At 1000 GMT, several surface craft sortied from both Bandar Abbas and Bandar Behesti naval complexes. In the early evening hours, several more surface combatants, including the new Chinese frigate and at least one submarine, the Kilo-class *Tareq*, sortied south from Bandar Behesti."

An aerial photograph of the Iranian submarine flashed on the screen.

"Excuse me," came an interruption from Dwight McDermott, the CIA liaison officer at Suitland.

"Yes, Dwight."

"We have word that two Kilos are gone from Behesti."

"Confirmed?" asked Winchell.

McDermott shook his head, "No, not confirmed, but very solid."

Everyone in the room knew the unspoken part of McDermott's statement. The CIA had a covert operative in Bandar Behesti, and they were not willing to discuss details.

"OK," Winchell said as he made a note on his papers.

"Two subs in the exercise."

He continued, "The Notice to Mariners indicated torpedo and missile exercises, therefore we were limited on use of our sub assets to surveil. However, air and satellite assets indicated the exercise was fairly routine, except that is for the attention Iran called to it. A bit cautious for them. As far as we can tell, there was no new capabilities in evidence. No new equipment. Just more of them showing off their intention and ability to interdict shipping into and out of the Gulf. They used two Iranian flag merchantmen as guinea pigs, a supertanker, *Haroot Farsi*, and a freighter, *Marat*. Both left port just in time to pass through the exercise area, ignoring the Notice to Mariners — obviously involved. But, all in all, not much new here. Most ships were back in port by last Friday. Anybody got anything to add to this."

"Yeah, a question, is that the same *Marat* the Iranians used to ferry the arms and Revolutionary Guards cadre to Bosnia? Sounds like the same. Any connection?" an analyst from 'Threats' asked.

There was a short silence until the head of the Shipping Registry section spoke up, "I don't have anything on the Bosnian connection, but we do show a *Marat* as logging in to El-Suwais harbormaster for passage through Suez yesterday. Bound for Bengazi, so the declared manifest stated."

Winchell started to speak but deferred to his boss, Captain Weston. She said, "Well, that's what these sessions are all about. If we have a merchantman with possible Revolutionary Guards connections on the move towards Libya and points unknown, we better get it on the Watch List. Dave, let's get a tasking message out; NRO, Sixth Fleet and NSA, at the minimum. Threats?" She caught the eye of the analyst who had spoken up about *Marat*. "You pull whatever you can find on this, past activity, collateral info, everything. Anybody have anything else on the Iranians, this morning?"

She waited without answer. "OK, Dave, let's move on. What's next?"

Lieutenant Commander Winchell signaled the petty officer at the computer to go on. A graphic showing the Far East came on the screen, and Winchell turned the page on his notebook to continue.

1045 EDT (1445 GMT), June 20, 1996
Southampton, Long Island, New York

Walid Mashadi watched as the real estate agent, Mrs.
Henry, smiled her vacuous smile and prattled on about the
house. He had given her enough hints already that the house
would be fine, but she seemed to be unable to take 'yes' for
an answer. Apparently she was amazed that anyone wanted
to rent this small and modestly furnished, by 'Hamptons'
standards, house for a full month. Walid knew from checking
around that vacation houses such as this on the 'wrong' side
of Southampton were primarily rented by the week or even,
for weekends.

As the agent mentioned the view of the back bay for
the second time, Walid caught a glance of his watch. It was
getting late. He had planned on finishing business on Long
Island and be on his way to New Jersey by now. He had an
appointment with the yacht broker in Atlantic City mid-
afternoon, which meant he had to traverse the length of
metropolitan New York to get there.

"This will be just fine," Mashadi said. "It is just a
place for our company's out of town guests to get away for a
few days while they are in New York."

"As I said, I do have quite a few houses that are much
more comfortable, you know, for your company's guests...."

"No, this will be fine." Mashadi knew that renting a

big, well furnished house would require more references and deposit than this house would.   He wanted as little trouble and traceability as possible.   After all, the house would probably not even be used in this operation, it was just a front in case they needed an excuse for being in the Long Island area.

"Fine, Mr. Dorleac, whatever you say," said Mrs. Henry addressing Mashadi by the name shown on the French business card he had presented her. She opened her briefcase on the kitchen counter and started to do the paperwork on the rental, June 25th through July 25th.

1230 Local (0830 GMT), June 21, 1996
State Dining Room, Marmar Palace, Tehran, Iran

Ayatollah Ahmad Jannati watched as people ended
their conversations and took their seats at the huge conference tables. He sipped spring water as the delegates moved
about trying to match chairs and place cards with their home
countries and organizations.

The placards read like a geography lesson of the
Middle East with a smattering of Western countries: Kuwait,
Saudi Arabia, Jordan, Egypt, Azerbaijan, Afghanistan,
Pakistan, Bahrain, Bosnia, Lebanon, Senegal, Iraqi Kurdistan
and several others. There were cards listing Germany, United
States, Canada, France and Britain, but Jannati knew that these
really denoted the Iranian activist who acted as the Hizbollah
front man for these countries.

Besides the nation states listed on the place cards, the
organizations read like a counterterrorist's nightmare:
Hammas, both factions of the Popular Front for the Liberation
of Palestine (PFLP), the Turkish Refah faction, the Islamic
Change Movement and a half dozen others. Jannati was
particularly pleased to see that Hammas, Islamic Change and
Islamic Jihad had accepted Tehran's invitation to participate
in this summit of Islamic revolutionary movements, because
they were Sunni, not Shi'i like Iran's ruling faction and most
of the others present here. Having the Sunni groups participate
here gave true legitimacy to Iran's role as leader of the Islamic

world, at least to Ayatollah Jannati's mind.

Many who came into the room came to the head table and gave their respects to Jannati who sat in the traditional garb of a mullah, and to Mahdi Chamran, who walked among them. As Iran's Chief of External Intelligence, Chamran was ostensibly the manager of this event. However, everyone attending, including Chamran, recognized that Ayatollah Jannati's senior position in Iran's theocracy made him the ultimate authority when it came to Hizbollah International and Iran's other foreign operations.

Jannati had already met many of the most important fundamentalist leaders as they trickled into Tehran over the past week and many were old acquaintances. They had all come to answer Iran's offer to fund their operations, and give the close cooperation and support that only a national government could give, the core concept of the 'state sponsored terrorism' that the Americans were always complaining about. In return, the two dozen groups represented would be asked to agree to unify their financial systems, standardize their training, recruiting and operations, and accept Iranian leadership on the international level.

The seating at the opening session of the conference was as carefully planned as the location in one of the most lavishly decorated of the three main royal palaces left over from the Shah's regime. To Jannati's immediate right, the two representatives of Hammas, Mustafa al-Liddawi and Imad Al-Alami, were given a position suitable to display the two Sunni leaders' presence to all in attendance. To Jannati's left beyond Chamran's seat was Egypt Jihad's Ahmad Salah and one of Hizbollah's most successful terrorists, Lebanon's Imad Mughaniyah. Ahmad Jibril from the PFLP and Turkey's Obdallah Ocalan headed the two side tables.

Jannati noticed that the Iranian senior intelligence officials, Muwahidli Karmani, Reza Salaf Alafi and Mohammed Gerhazi were spread out in the room at regular intervals. Karamani, the head of the Office of Revolutionary Movements, who had organized this summit, was talking to Ramadan Shallah from the Palestinian Jihad and a new man Jannati did not recognize who sat behind the placard of Islamic Change of the Hejaz. The Ayatollah noted with some interest that the most popular person in the room seemed to be Bakir Zuldikar, the financial chief of Iran's External Intelligence Office. These terrorists knew who paid the bills.

Chamran came to stand next to Jannati. He looked to Jannati and received a nod that indicated they should get started. Chamran took a fountain pen from the table and struck an empty glass on the table, the resounding chime ringing out over the murmur of the room. In the silence that followed, Chamran called out in Arabic, the common language at the summit, "Please take your seats, we are ready to begin."

When everyone had been seated and without introduction from Chamran, Ayatollah Jannati stood and slowly made eye contact with those at the tables. Then, in the deep baritone voice that had become so familiar to millions from his Friday noon sermons on radio and television from Tehran, Jannati began in Arabic, *"Bismallah al-rahman, al-rahiim.* Brethren! You, the vanguard of the Word of Allah in the world are welcome. You, the vanguard of the Revolution, are welcome."

Jannati paused a moment, then continued, motioning around the resplendent dining room as he spoke, "It is fitting that this, the first operational meeting of Hizbollah International should be held in this room — this room which has already been so important to the history of the world and played such a critical role in the history of the past half century of every country represented in this room."

Jannati again paused to let his bit of trivia have effect, "In this very room, forty three years ago, the then-leaders of the world divided up the planet. They decided who would have what government, who would be subjugated by whom, who would be forced to believe what. They decided that my country," he touched his chest, "would be ruled by the Shah. They promised that your countries," he pointed to both the Azerbaijani and the Kazaki, "would remain Communist. The world leaders assembled in this room decided that the Arab world would remain divided and secular."

The Ayatollah now slapped his palm on the table in front of him. "At this very table, in 1943, Winston Churchill, Josef Stalin and Franklin Roosevelt, at their infamous Tehran conference, decided the fate of the world. They decided our fate," he spread his arms to include everyone in the room, "without interest in the true Word of God, without asking the wishes of the People, without regard for anything but the national interests of the Great Powers; Russia, Britain and America.

"Today, you brethren are the leaders of the world — the Islamic world. And, you are meeting here at this table today to decide your own fate. To decide the fate of your own people. To decide the course of future history. And, to decide the fate of the so called 'Great Powers,' the 'Great Satan.'"

Ayatollah Ahmad Jannati continued on, explaining the need for coordinated action to remove the stigma of American intervention from Saudi Arabia, to remove the scourge of Western-leaning royalists from the Gulf States and to create a climate where Islam took its rightful, pre-eminent position in the center of world society.

Jannati droned on about the past successes of the various factions represented in the room. He listed the few governments that had become fundamentalist. He described the terrorist actions and insurrections that radical Islamic activists had brought about.

Jannati concluded his speech with a summation of the reasons for the creation of Hizbollah International. "We, in Iran, have been fortunate that through the enlightened leadership of Imam Khomeini, the Islamic Republic was born and has allowed us to form a society that allows the faithful to bask in the light of Allah. We seek to let you, the brethren who are the vanguard of Islam, achieve that same blessing in your own nations.

"It has been made clear to us, and to the world, that the Western powers, and particularly the United States, see our movement, see Islam, as a danger to their hegemony of the world. They have sought to confront and attack Islam and the aspiration of the Islamic people at every turn of the road.

"Now, with the international organization you brethren set up, with the decision you make at this table, the Islamic Revolution will be able to confront and successfully oppose those who would keep your people enslaved.

"The Islamic Republic of Iran pledges to you brethren its support, its wealth, its sons' blood. We shall take this battle to the seat of the 'Great Satan,' to the seat of the royalist states, to the seat of the secular powers who deny God's will. I wish you well, my brethren, you have a mighty task ahead."

The meeting of the Hizbollah leaders lasted four days.

In the end, the leaders approved an agenda that was precisely as outlined by Jannati. They would each commit to participation in a global anti-US Jihad; a confrontation with American interests wherever possible. Not only was the United States an actual, admitted enemy of the Hizbollah movement, but its power, wealth and heavy-handed record in the Third World, made it a delightful scapegoat for every woe that befell anyone. The lack of a significant Islamic community in the United States and its strong ties to Israel, as well as the House of Saud in Arabia, the House of Sabah in Kuwait and a dozen other anti-fundamentalist regimes made the United States a perfect focus for Hizbollah's attacks.

To carry out the Jihad, the summit approved the formation of an executive committee directly under Mahdi Chamran. The committee would consist of Usama bin Ladin, Ahmad Salah and Imad Mughaniyah. Promises were made that the Hejazi (Suadi), Egyptian and Lebanese members of Hizbollah International, the most active, experienced and capable, would take immediate steps to attack American interests. Iran, as the sponsor and ideological heart of Hizbollah, also promised to show its resolve by making a decisive blow against America.

It was recognized that Iran was in a different situation from the terrorist movements. Iran had to make sure its actions were not so overt as to bring about war with the United States. However, Iran's vast resources and proven willingness to take such overt acts in and against foreign nations left it a lot of leeway to show its commitment to Hizbollah.

At the end of the Tehran terrorist summit, the executive committee and several other key individuals agreed to meet again in Tehran on July 20th and discuss 'events' that would occur in the interim and future plans.

One very interesting aspect of the June 1996 summit of Islamic terrorist organizations was their willingness to let their purpose be known. The meeting was held in the wake of the world anti-terrorism conference held earlier that year at Sharm al Sheik, Egypt, and closely coincided with the superpowers' own G-7 summit in France at which terrorism was discussed. It was almost as if Iran and Hizbollah International were throwing down a gauntlet to the United States and its allies.

At a meeting between President Mubarak of Egypt and President Chirac of France in early July, the Egyptian president mentioned the Tehran summit to Chirac and expressed his concern at the escalation it signified. He blamed Hizbollah International for much of the fundamentalist violence Egypt was experiencing.

Also, in early July, Usama bin Ladin, the senior Saudi Arabian at the Tehran summit explained his view of the situation, "This is the beginning of a war between Muslims and the United States. This is not a declaration of war. It is a description of the actual situation. This does not mean declaring war against the West and Western people — but, against the American regime which is against every Muslim."

As a member of the executive committee of Hizbollah International, Usama bin Ladin's talk of 'war' with America had great significance. It was to have even greater significance when bin Ladin's comrades issued a threat by facsimile machine on the eve of the TWA 800 disaster.

2155 Local (1855 GMT), June 25, 1996
Dhahran, Saudi Arabia

The eight story building was one of many built to house military personnel at the sprawling King Abdul Aziz Air Base near Dhahran. The building's residents were technicians, military staff members and support personnel. They were primarily Americans.

Shortly before ten o'clock on this Tuesday evening, a large tank truck pulled to the curb near the building. The truck was out of place. This was not an industrial area. There was no need for fuel delivery or any other purpose for this truck in the residential complex.

Two Security Police approached the truck. They saw two occupants run from the truck to a waiting car. Another car nearby sped off into the night. Suspecting the worst, the Security Police turned to run and warn the residents of the Khobar Towers building. They were not in time.

At 2155, the contents of the tank truck exploded. The entire facing wall of the building disappeared. Every window for blocks around blew inwards, slashing residents with flying glass.

Over four hundred American, Saudi and allied service personnel were injured. Nineteen Americans were dead. The blast was so powerful that it left a hole in the Saudi soil 35 feet deep and 85 feet across.

Three terrorist groups claimed responsibility for the Khobar bomb. One was a Saudi group which supported their jailed leader, Sheikh Udah, and called for removal of American troops from 'holy' Saudi soil. It was believed that this claim was mere exploitation of the real terrorists' work.

Two Hizbollah groups, Hizbollah Al Khalij (Gulf) and Hizbollah of the Hejaz (Eastern Saudi Arabia), sent messages claiming responsibility on behalf of Hizbollah International. These groups demanded that US troops leave Saudi Arabia or more violence would take place.

Suspecting that Hizbollah was indeed the perpetrator of the blast, Saudi officials rounded up and interrogated every Hizbollah member or sympathizer they could find. For many months, a huge investigation involving Saudi police, the FBI and several intelligence agencies tried to piece together the case against Hizbollah.

Finally, in March 1997, Canadian authorities arrested a Saudi national, Hani Abdel Rahim Hussein Sayegh. He had been living in Canada since August 16, 1996, having entered Canada from the United States.

Sayegh claimed to have been in Syria on June 25th, the day of the bombing, but indications were that he had been the driver of the second car at the bomb scene. He did admit to being an associate of the Saudi Hizbollah members arrested by the Saudis. He admitted to opposing the Saudi family's control of his homeland, and that he had received training in Iran, but he denied he was a member of Hizbollah, or that he had any connection to the Iranian government.

Intelligence officials in Canada, the United States and Saudi Arabia had a different opinion about the man. Sayegh, they said, was a recruiter and operative of Iranian intelligence, working out of Iran's embassy in Syria. Sayegh would recruit

Saudi nationals, members of the Shiite sect, when they made pilgrimages to Shiite holy shrines. Then, he would arrange either religious training and indoctrination for them in Iran, or sometimes guerilla training in Lebanon's Beka'a Valley at camps run by Hizbollah with Iranian support.

Sayegh was the driver of a car near the Khobar barracks. He signaled the truck drivers with flashing headlights. They left the tank truck and fled. Sayegh and another operative, Ahmad Ibrahim Ahmed Mughassil, fled from Saudi Arabia to Syria immediately after the bombing. Sayegh continued on, eventually passing through Boston and winding up in Canada, claiming refugee status.

Sayegh's co-conspirator, Mughassil, was the leader of the bombing raid. Mughassil went from Syria to Iran after the bombing. There are widely published reports, which Iran officially denies, that Mughassil is a guest of the Iranian government and living at the Hizbollah training facility in the holy city of Qom.

Sayegh, at press time for this book, was still awaiting final action by the United States Justice Department, who had extradited him from Canada. The Saudi Arabian government, after much bickering with their US allies, had declared the Khobar bombing an internal matter, leaving Sayegh to the Americans. The Justice Department had dropped charges in September, 1997. There are rumors that Sayegh's long internment without prosecution in the hands of FBI and CIA handlers is indicative of his cooperation with US authoriites, or at least their attempt to turn him.

1630 EDT (2030 GMT), June 25, 1996
Atlantic City, New Jersey

The wire transfer from Switzerland had cleared into the yacht broker's account without a hitch. Walid Mashadi had wasted no time in coming down from New York to take title to the boat. The broker, a thin mustachioed man in white clothes and skipper's cap, met him at the dock. They headed down the far pier where the brokerage boats were moored.

The broker patted a plastic logbook and portfolio, which he handed to Mashadi, "Everything is in order. Title is registered in the name of your boss' company, Suli...Sulf...just can't get those French names down."

"Sulifont SKG?"

"Yeh, that's it. The boat had a full survey by a bonded surveyor. You should have no trouble insuring her. Like I said, if you want I can put you in touch with some good insurance companies."

Mashadi shook his head, "That won't be necessary."

"Whatever you say. She's fueled, tuned up, polished and ready for her new master." With this the yacht broker rounded the corner and gave an overly expansive arm gesture as if he was introducing Mashadi to his new boat for the first time.

He had already seen the boat before, which made the broker's gesture all the more trite. Mashadi had picked carefully — he had known the parameters of what he wanted.

When he heard the news that this broker had an offshore racing boat bought at a DEA auction, he came to check it out. It had been perfect. A custom made, twin engine cruiser, it could easily make fifty to sixty miles an hour in calm seas. It had huge fuel tanks for long range, apparently a necessity for the owners who had forfeited it to the federal drug agents. Even the color had been perfect — shiny, pitch black with blue pinstriping.

"You want me to go with you on a shakedown cruise?" the broker asked.

"No. I am quite familiar with this type of boat. I had one quite like it in Marseilles." Mashadi lied. "It will be OK if I keep it docked here for a couple of weeks? I cannot take her home to Virginia until about mid July."

"No problem. Glad to do whatever we can for a cash customer."

0915 EDT (1315 GMT), June 26, 1996
National Maritime Intelligence Center, Suitland, MD

The briefing had gotten another late start. Everyone, Captain Weston included, had been watching the Pentagon briefing about the Khobar Barracks bombing. After that, Judy Weston had started the briefing off with a reading of the first classified report of the bombing sent out by the intelligence staff of the US Central Command, the joint command with responsibility for the Saudi operations.

Weston followed up with the routine question of whether anyone on the naval intelligence staff had anything of any import on the bombing. The Khobar incident was outside of their area of responsibility, so nobody had anything additional.

Dave Winchell went through the usual discussion of the main intelligence topics, briefing them and waiting while they were discussed. Finally, he got to the last item, follow up discussion of the previous sessions' 'Watch List.'

"OK, let's turn to the Watch List," Winchell said. "We have two active items. The North Korean anti-ship missile shipment and the Iranian freighter, *Marat*. What do we have on the Koreans?"

A young lieutenant spoke up, "They transited the Malacca Straits Monday. Nothing out of the ordinary. We have nothing else."

"No one has any better idea on the customer for the

missiles? Pakistan? India? Iran?"

Nobody answered.

"OK, then it stays on watch. Next, the Iranian frieghter *Marat*. We had a full Watch on it. What's happening?"

"Sigonella had a P-3 sighting on it, 34-10 North 17-04 East. Tracking due west," came an answer.

Winchell turned to the petty officer on the computer and said, "Med map."

In a few seconds, a map of the Mediterranean Sea appeared on the projection screen. Winchell squinted at the tiny longitude and latitude marks then brought his laser pointer to bear on the map, southeast of the island of Malta.

It was Judy Weston who spoke next, "If *Marat* was supposedly bound for Benghazi as reported when she transited Suez, she's a bit lost. Wouldn't you say?"

"Yup," Winchell answered.

The Threats analyst chimed in, "And if *Marat* is working for the Revolutionary Guards again, she's not on track to head for Bosnia like last time."

"Well, assuming the worst, that *Marat* is a Guards asset and up to no good," Weston said, "where could she be heading out there. Who's she going to help?"

Winchell answered with his pointer on the map. "Best guess, Algeria. Algerian fundamentalists."

Weston turned in her chair to face Dwight McDermott, "The Algerian fundamentalists are a top priority for Langley, aren't they?"

McDermott answered, "Sure are. We'll put this into the hopper, and see what we can find out." He stopped, but continued again. "Oh, this *Marat*, she's the one we picked up with the Iranian naval exercise early this month, isn't she. Well, on that topic, you should know that of the two Kilo subs that left port, only one, the *Tareq*, has come in."

"But that's almost a month now," Winchell surmised. "Pretty unusual."

Commander Faulkner, the submarine intelligence chief now spoke, "Yeah, it is unusual for the Iranians. But the Soviets, err, the Russians, regularly deploy Kilos for two or three months."

"But, where does an Iranian sub go for a month away from port?"

No one answered.

"Well, if nobody has anything else on her, this sub better join her Iranian comrade *Marat* on the Watch List. What's her name?"

"*Noor*," Winchell answered at the same time as Faulkner.

"OK, put the *Noor* on the Watch List."

0145 GMT, June 30, 1996
Near the Equator, South Atlantic

Allah could not have been kinder to us, thought Captain Morteza as he peered through the periscope.

As expected, the summer seas in the equatorial latitudes had brought calm, almost placid ocean conditions. He could not see the stars, but the lights of the *Haroot Farsi* were crystal clear across an almost glasslike expanse of ocean.

It was, of course, not his first view of the huge supertanker through the periscope. He had followed the *Haroot Farsi* the entire trip from the Arabian Sea. The cruising speed of the huge tanker was much the same as that of the submarine while snorkeling. Following several hundred to a thousand meters in the wake of the supertanker had not only masked their passage from any listening submariner's sonar system, it also assured them that they were reasonably safe from someone noticing the wake they made at their snorkeling depth or seeing their snorkel itself from satellites or passing ships.

The schedule of transit for the supertanker from the ocean loading terminal at Khark Island in the Persian Gulf to Rotterdam had been carefully handled by the Iranian authorities. The crew of *Haroot Farsi* had been augmented by Revolutionary Guards. Morteza suspected that any regular able seaman who had actually been allowed to crew the tanker were right now sequestered below decks, to avoid explanations of this night's events. Like everything else about this mission, every effort was made to limit the number of people who knew about the *Noor* and its goal.

Morteza maneuvered the *Noor* to within 500 meters by periscope. *Haroot Farsi* was clearly at dead stop. Just as planned and in response to Morteza's short coded signal. The equipment the Russians had to accomplish refueling while underway was not in the cards for the Iranians this mission. It would be too obvious. However, what they had planned would probably work just fine. It had to, they had not even wanted to show their hands enough to test the plan out or train on it.

At 400 meters out, Morteza ordered over the submarine's P.A. system, "All hands stand by for refueling detail." They had trained at this, many times, but without surfacing, everyone had been drilled as to his duties.

"All stop. Blow ballast one, two, five, and six. Surface," Morteza cautiously ordered. The center ballast tanks had been cross connected to fuel pumps as suggested by the old Russian years ago. They would be refilling the center ballast tanks along with the main fuel tanks shortly.

Captain Morteza climbed the ladder to the conning tower and emerged in to the night air. It was not cold, but not warm either — much like the Gulf.

He did not need his binoculars to see that all was ready on the *Haroot Farsi*, now only a few hundred meters away. A string of inflatable rubber bumpers would cushion the submarine from the side of the tanker, riding low in the water with its full load of crude oil for the Europeans to refine. Two big spotlights illuminated the side of the tanker. They would stay on only while absolutely needed, always cognizant of the prying eyes in the heavens above them. A large black hose connected to the tanker's diesel fuel storage tanks already hung partially down the side. A metal gantry was poised to allow the replenishment of foodstuffs on the submarine.

Below him Morteza saw his men scurrying to their stations on the wet deck. He grabbed the microphone to the helm and prepared to bring the *Noor* alongside the *Haroot Farsi*. With any luck, he would be done and on his way, refueled and restocked, in less than twenty minutes.

July 1, 1996
Tehran, Iran

Press release from the Islamic Republic New Agency (IRNA)

AIRBUS-ANNIVERSARY-CONDEMNATION INTERNATIONAL CIRCLES URGED TO CONDEMN U.S. DOWNING OF AIRBUS IN 1988

BANDAR LENGEH, HORMUZGAN PROVINCE, JULY 1, IRNA — ON THE EVE OF THE ANNIVERSARY OF US DOWNING OF AN IRANIAN PASSENGER PLANE OVER THE PERSIAN GULF, THE BEREAVED FAMILIES OF THE VICTIMS OF THE CRIME CALLED ON INTERNATIONAL CIRCLES TO CONDEMN SUCH A SAVAGE ACT.

"THE ATTACK BY THE US NAVAL FORCES ABOARD THE FRIGATE USS VINCENNES ON A PASSENGER PLANE OVER THE PERSIAN GULF BETRAY THE FALSITY OF THE HUMANITARIAN CLAIMS RAISED BY US STATESMEN," THEY SAID IN A STATEMENT ISSUED HERE MONDAY.

THE IRAN AIR AIRBUS EN-ROUTE TO DUBAI WAS SHOT AND BLOWN UP INTO PIECES IN MIDAIR BY MISSILES FIRED FROM THE US NAVY SHORTLY AFTER TAKE-OFF FROM BANDAR ABBAS ON JULY 3, 1988. ALL 290 PASSENGERS AND CREW ABOARD THE PLANE WERE MARTYRED.

SOME 52 OF THE VICTIMS WERE FROM THIS SOUTHERN IRANIAN PORT CITY.

The official news organ of the Iranian government wanted to make sure that everyone remembered the Iran Air disaster. This official condemnation also made clear that the monetary compensation paid by the US Government had not cleared the atrocity from the Iranian psyche, nor absolved the command for retribution of the Holy Koran.

0815 EDT (1215 GMT), July 16, 1996
National Maritime Intelligence Center, Suitland, MD

"This couldn't have happened when the Admiral was in town, huh?" Judy Weston said. Nobody believed her show of concern. They all knew she enjoyed taking the point, relished it, in fact. The Director's mid-summer vacation was her time to really take charge. Today was her show.

Commander Joe Faulkner shrugged. "Not much choice. METOC put out a 'possible' on it when it passed the Bermuda SOSUS array on the eleventh. Then, right on time for a diesel boat, Norfolk reported it on the Shelf last night."

Dave Winchell spoke up, "But, it is still a 'possible.' And, a damn unlikely 'possible' at that." He drummed his fingers on the Admiral's conference table, where the four of them sat; Winchell, Faulkner, Captain Weston and Dwight McDermott.

"What on earth makes you think it is the Iranian?" McDermott asked.

"Simple head counting, and process of elimination." Faulkner answered. "That's my main job, if you'll remember — counting subs."

Faulkner stood up and moved to the world map. "We've got some dozen countries with operational Kilos or Foxtrots, that's what SOSUS thinks they caught a whiff of. But, we can eliminate half of those by simple geography, those in the Pacific, North Korea, China.…" He thumped the map several times. "Most of the rest are out of service — Libya, Egypt. You said Algeria is accounted for. Russia doesn't deploy their diesels anymore, and from what we can tell, all are accounted for in the Northern Fleet and nothing has been heard at Gibraltar or Dardanelles listening points. Castro's subs aren't even functional as tourist attractions anymore, they're so decrepit. All in all, I count one operational Kilo in any kind of range which is owned by any country that would want to come nosing around the East Coast."

"But, that's the key word — range. The Kilo is not a strategic boat. It's not nuke. It's a diesel, for christsake. What 7,000 miles range, max?" Winchell said.

"But, Iran is surely capable of having one of its ships give a thirsty pup a drink. They're an oil state — a crazy, pestilent, foolhardy, militant, oil state. They are precisely the one's who would try something funny with a boat. God knows what they'd try. Look at Khobar." Everyone nodded.

Weston asked, "So, what are you suggesting?"

Faulkner walked back to the table, "Intelligence wise — we ask for a tasking from NRO. A diesel boat snorkels. It's vulnerable to satellites, if we're looking for it. And, we have some idea of where it is. Between the Bermuda and Seaboard SOSUS hits, it looks like a track straight toward the Chesapeake, or Washington, DC for christsake. We'll ask Mr. McDermott here to see if his people at Langley can get some more on the out-of-port Kilo in Bandar Behesti. Maybe they can, maybe they can't. Then, operationally, we back up SOSUS' 'possible' with our best estimate, the Iranian *Noor*, we don't go overboard, but we recommend CINCLANT try to task some anti-submarine assets, hopefully some attack boats and ASW birds. It is nothing we didn't do every once and a while when we were staring down the Russkies in the

Cold War."

"OK, so what classifications do we put on this?" Weston asked.

Faulkner answered immediately, "Not much choice, between the SOSUS stuff and the covert from Langley. . ."

Faulkner was interrupted by McDermott. "Yeah, I was gonna remind you of that."

Faulkner continued, "We really have to make this Top Secret. It goes with the territory."

Weston said, "Yeah, so if we end up looking like fools by predicting the Iranians are coming, only the really important people will know about it. Huh?"

Faulkner responded, "I don't know. On this one, I think I'd be more comfortable looking foolish than if I turn out to be correct."

0305 EDT (0705 GMT), July 17, 1996
40°11' N 72°37' W, South-Southeast of Long Island, NY

"We have crossed the 50 meter contour, Captain," announced the navigator from his plotting board. They had run a continuous navigational trace ever since the hard right turn they had made six hours before, in conjunction with the switch from diesel to electric for two hours thereafter. If they had been tracked by the American underwater sensing devices, they hoped the quick turn from a noisy westerly track to a quiet northwesterly track had broken the trail. When running on full electric, the Russian Kilo was one of the quietest submarines in the world, quieter than most nuclear submarines. They would see.

"Thank you. Slow to five turns. Make your depth twenty-five meters. Standby to go to periscope depth."

"Slow to five turns, depth two five," repeated the helmsman.

Major Mohaddessin entered the control room and stood next to the navigator at the chart table. "How are we doing?" he asked.

"Everything is as planned," Morteza answered. Then, turning to the navigator, he asked, "Does inertial still match GPS data."

The navigator read the digital readout on the satellite positioning system and quickly compared it to his marks on the chart. The German GPS system had been purchased ostensibly as an oilfield surveying tool.

"Yes, Captain. Exactly." The navigator sounded pleased with himself.

"Are your men prepared?" Morteza asked Mohaddessin.

"They have been prepared for days," Mohaddessin laughed.

After a minute of silence, the navigator announced, "Two minutes to the rendezvous point."

"Sonar, anything?" Morteza asked.

"Negative, nothing close, Captain. Small craft at great distance, 320 to 010, very faint. Commercial shipping at 270 and 095, great distance."

"Periscope depth," Morteza ordered.

"Periscope depth, aye," the helmsman responded.

Morteza waited for the proper report, "Periscope depth, Captain."

"Up periscope," Morteza ordered.

Captain Abdi Morteza rotated completely around several times as he peered through the eyepiece of the periscope, quickly scanning the entire horizon for nearby ships the sonarman might have missed. There were no surface ships close by their position. On the far northern horizon, he could see the halo of light from the Long Island coastline. There was nothing nearby though.

Captain Morteza did one more careful sweep of the horizon. He checked his watch.

"Down periscope," the Captain commanded, not wanting any more exposure on the surface than absolutely necessary.

The navigator plotted the latest GPS numbers on his nautical chart. Captain Morteza stepped over and watched the pencil marking mix with many other critical pieces of information on the chart. Beyond the nautical information on the standard coastal chart were several red lines that represented the prescribed airways routings into and out of the New York City area. A green circle marked his first objective - a rendezvous point about 50 kilometers from the coast. A blue circle marked his second objective, for the coming night — a rendezvous point was 75 kilometers out and over an underwater canyon with just over 100 meters to the bottom. Morteza picked off the heading change needed to move the vessel into the green circle.

"Come right to heading three one nine," Morteza commanded and listened for the response from the helmsman to confirm the order. He also checked his wristwatch as well as the ship's chronometer to verify the time. He ran his right index finger down the timetable pasted to the nautical chart. They were nearly in position and essentially on time to their rendezvous with destiny.

"Rendezvous area," the navigator announced.

Morteza went back to the periscope.

"Up periscope. Extend the radar and countermeasures antennae, and the infrared beacon mast, but keep the radar on standby. Radio, begin scanning. Major, prepare for debarkation."

Major Mohaddessin went aft.

Once again, Morteza scanned the horizon. "All stations on the phones," Morteza ordered. In the close confines of the control room, the phones were unnecessary except to contact engineering, but Morteza would soon be going topside, and would need everyone's constant input.

"Radar, give me two sweeps every minute. Twenty kilometer range."

"Aye."

Morteza checked the ship's clock on the bulkhead behind the navigator, 0726 Greenwich Mean Time.

"Radar?" Morteza anxiously awaited the report.

"Captain, one radar contact within five kilometers. Three zero zero degrees, small contact. Multiple contacts west and north, range 10,000 meters and greater."

Morteza turned the periscope to 300 degrees and watched. After what seemed like an eternity he saw it. Two strobes of red light, followed by a single strobe, then nothing for thirty seconds, then two reds, then one, then nothing.

"That is it. Bring us up very slowly to reconnaissance depth. New course, 300. Secure the beacon. Make your reports to the conning tower," he commanded. The unusual but practiced special depth would expose only the top half of the conning tower. Most importantly, it kept the entire hull below the surface, and yet kept waves for getting them wet. They did not need to give any observers, visual or electronic, more of a target than absolutely necessary.

Morteza grabbed his binoculars from the navigator's shelf, moved quickly to the conning tower access and vitually jumped up the narrow ladder. Mohaddessin and his men moved aside into the recess. They let Morteza climb past them as they had drilled a dozen times.

The usual splash of seawater flowed in as Morteza cracked the hatch. He climbed out into the evening air. The smell of cool, sea air filled his lungs.

Morteza quickly surveyed the horizon, and then the air above. He normally would have had a lookout with him, but tonight the Revolutionary Guards would serve that purpose.

The lights of New York were reflected in an aura

across the northwestern sky. There was some haziness down low, but the sky above was clear. Morteza could see no surface ships. He felt Major Mohaddessin move next to him. The major had the night vision glasses, already scanning the northwestern quadrant.

Looking west they saw the red lights blink again. "There," Mohaddessin said. Morteza was already giving the helm orders to intercept the red lights.

The lapping sounds of the small waves against the partially exposed conning tower made the scene seem far more peaceful that it was. Morteza felt a churning in his stomach as he approached the boat ahead of him.

Mohaddessin was looking through the night vision glasses as he described. "One small craft. One person on board. Correct lights. That is our contact."

Morteza nodded and ordered, "Slow to steerageway. 305 degrees."

Morteza could now see the boat himself. It was a strange sight. They were rendevousing with a sleek, black racing boat. A rich man's boat. It somehow seemed out of place on this military mission. The person on the boat acknowledged their presence with a wave of a regular flashlight and the red lights stopped.

The Guards were ready. When the black boat pulled alongside the conning tower, one of them first threw the rope ladder over the side, then climbed down the ladder outside the conning tower and jumped aboard the boat. Then the bundles of equipment were tossed to him. Two special, green cases were gently lowered to the bobbing boat. The second man went down and boarded the boat, leaving only Mohaddessin with Morteza on the conning tower.

"If God is willing we will see you tonight. Don't get

caught by their Coast Guard." Morteza put a hand on Mohaddessin's shoulder.

"We'll be fine. *Insha'allah,"* Mohaddesin said as he swung over the gunwale to board the boat.

"Welcome to America," Walid Mashadi said as Major Mohaddessin stepped beside him. Mashadi was already pulling away from the submarine, revving the huge V-8 engines of the boat to full power.

"Major Ali Hassan Mohaddessin."

"Walid Mashadi. But you can call me Pierre Dorleac. That is my name if we get stopped. You have your papers?" Mashadi asked.

"Yes, everything."

"All right. We should not have any trouble. I have made this run from New Jersey to Long Island twice now and nobody interfered or asked questions. It is a very open country. But if they do, we just say we are merchants, you know, your cover. We are going to a vacation house on Long Island. Return trip tonight. God willing. Have your men store the equipment in the engine compartment, way up front, there is plenty of room. This used to be a drug running boat."

"Really?" Mohaddessin looked behind them. The *Noor* was no longer visible. Hopefully he would see her again later tonight.

2025 EDT (0025 GMT), July 17, 1996
40°38' N 72°39' W, Offshore, Moriches, Long Island, NY

"Everything has been closed?" asked Major Mohaddessin as he felt the nervous energy of impending battle.

"Yes," answered Mashadi who remained at the controls of the boat. "I mailed a letter closing the rental contract with payment in full, plus I told her there was a gift at the house — a cash bonus. She will feel amply rewarded. The yacht broker was already expecting me to be gone. So there will be no questions, no suspicions."

"Good. Then, we are clean ashore."

"Yes." It was not the first clandestine activity Mashadi had managed for Tehran. He was getting good at the preparations.

One of his Guards sergeants had the radio operating on the air traffic control frequency. Mashadi was acting as their interpretor. The four men sat in the small deck area of the racing boat. Mohaddessin was scanning the horizon with his binoculars. The other sergeant sat in the passenger seat, an assembled and ready SAM launch tube on his lap.

"Major, we have Kennedy control frequencies loud and clear," the sergeant said.

The moment of long awaited retribution for the loss of so many lives of the faithful would soon be upon them. They would also have the double honor to strike a mortal blow into the heart of the 'Great Satan.' Major Mohaddessin felt the adrenaline start to rush.

Mashadi reported, "Two American flag aircraft, just cleared Kennedy control, course 090. Trans World Airlines Eight Zero Zero and followed by, it sounds like Nine Zero Zero."

One of the Guards announced, "Estimated time to target area...," he paused to check a map by flashlight, "three minutes."

"There is an El Al flight directly behind them," Mashadi now announced.

"Ha!" Mohaddessin laughed. "That would be nice to, but would not serve our primary purpose." He continued to search the sky above them. "I have it!" Mohaddessin shouted. He was looking northwest.

"Up there," the sergeant with the SAM said.

"That would be a perfect shot, but we do not know what it is and it might be too high. The other one, there," he pointed. "That's the one. It would be one of the Trans World flights. It appears to be low enough for our range."

The sergeant followed Mohadessin's direction and brought his own binoculars up to view the approaching aircraft. He could see the running lights, and in the last light from the twilight sky, he could barely make out the profile. It appeared to be the guppy-like shape of a Boeing 747, its white underbelly dimly lit by the reflected light of late sunset. The plane was now just to the west and would be passing almost directly above them if it continued on its present course.

"Are we agreed?" asked the sergeant.

"Yes. You are cleared to fire," commanded Major Mohadessin.

The sergeant backed up against the rear side gunwale

of the boat so the backblast of the shoulder-fired missile would miss the boat. The loud bang announced the missile launch. The slender green missile leapt into the air well above them, then a long flame erupted from the nozzle at the tail. The small missile snaked skyward toward the large silhouette and its flashing lights, now more than 12,000 feet above them.

The tiny deck area of the boat was filled with the puff of acrid white smoke from the launch. Mohaddessin turned his attention to the white trail now pointing directly toward the aircraft. He brought his binoculars up, the airplane was now slightly northeast of them. The missile trail made an arching concave curve toward it.

He noticed a small flash on the right side of aircraft near the wing root. Nothing happened for what seemed like an eternity, then he noticed that the silhouette had changed — the guppy no longer had a bulbous head. The entire forward section of the plane had fallen away. The remainder of the plane continued forward and down.

"Ahhh! Yess!" Mohaddessin shouted. "It is going down. Totally destroyed." At that moment, the rear half of the aircraft exploded into a fireball of red and yellow. Several additional spurts of fire ballooned from the main fireball. Mohaddessin no longer needed the binoculars. The dying 747 could be seen for miles around.

"Allah, the Merciful, the Compassionate. Have mercy on their souls," was Mashadi's solemn reaction. The two Revolutionary Guards mumbled the appropriate response to Mashadi's supplication to Allah.

"Let's go," Mohaddessin ordered Mashadi. "This place will soon be covered with rescue boats."

Mashadi revved the boat back to full power and turned to the south. When he had the boat headed away from the blazing pyre behind them, Mashadi asked Mohaddessin, "Do you think anyone saw us?"

"They certainly saw what we did. We will have to see if anyone follows us south to the rendezvous."

Mashadi looked back over his shoulder at the fire now spreading on the water. "I think they will be too busy to follow us."

Mashadi took them to the planned escape course, due south on the boat's magnetic compass. They would take that course at best possible speed to clear the crash area and shore-based surface radar, then they would turn to a different course to rendezvous with the *Noor*.

2015 EDT (0015 GMT), July 17,1996
The US Senate Chambers, Washington DC

At the same time as TWA 800 was taking off from JFK on Long Island, the US Senate was taking a vote on the new, expanded, economic sanctions legislation against Iran. The bill would punish investors in Iranian enterprises who also did business in the US among numerous other tough measures. The bill passed on a simple voice vote.

The US House of Representatives had already, in June, passed a stronger measure. A compromise bill, with the stronger terms passed both houses a few days after the TWA 800 disaster. It was immediately signed into law by President Clinton.

2015 EDT (0015 GMT), July 17, 1996
20,000 feet over Long Island Sound

Copilot Lieutenant Junior Grade Michael Armstrong, USN, checked the instrument panel to verify what he already knew. The Lockheed Electra P-3C Orion, complete with its Update IIIR modifications, was humming perfectly. The Tactical Situation Display told him they were a hundred fifty miles out from their assigned training area for this evening — a special training area set up for the night one hundred miles southeast of New York Harbor. The area had been given a special designation, WX 7-1, for the night's simulated combat exercise. These training missions were important, but they had become too routine, almost boring. Tonight, they were set to drop a sonobouy pattern across the operations area to assist the USS *Trepang* in locating and engaging the USS *Albuquerque* in its exercise role as an aggressor submarine. Armstrong glanced at his communications panel and switched to pilot only.

"Are we going to give 'em any surprises tonight," he asked the aircraft commander and pilot, Lieutenant Peter Hastings, USN.

The veteran P-3 pilot switched his communication panel. "Not tonight, Mike. I don't think the guys are quite used to the new software, nor those new poppers they gave us. We're gettin' close to the airways. You'd better give center our entry call."

Armstrong nodded his head as he reset his panel to

contact the Navy Fleet Air Control and Surveillance Facility (NAVFACS), code name, Neptune, in Virginia Capes, Virginia. It was this Navy center that would coordinate the P-3's location and mission with civilian air controllers in New York and Boston. "Neptune , this is Echo Tango One Seven, with you at angels two four."

"Echo Tango One Seven, Neptune, roger. Confirm your position."

Armstrong glanced at his navigation display. "We're two two four at 12 miles off Groton."

"Roger, One Seven. We have you. Whiskey One Oh Five is hot below angels six. One Oh Six and One Oh Seven are cold. Squawk Mode 2. You are cleared to enter Whiskey Xray Seven One. The area is hot for you, 10,000 feet to the surface."

"Negative Neptune, we're EMCON One," responded Armstrong confirming that the evening's exercise was a simulated combat mission, and they were required to avoid any electronic emissions, or EMissions CONtrol level One, the most stringent, once the exercise began in another 20 minutes.

"Tango One Seven, Neptune, roger. We will inform New York Center. Maintain at or above angels twenty until entering Whiskey One Oh Five, and at or above angels eight until entering Whiskey Xray Seven One."

"Tango One Seven, wilco," Armstrong answered, then checked the aircraft's IFF transponder master control knob in Standby.

The P-3 crew communication link came to life in Hasting's and Armstrong's earphones. "Flight deck, Tac-O. I just got a Pinnacle Blue on secure comm from Homeplate. It's a tasking message ordering us to identify and track a possible Kilo or Foxtrot contact across a line running from point 40-72 to 38-73."

Armstrong answered, "That'd be *Albuquerque* streaming a decoy."

"I don't think so, Mike," said Lieutenant Jeremy Travant, USN, the Tactical Officer, or Tac-O. "This isn't an exercise, now. This Pinnacle Blue is a Top Secret message from SUBLANT forwarded through the squadron, and they are calling *Trepang* and *Albuquerque* on VLF to help, as we speak. The same message directs *Wyoming* to depart the area at best speed. The boomer must be around here somewhere. With this kinda message, SUBLANT probably has a SOSUS track on a possible bad guy."

"Exercise is off," commanded Hastings.

Armstrong cut in, "A Kilo or Foxtrot, what in the hell would they be doing here. A little out of their territory."

"Maybe Cuban," Travant suggested.

"And maybe the SOSUS guys have been smoking something funny. That's silly," Armstrong added.

The crew remained silent as each of them considered their next set of actions.

"Should we call NAVFACS and inform them?" Armstrong asked.

"Negative," interjected Hastings. "If we are under a TS tasking order, we don't tell nobody that ain't already involved. Tac-O, plot the northernmost point and give me a vector. Tell Van Dyke to get ready with a double picket string, active and passive. We'll lay the poppers first along the eastern boundary. Then, send a confirming message to Homeplate. Then, you and Morris try to reach *Trepang* and *Albuquerque* on Lantern and HF. Let's coordinate, and let's find this guy. And, Jerry, have someone bring a copy of that Pinnacle up here, I want to read it all."

"Aye aye, sir."

The Tac-O had just finished responding when a whine went off in the cockpit. Hastings reached for it, switching a toggle off, then on again. "IR Threat detected?"

The pilots had only a moment to think when an orangish-red light flared below them filling the cockpit with the eery strange glow.

"What the hell?" Hastings muttered.

"Flight deck, Tac-O, we have...."

"I know."

Hastings pushed the throttles forward and took the plane into a sharp bank to the left. In a few seconds, he could see a massive fireball boiling below him.

"Mary, Mother of God. What...?" Armstrong said as he looked across the cockpit at the scene below them.

Hastings and Armstrong could see the objects within the fireball streaming toward the ocean, falling in an arc to the northeast.

"What is it?"

"Somebody's lost it, something real big."

Seeing that their turn would bring them into the smoke cloud rising from the fireball, Hastings leveled his wings, headed due east.

Armstrong was already rolling the frequency on the communication unit to the civil emergency frequency — 121.5 MHz.

The voice of another pilot filled their ears. "...over the site with that airplane or whatever. It just exploded and went into the water."

Hastings switched back to crew only. "They already have it. Sounds like a bird went down."

They were under their own emergency. A Pinnacle Blue, or more formally an Operational Report 3 - Pinnacle Blue, was the most serious Navy operations message. Something felt very threatening about the events surrounding the single P-3C aircraft diverted from a training mission to what was probably a national security situation. Were they at war? Was their mission connected to the explosion of the airliner? The possibilities became to much for him to worry about.

The silence was broken by Lieutenant Hastings, "Tac-O, you have my vector, yet? Not anything we can do here. We have a priority mission."

"Roger, lieutenant. Vector one six zero. Maintain this altitude. Whiskey One Zero Five is still hot below us up to 6,000 feet."

Hastings switched to copilot only and asked, "What do you think happened?"

"God knows."

"What about the IR threat detect we had?"

"Coulda just been the first trouble that caused the fireball. That sure was enough heat to set it off."

"Of course."

Hastings took one last look down to his left at the flames that now spread out across the ocean below him and banked to the right toward the submarine contact report location.

2028 EDT (0028 GMT), July 17, 1996
Gabreski Airport, Westhampton Beach, NY

"Jolly One Four, executing missed approach," broadcast Captain Chris Baur as he followed the appropriate procedure.

The Sikorsky HH-60G Pave Hawk combat SAR helicopter responded smoothly and promptly to the collective input from Captain Baur. The aircraft climbed straight down Runway 24 at the Francis S. Gabreski International Airport.

"Looks like you guys are going to get an easy go tonight," said Major Michael Noyes, the instructor pilot for the 102nd Rescue Squadron helicopter's night training mission. "Perfect night. You're going to get off easy on the night pump."

"Hey, us old men need a few breaks," answered Major Frederick 'Fritz' Meyer, the 56 year old pilot of the Pave Hawk.

The big event for this evening's two hour mission was their requalification for night water rescue operations as well as the requisite night, lights out, combat aerial refueling matching them with their sister squadron's HC-130P Combat Talon aircraft, just about the hardest flying task for combat Search And Rescue pilots.

"What the hell is that?" asked Baur.

The three pilots stared out the windscreen almost directly in front of them. An organish-white streak arced across the sky high above them.

"What's the Navy doing firing off stuff so close to shore?" asked Captain Baur.

No one answered as they continued to watch. A small bright ball flashed at the left end of the streak. Then, several more, larger flashes stepped across the sky to the left, or east, and began falling. An enormous fireball, many times larger than the Sun, erupted above them.

Streamers of flaming debris fell from the explosion. It looked like some really strange 4th of July display.

"Jolly One Four, state your intentions," radioed Islip Approach Control as the New York Air National Guard helicopter continued to deviate from the prescribed missed approach pattern.

The three pilots looked at each other, then looked back to the east. "Islip, we have...," Meyer's broadcast was cut off by an even larger explosion within the explosion. It had to be a very large aircraft high above them less than maybe ten miles away. "Jesus," the helicopter's radio broadcast with neither pilot thinking about a transmission.

"Jolly One Four, your intentions," demanded the controller.

"Islip, I think we've a jumbo mid-air. Stand by." Meyer switched his thumb to the intercom. "Get the nose up, Chris. Let's keep this guy in sight."

The helicopter responded.

"Jolly One Four, do you have a problem?"

As they watched the fire spread across the night sky, the pilots remained transfixed on the scene playing out above them frozen like rabbits in the headlights and ignoring everything else around them.

The experienced rescue crew kept their objective in

sight. The entire crew knew without discussion or conversation, they now had real work to do, and they were now witnesses to a tragic disaster.

The radio blared, "Mayday, mayday, mayday. We have a large airliner that has exploded in mid-air off Point Moriches, Long Island."

Meyer, Noyes and Baur knew they were not the only witnesses to this disaster.

"Islip, we're switching to Tower." Without waiting for an answer, Meyer switched the radio to the airport tower's frequency. "Gabreski," radioed Meyer, "notify all sea and air rescue units in the vicinity. We've got an airliner crash at sea." In the background of his attention, Meyer heard Gabreski Tower responding to the call. Again, he slipped his thumb across to the intercom. "Chris, let's get out there, pronto." Meyer turned in his seat to look back at the professional expression of Noyes. "Let's get ready to search...," he stopped, thought, then continued, "there aren't likely to be any survivors, but we owe it to them to try."

The size of what they saw was so far beyond anything they had ever trained for, none them really knew exactly what if anything they could do. They had trained more times than they wished to count the rescue of a downed fighter pilot at sea, in the mountains, in a snow storm, but always one or two men. The jumbo jet carried hundreds of people. Meyer thought about returning for a couple of pararescuemen, but that would take too much time. If there was any hope of saving someone out of that conflagration, it had to be done immediately.

Meyer glanced back and forth between the radio and the falling debris splashing into the water some of it still burning brightly. He switch their UHF radio to the 106th

Rescue Wing's Operations control frequency. "Control, Jolly One Four."

"Jolly One Four, this is Control, go ahead."

"We've just seen what looks like a mid-air with a jumbo jet. We're enroute to the site to see what we can do. We've notified Gabreski for sea rescue. We need some help."

"Roger, One Four. We just received the same report from King Seven Four. Do you have any paras with you?"

"Negative. We're proceeding direct."

"Roger, we'll get them ready for you, if you need them."

Many actions began to click away behind them. Their attention remained riveted on the splashes of all sizes in the water now blazing with burning jet fuel. The nose of the HH-60G Pave Hawk helicopter dipped toward the crash site to maintain the 145 knots of airspeed Baur commanded.

A white object flashed past Meyer's side of the aircraft. "We're in the debris pattern," announced Meyer. "Turn around."

Baur did not hesitate as he rolled the agile Sikorsky helicopter hard left. Without commands, Chris Baur moved back about a mile, then slowed the aircraft turning back to the right to give his commander the best view possible of the crash site. They watched in silence as the bits and pieces of what was once one of the largest airliner ever built fell into the ocean. 'Fritz' Meyer remembered his first ride on a chartered 747 taking him to Vietnam 25 years earlier.

The crew of the 106th Rescue Wing, HH-60G Pave Hawk helicopter was the first rescue unit on the scene. They used their night vision goggles, Pave Low FLIR and other sensors to search for survivors. High-speed boats headed toward them from several areas of Long Island. The bodies and body parts floated among the parts of the aircraft still floating. Pockets of burning fuel made the search process more difficult; not bright enough for unaided eyes and too bright for the sensitive night vision goggles. The debris field was several miles long. As they circled the debris field, they marked the boundaries as best they could with their sophisticated navigation system. The investigators as well as salvage operations would need the information.

The finality of the event sank in deeper and deeper as every object they could find bobbed on the gentle swells of the Atlantic Ocean. Nothing moved on its own. The few intact bodies they found floated lifelessly with most of their clothing stripped away by the high velocity air stream that tore the airliner apart. Hopefully, 'Fritz' Meyer told himself, it was a quick death.

As the surface rescue units increased in number and the search process took on a methodical character, Meyer's mind turned to other questions. What had happened? The airliner was on an instrument departure. A mid-air was certainly possible, but highly unlikely. Had there been something wrong with the aircraft? When was the last time anyone saw a modern airliner explode in mid-air? Had the jumbo jet been shot down? If it had, where was the shooter?

The veteran pilot checked the clock on the instrument panel in front of him. It was nearly 2100, not quite 30 minutes since the explosion. They still had 90 minutes of fuel on-board. They continued to search for any signs of a survivor.

The HC-130P assumed the role of on-scene commander as was their practice. They dropped flares to light the site as the fires died out.

Several private craft joined the professional boats in the search. They used every tool available to them, but as time rolled on, the conclusion became unavoidable.

"We'd better go home," said 'Fritz' Meyer with heavy solemnity.

Chris Baur banked the aircraft gently to the left. "Control, Jolly One Four."

"Control, go."

"We're at Bingo fuel and RTB. ETA 20 minutes."

"Roger, Jolly One Four. Good work."

None of them felt good about what they had done. They had not been able to save anyone.

The fires had gone out. The sea was filled with red, blue and yellow flashing lights as well as numerous steady red, green and white lights. Each of them remained silent captured by their thoughts, images and concerns. Only the routine air traffic calls broke their silence.

2315 EDT (0315 GMT), July 17, 1996
39°51' N 71°58' W, South-Southeast of Long Island, NY

Major Mohaddessin checked his watch — 15 minutes until the first rendezvous window. He then checked the handheld GPS receiver. They were precisely where they were supposed to be, 500 meters from the exact rendezvous location 75 kilometers from the coastline, in International waters. "We are ready. Lights out," he commanded. He looked down before the lights went out to see the precise location of the spare missile, just in case they needed it before they made good their escape.

Mashadi turned off the boat's running lights.

It took only a few minutes of darkness for their eye's natural night vision to reveal the blanket of stars above them blossoming into full glory. The starlight was sufficient to see the deck details as well as each other.

"Do we need the night vision devices?" one of the sergeants asked .

"If you wish," answered Mohaddessin, "but, it is not necessary. We still have several minutes until the beacon appears."

The ocean swells gently undulated the boat. The moderate breeze prevalent all day slowly pushed them toward their rendezvous point and produced sufficient wavelets for the lapping sounds against the hull of the quiet, dead calm, boat to dominate their hearing. The four men waited patiently scanning the horizon and well as the sky above them. They were professional warriors. However, they were not sailors, and the isolation of nothing but ocean in every direction and only the stars above them to provide orientation gave them all a disconcerting apprehension.

Mohaddessin lifted the cover of his luminous dial watch — 2331. He picked up the night vision goggles and slipped the straps over his head. The others followed his lead. The starlight was perfect. He could see the horizon. Excellent, he said to himself. On his first scan to the east, he saw the dim winking light — three short pulses, ten seconds, then two short pulses. He lifted his goggles to confirm that it was an infrared beacon. It was. He could not see it with just his eyes, and it was clearly distinguishable with the night vision device. That was it. "There she is," he said softly as if someone might over hear them. He did not need to command them.

The engines started promptly. As Mashadi, slowly moved the boat toward the beacon, Major Mohaddessin entered the small cabin beneath the forward deck. With a small infrared light, he scanned the cabin. The spent launch tube lay on the right bunk. He looked down the rectangular hole of the removed deck panel and checked the small explosive charge stuck to the hull under the cabin deck. The two conventional water proof fuzes were cut to similar lengths. They would have ten minutes plus or minus a few seconds to get aboard *Noor* and back away from their escape vehicle before the charge blew a small hole in the hull, scuttling the boat. One of his men had already used a portable drill to drill thumb sized holes in the upper deck areas, to speed the scuttling process. They wanted to entire boat and all its contents to sink to the bottom — no floating fragments to be perchance collected. He estimated the boat would be out of sight and on its way to the bottom in less than five minutes, plenty of time for them to enter the submarine. They had carefully calculated the rendevouz point based on time, distance and the depth of the ocean. They were over an undersea canyon. The boat with its incriminating contents would come to rest in 100 meters of water, beyond the reach of most divers, assuming they even knew where to look.

They approached the beacon mast. Several other posts occupied the space to the left of the beacon. Major Mohaddessin pointed his infrared flashlight at the left most mast, the optical periscope. He blinked the light three times, waited for ten seconds, then flashed it once. The six masts began to rise up out of the water. In less than a minute, the upper portion of the conning tower appeared before them just as it had disappeared in the early morning hours.

Ali Hassan checked the boat's rubber bumpers. They pulled along side. One of the Revolutionary Guards operatives slung the carrying strap of the spare missile over his shoulder while another grasped the rope ladder dangling from the submarine's conning tower. Ali Hassan waited for his men to disappear down the access hatch. He looked up to see the concerned face of Captain Morteza. "Ready?" he called to the Captain.

"Ready. Move quickly. Every second is more exposure."

With the small infrared flashlight in his teeth, Mohaddessin reentered the cabin, held both fuze lighters in his left hand, put his right index finger through the two rings and pulled. Both fuzes lit. He dropped the rings and moved quickly to the submarine. Ali Hassan joined the Captain on the bridge. No commands were necessary. The submarine was backing away from the boat.

"You were successful?" Morteza asked as Mohaddessin looked over the gunwale of the conning tower.

"Completely," Mohaddessin answered.

"No sign of anyone following?"

"None."

"Well, we have not been so successful. Either they suspect a submarine, or we have had the misfortune to land in the middle of an anti-submarine warfare exercise. It was a close call whether I would surface to pick you up. The more time we spend on the surface the worse it is."

"I just want to make sure the boat sinks."

Morteza nodded his head.

The submarine was perhaps 100 meters away when they heard a dull thud along with the small flash of light. The submarine continued to back away another 50 meters when the black boat slipped beneath the surface. Mohaddessin went down the hatch.

"Prepare to dive. Secure radio, radar and beacon. Rig for silent running. Right full rudder. Come to new course 140. Ahead standard electric," Morteza ordered through the phone circuit before he pulled the hatch down above him and went below.

When he reached the control room Morteza took a quick view of the chart. "Submerge. Make your depth 75 meters."

Morteza studied the navigation chart. They were on track. They headed toward the suspected American SOSUS sensor line at the shortest distance and angle possible, to limit the time they might be detectable. Once clear of the Continental Shelf, he planned to turn *Noor* south toward their refueling rendezvous in the Central Atlantic. As soon as they cleared the SOSUS line, Captain Morteza would take *Noor* deep. Once below the thermal incline, the layer of rapid temperature change that tended to reflect sound waves like a mirror, they would be able to increase speed and avoid detection by the Americans or anyone else in this big ocean. Deep water felt like a safe haven to a submariner.

0015 EDT (0415 GMT), July 18, 1996
40°38'N 72°40'W, South of Center Moriches, NY

A flotilla of vessels had converged on the TWA wreckage -- dozens of boats, private cruisers, Coast Gaurd cutters, National Parks Service patrol boats, police boats from Suffolk County and as far away as New York City. Overhead, Coast Guard, National Guard, police and television station helicopters circled and flashed their NightSun™ lights on the carnage and confusion below. The fire on the water had died out now, and the hopes of finding survivors was dying also.

The early word of dozens of bodies in the water a mile west of the raging fire on the water had led would-be rescuers to hunt there for possible survivors, without any luck. Well-intentioned on-lookers pulled bodies and wreckage from the water and took them to the nearest dock.

Chaos was the only word to describe the scene. It would not get much better before dawn, when the Coast Guard finally got control of the area and implemented the federal agencies' orders to keep private craft away and control the official vessels' actions.

0055 EDT (0455 GMT), July 18, 1996
39°44'N 71°51'W, South of Montauk Point, NY

"Captain, Sonar. I have active sonar at two zero zero. Long range."

"Identify," he demanded. He knew this would be a difficult thing to accomplish. His sonarman had little experience. If the sonar was not one of the ones the Americans used in the Arabian Sea, he would have little chance of identifying the sonar platform just by the sound of an active sonar. This was one area where the Russian training had been very weak, and the Iranians did not have the forty years of Cold War experience the Americans and Russians shared in submarining.

"Another active ping. Two two seven. Similar but different frequency. I believe they are sonobouys, Captain."

"Sonobouys? Why would they be laying sonobouys?" Morteza muttered to himself. He bent over to look closely as the navigator marked the sonar bearing on the chart in colored pencil.

"Any clearer idea on range?" Morteza shouted to the sonarman.

"Captain, they are far out, maybe in the convergence zone. We had the American S-3's drop them on us, almost directly, last year in Hormuz. It was much stronger than this."

"What does this mean?" Mohaddessin asked. The Revolutionary Guards officer was now totally out of his element.

"It is as I told you, either they suspect us or they are having an exercise. The American anti-submarine aircraft, both fixed wing and helicopter, drop sonar pods, sonobouys, that radio submarine positions back to their aircraft and to surface ships. They have passive ones that just listen and active ones, that ping and wait for a reflection, much like underwater radar. They lay a pattern of the passive ones to listen, and then a line of the active ones to herd an enemy sub into the passive field for the kill. They can track a submarine very accurately from the air."

"Then, they know about us? Have we been located? Did they see us and send the plane?"

"No, not located. They are too far off. And, this is too quick, no Navy could react this fast, when they had no idea we were coming. They had to already be doing the sonobouy drop. But, the question is — why are they dropping them? It is in the busy shipping channels, the busiest in the world. Middle of the night, no sign of military surface vessels, so far. They must be looking for something, either us or one of their own submarines on an exercise in the area. Either way it is not good news. Perhaps they heard our approach, down in the sea lanes to the south. Maybe they knew we were approaching, and they are defending New York harbor with a pattern of their sonobouys."

"Will it change our plans?" Mohaddessin asked.

"No. It will just require more caution. Sonobouys mean military anti-submarine aircraft in the area."

"Sonar? Report."

Sonar answered, "We have active sonobouys, five in all now. And, there are multiple high-speed craft to the north and northwest. Like before. Distant. Probably rescue vessels for the crash."

"Very well. Give us five-minute marks on the outer bearings of the sonobouys. Navigator, I want a dead reckoning trace on the sonobouys. I want to know where they are. Maybe that will tell us why. If they are looking for us and there are military aircraft up there, they may have seen the missile shot. If so, we may still be tracked down. This has been too easy, so far."

Morteza reached for the submarine's intercom. "Engineering, report on batteries."

"Captain, we have seventy percent charge. Two hours, plus a bit more, remaining at this speed."

"Very well." Morteza ran his fingers through his close cropped ebony hair. His best speed on electric drive was seven knots. In two hours, he could only put another twenty-four kilometers between the location of the submerged escape boat and the *Noor*. Then, he would be forced to put his snorkel up on the surface, recharge his batteries and make his high speed diesel-powered run to the open Atlantic.

They needed every advantage they could find now that the American Navy might be looking for them. He reached for the intercom, again. "This is the Captain. I must ask each of you to maintain maximum silence for the next several hours. We must make no noise that might help the 'Great Satan.'" Morteza did not smile, although he was happy with his derogatory reference to the enemy.

106th Rescue Wing
New York Air National Guard
US Air Force
Westhampton Beach, NY 11978

Release 96-10
Air Crews on Scene Minutes After Explosion

Gabreski ANG Station, 17 July 96 — While performing a local training mission here NY Air Guard fliers aboard an HC-130 air tanker and an HH-60 rescue helicopter witnessed the explosion of TWA Flight 800. The aircraft, designed for search and rescue, were on scene within minutes and immediately began operations. They did not find any survivors among the more than 200 people on board.

The HC-130, call sign King 74, was just leaving the ocean training area known as 'Jaws' when the explosion occurred. King's crew called in the report to the Gabreski tower and flew to the scene. When they arrived a minute later they found smoke, burning fuel, and aircraft debris still raining from the sky.

The HH-60, call sign Jolly 14, was on an ILS approach to runway 24 at Gabreski. It had just cleared below 200 feet when the pilot called out the altitude. All on board glanced up and were looking out the front of the helicopter when the explosion occurred. Believing they might have witnessed a mid-air collision, the pilot radioed the tower and flew to the scene. They arrived in under five minutes. Upon arrival, the

Jolly 14 crew had to bank the helicopter because of falling debris, they circled around and began to identify the forward edge of the debris field and then initiated a search along the two and a half mile area. "The fire was burning on an area the size of a football field," said one of the crew.

The debris field was so large that the crew asked Gabreski tower if any aircraft were missing and found out that a 747 from JFK had dropped off the radar screen. "We were silent witnesses to a horrible tragedy," said one of the Jolly 14 crew.

As the King 74 crew continued searching from 1,500 feet, the Jolly 14 crew flew back to Gabreski and picked up two pararescuemen, one of who had just parachuted from the HC-130. They too had seen the fireball and had dressed in their wetsuits anticipating the pickup.

After flying back to the scene, the Jolly 14 crew resumed its search for survivors. Darkness had set in so the crew donned night vision goggles. The pararescuemen, in scuba gear, sat in the doors in the back of the aircraft. They flew a grid search pattern back and forth across the debris at 100 feet. They would hover when they thought they saw something, but they did not find any survivors.

The task force on the water grew when the Coast Guard arrived on scene, followed by scores of civilian boats on the water that night. King 74 dropped illumination flares, which can light up a 2-square mile area for 20 minutes. Using chemical light sticks the PJs marked where the bodies could be found. Only when they ran low on fuel did the tired and disappointed crew return home to Gabreski.

King 74 also returned to obtain fuel, additional flares and pararescuemen, then took off again to assist the Coast Guard in the search area. Between midnight and 3 AM, they dropped an additional 79 flares.

Assisting in the effort were four other members of the unit. Three PJs and a life support specialist took the unit's Boston Whaler to find survivors. Although they didn't find anyone alive they did recover the remains of three people.

July 22, 1996
Tehran, Iran

Ayatollah Fazel Lankarani and Ayatollah Yousef Saneii, well-known government clerics, issued a *fatwa* [religious edict] and described suicide-assassination operations as esteemed deeds for all Muslims. The edicts by two high ranking government clerics, were published in an issue of the daily newspaper <u>Jomhuri-e Eslami</u>. The edicts were issued in Arabic and Farsi language.

At the same time, the Executive Committee of the recently revamped Hizbollah International met in Tehran. The head of Saudi Hizbollah, Usama bin Ladin, was congratulated on his operatives great successes since the last meeting. He, in turn, thanked Mahdi Chamran for his continuing support and congratulated Chamran on the Islamic Republic's accomplishments in recent weeks.

It was one of Usama bin Ladin's men who had sent the warning by facsimile the night before the TWA disaster and an affiliate of bin Ladin's who had claimed credit for the 'bombing' of the TWA flight. Iran, itself, could obviously not take credit for the TWA event, that would be admitting an act of war against the US, but if a Hizbollah faction took credit and the US suspected foul play, the effect would be the same on the United States leadership. That did not matter, anyway, this was a matter of principle and a matter of perception, by the Hizbollah International leadership. The

Iranian operatives had proven the point, Iran could effectively challenge the United States on their home turf and avenge the acts of the 'Great Satan.'

The Iranian intelligence officials backing Hizbollah International would soon part company with Usama bin Ladin, however, over the issue of bin Ladin's support of the Taliban militia in Afghanistan. The Taliban movement was one of Usama bin Ladin's prime beneficiaries and tools. When, in late 1996, the Taliban threatened Tehran's allies in power in Kabul, an open rift between Tehran and bin Ladin formed. Usama bin Ladin moved his power base to the hills of southern Afghanistan and his open and notorious threats to send Americans home from the Middle East in coffins were not in keeping with Iranian diplomatic interests. By August 1998, the official Iranian news agency was one of the first news organizations to name bin Ladin as the likely culprit in the East African US Embassy bombings and bin Ladin's Taliban compatriots had taken eight Iranian "diplomats" hostage amid fighting in northern Afghanistan.

1530 EDT (1930 GMT), July 23, 1996
The Pentagon, Washington, DC

Kenneth H. Bacon, the Assistant Secretary of Defense for Public Affairs, held a news conference with the press representatives at the Pentagon on the TWA 800 disaster, terrorism and the Saudi Arabian bombing situation:

Mr. Bacon: "Welcome to our briefing.

"I, first of all, would like to welcome Mark Brzozowski back. Colonel Brzozowski, as you know, was in Tuzla running the JIB there — the public affairs operation. Did a great job. We were able to pry him back here from General Nash's hands only by sending Lieutenant Colonel Donna Boltz over as his replacement. We're glad to have him back. He's tanned, rested and ready after his leave, and here with us. So welcome.

"With that, I'll take your questions — on Mark Brzozowski or anything else."

QUESTION: "What part is the military taking in this investigation, specifically in the crash investigation?"

ANSWER: "We're supporting the FBI and the NTSB, and the primary role the military is playing is to provide naval support to the people who are trying to locate and retrieve parts of the plane. And as you know, we have a fairly long list of equipment that the Navy's provided to the National Transportation Safety Board, which we can give you. I can give it to you now, or we can give it to you later."

QUESTION: "More specifically, have you been asked to simulate missile firings from the area or test where missiles might have been fired or angles at which they might have been fired from the sea?"

ANSWER: "No, I'm not aware that we've been asked to do that. I think it's premature right now. There's still, as I understand it, three main theories of what caused this. Until we get more information to allow people to narrow down and focus on just one of those theories, I think it's premature to start doing the type of simulations you asked about."

QUESTION: "Have you been asked to take part in any chemical testing or anything like that?"

ANSWER: "Not that I'm aware of, but remember, the FBI and other agencies have ample skill and experience in those areas."

QUESTION: "I understand. I'm asking if you, to your knowledge...."

ANSWER: "I'm not aware that we've been asked. I would frankly be surprised if we'd been asked to do that, but we stand ready to provide any assistance we can."

QUESTION: "Can I do a follow-up on that particular question? One of the investigative reporters from ABC reported there were military exercises taking place in the area at the same time. The flare that people saw going upwards could have in fact been coming downwards from a C-130, or been something else coming up from the ground as part of that military exercise. Was there a military exercise in the area? And if so, were any kind of pyrotechnics or flares used?"

ANSWER: "I'm not aware that there were any military exercises in the area. I've been told by the Joint Staff that there were not. There was a P-3 flying down south to participate in an exercise, considerably south of Long Island. It was flying over the location of TWA Flight 800.... It was about 3,000 feet over it, and it was several miles south of TWA 800 when the disaster took place."

QUESTION: "Did it drop any flares?"

ANSWER: "It did not drop any flares."

QUESTION: "It didn't see anything?"

ANSWER: "No, nothing of note."

QUESTION: "Do you have information on the National Guard exercise involving a helicopter and a C-130?"

ANSWER: "I know there was a C-130 in the area. I don't have information on a National Guard exercise. As I say, I'll double check this, but my understanding from the Joint Staff was there were not exercises taking place at the time, but I will double check."

QUESTION: "They're not calling it an exercise. They're calling it a training session or something, just where two aircraft from the Air National Guard...not a formal exercise."

ANSWER: "I'll check on that."

QUESTION: "To follow on Charlie's question about missiles, apart from simulating, what have you done to eliminate the possibilities that any missiles might have been fired, any missiles might be missing from any military arsenals, or any missiles might have been detected in flight?"

ANSWER: "This is replowing old ground that people have been over for the last week or so, but we have made available all our radar tapes or sightings to the analysts who are looking into this crash. We have not seen any signs on those radar tapes from our own analysis or from their analysis of something that looks like a missile. Now, this is a theory, and the idea that a missile may have been involved is one of three theories that the investigators have said they're holding open now.

"There are, as I understand it, and the Pentagon is not doing this investigation so this comes from watching what you and others and CNN and ABC, and all the news media have been reporting, there are some eyewitness accounts that make it sound as if a missile could have been involved. There is precious else to support that at this stage. But, until the investigators have more information about what might have caused this disaster, I don't think they're willing to rule anything out, and I think that's reasonable on their part."

QUESTION: "How does the military interpret those eyewitness accounts? As erroneous? As inconclusive?"

ANSWER: "It's not our job to interpret them. We are clearly doing what we can to support the investigators. Until there's more information, it's very difficult to comment with any authority or knowledge about what happened. That's why there's still three theories, because the investigators have not been able to find enough information to allow them to focus on one of the three possible causes of this. There may be more possible causes when they get into it, but they've narrowed it down, as you know, to three."

QUESTION: "When you say your radar doesn't show any missiles, are you discounting that one of the three?"

ANSWER: "You're trying to force me to make a judgment. I'm not going to make a judgment. I'm not an investigator. The FBI is investigating this. We provide information to the FBI and the National Transportation Safety Board as requested.

"I think we have to wait until we get more evidence before anybody can talk with knowledge about what happened."

QUESTION: "Some experts say the radar would not have

picked up a shoulder-fired missile as small as a Stinger-type or something comparable. Do you have any word from the radar people in DoD or air traffic control either affirming that or negating that statement?"

ANSWER: "It would have been difficult for these radars to have picked up a shoulder-fired missile."

QUESTION: "Can you possibly elaborate just a little more on that as to what would differentiate the types of radar that would pick up that type of information and whether civilian radars do or don't? If you could give us a little bit more background on what determines the ability of a radar to provide reliable information of any type?"

ANSWER: "Without trying to take sides on whether or not a missile was involved, because I really don't know, and nobody knows right now, and I want to stress that for the third or fourth time.

"The two arguments against a missile being involved are, one, range; and two, lack of signals on a radar. I'm not an expert on radars, so I can't give you a detailed explanation of what sort of radars might pick this up, and what sort of radars might not pick it up, but nothing in the radar leads anybody to believe that there was a missile involved.

"The FAA radar probably could have picked this up. There were other radars involved that would have been extremely unlikely to have picked it up, in fact didn't. No radar has picked up anything that looks like a missile trail at this stage. So, those are the two arguments against missiles being involved. Range. This plane was generally outside the range of any shoulder-fired missile in the general inventory. Then, you could ask other questions. Could it have been fired from the water? That is a question they're looking into.

"I'm just not in a position to comment in any way as

to what caused this crash, and you shouldn't be asking me. You should be asking the NTSB. You should be asking the FBI. They're the people doing the investigation."

QUESTION: "Some of the DoD people are finding the wreckage. I understand, the main section, the fuselage has been found. Do you have any knowledge as to the condition of that fuselage, what the damage might indicate?"

ANSWER: "No."

QUESTION: "Nothing from that?"

ANSWER: "No, but that's exactly the type of information that will come from the National Transportation Safety Board and the FBI. We're basically working for them to help them complete their investigation."

QUESTION: "Any news on the black boxes?"

ANSWER: "No."

QUESTION: "In this report this morning, can you make any comment at all about a boat that was rented in the afternoon and then returned, and people left without getting their deposit?"

ANSWER: "I think you should ask the FBI or the Coast Guard about that."

QUESTION: "Maybe you can help me with this, though. Is there a worldwide alert that there might already have been planned and in place other terrorist attacks against US assets abroad and in this country? Is there any kind of alert?"

ANSWER: "Not that I'm aware of. We, as you know, after the OPM SANG bombing in Saudi Arabia last November, have had our troops in Saudi Arabia and some other areas on high alert. They've been on very high alert in Bosnia and some other parts of the country. Certainly all our troops are aware of terrorist threats now, and that was true before the TWA 800, but I'm not aware of any specific alert. Whenever there's a disaster like this, reasonable people look at their security arrangements and take steps to improve them, and I assume that's going on in the commercial sector as well as the government sector, not just in this country, but all over the world."

QUESTION: "There's been no heightened alert attributable to the Khobar bombing and the possible sabotage...."

ANSWER: "We are at the highest possible level of alert in parts of Saudi Arabia and other parts of the world."

QUESTION: "A senior defense official called that a "critical" state of alert. Is that correct?"

ANSWER: "We can't be at a higher level of alert than we're at, Charlie."

QUESTION: "There's been speculation on the possible shoulder-fired missiles. Have you done anything to intensify or reintensify efforts on behalf of the State Department and this building to reacquire Stinger missiles which were passed out in Afghanistan?"

ANSWER: "That's an interesting question. We made a very concerted effort after the Afghanistan War to reacquire or collect as many of these Stingers as possible. I'm not aware that there's been a new effort since this disaster took place. The question you asked, of course, presupposes that a missile was involved, and we don't know that.

"Stingers aren't the only shoulder-fired missiles available in the world today. They are fairly common weapons around the world."

QUESTION: "Can you give us a breakdown on numbers of missiles that might have been, that were sent to Afghanistan, and the number that have been reacquired...."

ANSWER: "We'll check and see if we have that. I don't have the numbers at my fingertips. If we have them, if we can get them, we'll provide it."

QUESTION: "The State Department said it would pay for the trips of family members back to this country who are living in Saudi Arabia. Does that apply to DoD military family members? And what is the building policy on whether or not they should return home or stay there?"

ANSWER: "Overall, we are still working out the final details of the return policy, but yes, we will pay. What the State Department announced, the policy they announced authorizing a return means that any government employee, any dependent of a government employee who comes back will come back at government expense, so that will be done.

"As I say, details are still being worked out. I would expect that the final details will be resolved quickly, maybe even today; probably, more likely, tomorrow. And we would hope that the first people volunteering to come back will come back next week some time, I would guess."

QUESTION: "Are you encouraging people to come back, or not discouraging, or...."

ANSWER: "I think before I can respond completely to that we ought to have our policy in place. When it's in place it won't be a secret policy, but I would just like to wait until all the policymakers and lawyers and others, the CENTCOM people and others have gone through it and worked out the final details."

QUESTION: "Can you tell us how many dependents might be involved in this?"

ANSWER: "Yeah, there are about 1,000 DoD civilian and military dependents, and it's about a two-to-one military to civilian ratio. I don't have the exact numbers, but...."

QUESTION: "In Saudi or all of CENTCOM?"

ANSWER: "That's in Saudi Arabia."

QUESTION: "While we're on the subject of Saudi, has anyone released what type of explosive was used in that bomb?"

ANSWER: "No. It's not been released yet."

QUESTION: "Has Secretary Perry received any new security recommendations from General Peay or anyone else in the theater regarding force protection in Saudi and did he discuss any of this morning on the Hill?"

ANSWER: "He received from General Peay today the recommendation for protecting the forces in Saudi Arabia, including a possible relocation of forces. That is now under review, the General Peay/CENTCOM recommendations are under review. We've already started discussing this with people in Saudi Arabia, and we'll discuss it further with them as we reach our own conclusions on what to do."

QUESTION: "Is the relocation Riyadh as well as Dhahran?"

ANSWER: "That's exactly the type of question that we'll answer as we go through General Peay's recommendations and make our own decisions about what to do."

QUESTION: "Can you say whether there's anything besides force relocation being discussed at the moment?"

ANSWER: "Yes, in short, there are other things being discussed, but they're of the type we've already discussed here. They're passive defense measures and active defense measures. We've talked fairly extensively about some of the passive defense measures that took place before the Khobar Tower bombings and some that have taken place after the Khobar Tower bombings. We've also talked a lot about creating an intelligence fusion cell and doing some other things to improve intelligence collection and dissemination."

QUESTION: "When would you expect that fusion cell to be up and running?"

ANSWER: "I think basically it's pretty much going. It's a question of improving what's already there and making it more helpful, more robust."

QUESTION: "Is this plan from General Peay and the Saudi leadership; have they generally agreed on this plan; and, would it entail the movement of, as you said, 3,000 to 4,000 military personnel?"

ANSWER: "I'd rather hold off until the plan is actually evaluated and complete. I know it's unsatisfactory to you. The Saudis have used the figure 3,000 to 4,000 troops, we've used the figure 3,000 to 4,000 troops, I don't think there's going to be a huge change in that; but that's what we're looking at, in that area, and we'll work out the final details quickly."

QUESTION: "This plan that's been proposed to the Secretary has generally been approved by the Saudi leadership. This isn't...."

ANSWER: "We've been talking with the Saudis about this. The Saudis first proposed relocation in November, so this has been a continuing dialogue with the Saudis. General Peay did not submit a plan that had been chopped by the Saudis. The Saudis are very aware of what's in the plan. There's a dialogue going on. That dialogue will continue. We expect support from the Saudis for this plan."

QUESTION: "Just to clarify something. You said the Saudis proposed relocation in November."

ANSWER: "The Saudis first brought up the idea of relocation in November."

QUESTION: "Do you know if this proposal is for forces in Riyadh or forces in Dhahran or both?"

ANSWER: "Riyadh."

QUESTION: "On Friday or Thursday of last week, at a terrorism task force on the Hill, the House side, several expert witnesses testified that the Saudi Arabian government was much weaker than was generally thought. Does the United States have full confidence in the Royal Family to protect American citizens in the Kingdom and the basic confidence of their security apparatus there?"

ANSWER: "We have confidence in the Saudi government. We're working very closely with the Saudi government. Saudi Arabia has been and generally is a very secure place, but it's facing a threat; we're facing it together. Clearly in the last nine months or so there's been more terrorist activity there. The Saudis, as I said are working very diligently to deal with this, as are we. We're partners in this."

QUESTION: "In the last briefing, I asked you if DoD had any block seats filled with DoD personnel, and you were going to check. Did we ever get an answer on that?"

ANSWER: "I believe there was only one DoD employee on the plane — a civilian employee. We did not have a block of seats on the plane."

QUESTION: "All the previous questions about detection dealt with radar. What about satellite? Has anything turned up on military satellite?"

ANSWER: "Nothing significant."

QUESTION: "Nothing significant?"

ANSWER: "Nothing helpful."

QUESTION: "What was there that might even be...."

ANSWER: "We have, as you know, ways of detecting all sorts of things, and we did detect an event that we believe was the explosion of the plane. But, it doesn't add any new information. We already knew the plane exploded. We didn't need outside monitoring sources to tell us that, and it didn't provide any information that would help lead investigators to a conclusion as to why this happened."

QUESTION: "Nothing that preceded the event?"

ANSWER: "No. Nothing that preceded it."

QUESTION: "The only strong indication you've had that we've heard about until now was that people saw what they believed was an explosion. Now you're telling us that the satellite saw something that appeared to be an explosion...."

ANSWER: "We know the plane blew up, right? And we know it fell into the water."

QUESTION: "People say they saw something that appeared to be an explosion. There's been no...."

ANSWER: "The plane's in parts underwater. People saw it blow up. I don't want to get into semantics about what happened to the plane. Something happened to the plane, and it fell into the water. That's what we were able to confirm." (Laughter)

QUESTION: "Olympic security. Is there any discussion going on for providing any additional military or reserve personnel for all types or any types of security down there? Also, is there any discussion about bolstering self-protection forces around areas where US troops are residing around the Atlanta area?"

ANSWER: "We have taken prudent and thorough security measures working with local and state and federal authorities. We aren't primarily a law enforcement or a protection agency domestically. What we've done is in support of other authorities, and we've done what they have asked us to do. We've also taken, we believe, prudent steps to protect our own soldiers down there, some of whom are living in an area close to the Olympic operations."

QUESTION: "Were any changes made in your thorough measures working with the local authorities, any changes made since the Flight 800 disaster?"

ANSWER: "I'm not aware that they have been. They may have been, I'm just not aware of them."

QUESTION: "A quick follow-up to the TWA issue again. The radars that you referred to, can you comment more on this? Are they at military facilities in the area?"

ANSWER: "The main radar, of course, is the FAA radar. Then, there was a fleet air support facility called the FASFAC which is down in Norfolk, I believe, but it basically used the FAA radar. It just had a relay that brings FAA radars into its facility so it can monitor naval air traffic in the area. There was a NORAD radar that picked up something. There was a naval radar in the area. There were several military radars, but as I say, they didn't, they have not produced anything that would help investigators determine what happened, nor would they produce anything that strengthens one of the various theories about what happened to the plane."

QUESTION: "Is that naval radar in the area of the P-3?"

ANSWER: "No, there was a ship in the area about 180 miles away."

QUESTION: "They're automatically recorded on videotape, aren't they?"

ANSWER: "The ship didn't record it because its radar was on low, and it was out of the range of the radar."

QUESTION: "What about the others? The FAA and the others?"

ANSWER: "Yeah, they did record it. They have the tapes and they're able to analyze the tapes.

"I want to follow-up on two things that came up earlier. There was a New York Air National Guard unit, the 106th Air Rescue Recovery Wing in West Hampton Beach, New York, had one HC-130 and — is this two helicopters — in the air about ten miles away from the scene of the crash when it occurred. They witnessed the accident, and they were the first on the scene to provide assistance. They stayed on the scene for about two hours, and then returned to their base. Later the HC-130 went out again and worked until about 3 a.m. deploying flares to help ships."

QUESTION: "Which unit was that again?"

ANSWER: "It was the 106th Air Rescue Recovery Wing from West Hampton, New York. The flares that are used by this National Guard unit are gravity type flares that are dropped from the plane and float on the water. That's what they were using to help illuminate the crash scene after...."

QUESTION: "Were those the flares that people saw, or they dropped them after the...."

ANSWER: "They dropped it afterwards."

QUESTION: "They didn't drop any before, during the exercise?"

ANSWER: "Not that I'm aware of. We've checked pretty closely what was going on in the area around the time.

"The second thing, on the Stinger missiles, the DoD wasn't involved in the Stinger missile program in Afghanistan. It was other agencies that were involved, and they might be the people with whom you should check."

PRESS: "Thank you."

0331 GMT, August 12, 1996
Near the Equator, South Atlantic

The anticipation of the fresh sea air kept Captain Abdi Morteza one step short of eager. It had to be even worse for Major Mohaddessin, his two Revolutionary Guards, Mashadi and those younger members of the crew. The last time they felt the ocean's salty breeze was the glorious night of their victory, and even then, it was only five of them.

They were nearly a week late reaching their rendezvous point with their return trip refueling ship, the freighter, _Marat_. He knew the _Marat_'s captain had to be very nervous wandering around the mid-Atlantic not actually knowing whether the meeting would ever occur. For all he knew, or anyone else for that matter, the Americans had quietly dispatched the attacker in their territorial waters.

Their retrograde maneuvering away from New York City with at least one anti-submarine aircraft and one or more American attack submarines looking for them required a very slow, careful transit. They stopped cold several times, staying as quiet as they possibly could, to listen for any trailers stalking them. They listened to radio traffic, including the _Marat's_ coded position data, but the _Noor_ had not transmitted a radio signal in over two months. Avoidance of detection had been the paramount objective, once their primary mission had been accomplished.

"Up periscope," ordered Morteza.

The gush of hydraulic power drove the thick shaft

upward. The Captain quickly scanned the horizon completely around him. The running lights as well as the brilliant deck lights of the *Marat* provided the only element of humanity in the middle of the dark ocean.

Morteza chose to remain submerged longer than usual although the urge to surface grew stronger with each moment. He grasped the handset. "Refueling crew standby. Surface the ship."

"Surface the ship," repeated the helmsman.

"Lookouts up," commanded the Captain. "Engineering, get as much of a battery charge as possible while we are refueling."

As they broke clear on the surface, the undulating swells, the initial splash of residual water and the gush of fresh air greeted the few members of the crew designated to be on deck for the night replenishment. Captain Morteza wished he could allow the entire crew a brief moment in the fresh air, but they still had several weeks of vulnerable transit before they reached the safety of Iranian waters.

"Allah be praised," shouted a man from the main deck of the *Marat*. His attire meant he was probably the captain of the freighter. Only a handful of other men could be seen on the larger ship. The *Marat* was quite a bit smaller than the *Haroot Farsi*, but still dwarfed the *Noor*.

The same precautions, Morteza told himself, had to be taken to protect the secrecy of this mission, then he nodded his head and said almost to himself, "Allah be praised." He was tired. The adrenaline of combat had worn off. He longed for home, although he could not confide in anyone.

"Where have you been?" shouted the dark, bearded man wearing a maritime captain's brimmed hat.

Morteza watched the crew tie off the ship against the

bumpers, connect the fuel hose and begin pumping. "We had to take extra precautions as we departed."

"We had only one more day before we were required to depart. You were lucky."

Abdi Morteza did not feel particularly lucky, nor conversational. The chronic fatigue of a ship's captain and especially a warrior at sea would not dissipate. "We shall be topped off in short order and be on our way."

Another bearded man, this one younger and wearing the camouflage field uniform of the Revolutionary Guards came to the railing. "Congratulations to you from the Leader of the Revolution and our faithful people. Allah is smiling," the man said.

"Thank you," was about all the *Noor*'s Captain could say.

The men completed the refueling. Confirmation of the replenishment was communicated by the Engineering Officer. With the added range of the ballast fuel, they now had enough fuel and supplies to complete the remainder of the voyage with some margin.

"What message do you want me to send?" asked the Guards officer aboard the *Marat*.

"Make sure you use the proper code words. You may tell Tehran we have made good our escape, mission accomplished. We shall arrive home in 26 days, more or less."

"Very well, Captain. You shall have a hero's welcome upon your return. You have brought glory to Allah and to the revolution."

Captain Morteza did not feel glorious. Although the thought of being the instrument of retribution for his country and his faith had appealed to him, the deaths of perhaps hundreds of people left a very sour taste in his mouth. Besides, he already knew there would probably be no public hero's welcome, theirs would be a silent honor, inasmuch as they had been successful in keeping their identities unknown.

"May I have a word with Major Mohaddessin?" asked the Guards officer.

"We must depart," shouted Morteza, not wanting to spend any more time on the surface than necessary. It would be so tragic to lose the ship after so much work. He was certain the Americans were still looking for them, if they even suspected the *Noor* might be involved in the TWA 800 crash. The deck crew had closed the hatch behind them.

"It will only take a minute, Captain," the man pleaded.

"Lookouts below," said Morteza, then into his phone he said, "Major Mohaddessin to the bridge immediately."

As if the Guards major had been waiting a few steps below, Mohaddessin appeared on the narrow conning tower bridge. The two warriors nodded to one another, then Morteza nodded toward the deck of the *Marat*.

"Ahmed," shouted Mohaddessin.

"It is an honor, Ali Hassan," shouted the other man.

"We don't have much time."

"Your name shall be etched in stone for all history. You have brought honor to Allah and to our family."

Morteza looked at both men as he realized they were probably brothers. The family reunion was touching, but survival and safe arrival was more important. He waved Major Mohaddessin below.

"Allah be with you," shouted Ali Hassan.

"Allah be with you. I shall see you at home."

"Your brother?" asked Morteza. Mohaddessin nodded. "We must go," he said extending his hand toward the hatch as if inviting him into this house. The Guards major did not hesitate even for his brother.

Captain Morteza gave the appropriate commands. The *Noor* pulled away from the *Marat*. They submerged to snorkeling depth to complete the recharge of the batteries. Once they were well clear of the freighter and the batteries fully charged, Morteza stopped to listen — still no trailers they could detect. For the first time, Abdi Morteza allowed himself to think they might actually get away with this bold stroke at the heart of the 'Great Satan.'

0830 EDT (1230 GMT), August 14, 1996
National Maritime Intelligence Center, Suitland, MD

Captain Judy Weston was not in her usual chair as the weekly staff meeting came to order. She was standing at the podium, glaring at everyone to quickly take their seats.

"Come on, everyone. Let's get with it. Lots to do," she exhorted everyone.

The group of assorted naval officers, analysts and staff members reluctantly left the coffee pot and donut box to find their chairs.

Finally, Captain Weston said, "Thank you." She nodded to the lieutenant at the staff officers' entrance to the conference room. The lieutenant opened the door.

The assembled analytical staff of the National Maritime Intelligence Center was surprised to see the admiral, the center commander, stalk into the room. Unprepared naval personnel were barely able to shuffle to their feet before the admiral announced, "As you were."

The admiral looked the crowd in the eye and spoke firmly. "I don't usually get a chance to meet with you in a working meeting like this. But, there has been a matter of critical importance come to my attention that I wanted each of you to hear directly from me. It is a little out of the ordinary, at least for these post-Cold War days, but those of you who have been around for awhile remember the drill."

He paused to scan the room to ensure he had everyone's attention. "The National Command Authority," he continued, using designation of the DoD/Joint Chiefs of Staff when acting on presidential authority, "has made a classified declaration of national emergency, of sorts. Certain recent events, namely the Khobar Barracks bombing and the downing...ahh...crash, of TWA 800, have necessitated this declaration in order to protect information which the NCA has deemed to be critical to the national interest. This critical information involves the potential threat to the United States from terrorist attack and state sponsored terrorism. Much of it involves matters not of immediate concern to Naval Intelligence, namely the possibility of terrorist action in the TWA incident. However, some of it does."

The silver haired officer continued to keep eye contact with the group before him. "There are three matters of intelligence information which involve us here. Two of them were common knowledge with this group, having been discussed before you in the last two months. One involved a few of you here on staff. These three items of intelligence and all information relating to them have been reclassified Top Secret with a new compartment designation — HIJACK."

"Those items are anything to do with an Iranian submarine *Noor* and all its activities after June 1, anything to do with a Iranian merchantman *Marat* for the same time frame, and all information regarding a SOSUS track identified as a possible Kilo/Foxtrot boat on July 16th along with any reaction we may have had to that track.

"All information regarding any of these three items and under the designation, HIJACK, will be collected and given to Captain Weston. There will be no discussion of this directive, or what might have caused it at all, even among you within these walls. Managers with people involved or affected will give as little information to your people as possible, if you need assistance in getting the point across, well, let Captain Weston know. The very existence of this security directive itself is classified Top Secret. You will not discuss it.

"I know how unusual this all seems especially with respect to the tragic events of the evening of July 17 [th]. It is not the usual method of doing business, especially in these walls where our main purpose is to discuss and handle critical intelligence data. However, rest assured that it is important. Also, take note that any violation of this directive or my orders will be a violation of the National Security Act and subject to the appropriate criminal penalties. Specific personnel will be read into HIJACK in accordance with established procedures."

The admiral looked down at Captain Weston, then back to the staff members. "I hope you all understand the importance of my coming here to tell you this." Several nodding heads indicated they did.

"Very well. Carry on, Captain Weston," the admiral said as he marched out.

September 5, 1996
US House of Representatives, Washington, DC

Jim Hall, Chairman of the National Transportation Safety Board, testified before the Committee on Transportation and Infrastructure Subcommittee on Aviation, House of Representatives regarding HR3923, Aviation Disaster Family Assistance Act of 1996. The legislation, among other things, provided additional annual appropriation to the NTSB to help cover the huge costs of the TWA investigation and the follow-up to the earlier ValueJet crash.

Hall stated,"Good morning Mr. Chairman and Members of the Committee. I am pleased to be here today to present my views on HR3923, the Aviation Disaster Family Assistance Act of 1996. Mr. Chairman, the testimony I am presenting are my personal views, and do not reflect a Board position.

"First, I would like to give you and the Committee an update on the status of the investigation into the tragic loss of TWA Flight 800. As you know, Flight 800 disappeared from radar screens at 8:31 PM on July 17, 1996. Carrying 230 passengers and crew, the flight was bound for Paris, France. The aircraft suffered a catastrophic explosion or explosions, and evidence indicates that this explosion likely involved the center fuel tank, which was empty at the time of takeoff. Because of immediate and intense concern that this tragedy could have been an act of terror, the NTSB, while leading the investigation, has been working closely with the FBI and other Federal and state agencies in trying to uncover exactly what happened to Flight 800.

"The tragedy occurred at dusk in clear weather and wreckage fell in an area approximately 6 to 9 miles off East Moriches, Long Island. Coast Guard search and rescue vessels and aircraft were on the accident scene within minutes. They were assisted by numerous private vessels; but, unfortunately, there were no survivors. The wreckage sank to the Ocean bottom at a depth of approximately 120 feet, and it was spread out over 5 1/2 square miles. The NTSB called in the US Navy Supervisor of Salvage to coordinate the recovery efforts.

"If I could make a personal statement, the officers and crew of the Navy ships, USS *Grasp*, USS *Grapple*, USS *Oak Hill* and the *Pirouette* have done an extraordinary job under the most difficult conditions. Operating on a 24-hour-a-day basis, they have worked in an extremely dangerous environment, and from the beginning, the top priority has been the recovery of victims. The divers want nothing more than to recover every victim, and to date 211 have been recovered. This is an extraordinary accomplishment, under the circumstances, and we pray that more victims will be recovered.

"To date the investigative team has been unable to determine what was the likely cause of this accident. Although there have been tantalizing bits of evidence, there has been no so-called 'smoking gun.' Our investigation is on-going, and with about 75 percent of the plane recovered, we expect our efforts to continue in the coming weeks until we have brought to the surface and examined every piece of wreckage possible.

"Let me now address the issue at hand and relate this

bill to the efforts made on behalf of the family members of Flight 800. First, I personally supported this bill, not because it gives the NTSB more responsibility — we are a small agency with a targeted mission — but because it's the right thing to do. Something needs to be done to better coordinate services for family members of victims of air disasters. Let me describe briefly some of the challenges we faced in New York.

"The NTSB Go-Team arrived on-scene on Thursday, July 18, 1996, at 6:15 AM. Our Regional Aviation Director from Parsippany, New Jersey, had been on Long Island since 10:45 PM the previous evening. He had been doing groundwork for the arrival of our Go-Team and had been performing preliminary investigative activities.

"Early Thursday evening, the NTSB's Director of Government and Public Affairs arrived at the Ramada Hotel at Kennedy International Airport, met with local officials and briefed the approximately 400 family members who had already gathered at the hotel on the status of the investigation. It was clear at this session — as it was clear at the ValueJet tragedy — that at times like this the only two agencies that family members really want to hear from are the NTSB and the medical examiner's office. As the sole agency responsible for the investigation, family members want to hear directly from us, and, frankly, it is our responsibility to give them accurate and timely information.

"The tragedy on Long Island presented us with unprecedented logistical challenges. Family members were located at Kennedy International Airport; the staging area and temporary morgue were 1 1/2 hours away at East Moriches, New York; the NTSB command post was at the only available hotel at Smithtown, New York — 1 1/4 hours away (almost an hour from East Moriches); and the hangar where the reconstruction of the shattered aircraft would be reconstructed was not really near any of the above — at Calverton, New York.

"The logistics of the accident made even very basic communications difficult. Couple this with the very aggressive media market in New York, the numerous governmental jurisdictions involved, and the magnitude and multi-national aspects of the tragedy, and there is little wonder that some family members felt frustrated.

"When President Clinton visited the family members on July 25, 1996, he named the NTSB as the sole agency authorized to speak to the family members, and he gave the NTSB much needed support from FEMA to get the mission accomplished. I want to thank the President and FEMA Director James Lee Witt for their concern and their prompt action. With the additional support and resources, the NTSB was able to establish twice a day group briefings that were simultaneously translated into both French and Italian. The briefings and extensive one-on-one meetings went until Friday, August 2, 1996, when fewer than 15 families were left at the Ramada Hotel. At that time, under the advice of the Red Cross and State mental health professionals, the family members remaining were encouraged to return home to a more supportive environment. A follow-up network, including an 800 number, was put in place."

This testimony by Chairman Hall on the TWA 800 investigation was supplemented on March 11, 1997 with the following testimony before another congressional committee, the Committee on Appropriations, Subcommittee on Transportation and Related Agencies. This testimony was regarding the Fiscal Year 1998 Budget Request for NTSB in which Chairman Hall reported on many accidents and projects which NTSB were pursuing. In regards to TWA 800, Hall's testimony was:

"On July 17, 1996, TWA Flight 800 tragically crashed into the Atlantic Ocean near East Moriches, New York, killing all 230 people on board. The aircraft wreckage in this accident was ten miles off the coast at a depth of 120 feet, making this investigation anything but typical.

"To ensure the safety of the divers and to identify the location of the wreckage, the area had to be thoroughly mapped before the full scale underwater recovery effort could begin. Heavy wreckage was not lifted from the ocean floor until early August. By the end of October, the divers had cleared the debris fields of all large pieces of wreckage. On November 3, scallop trawlers were brought in to drag the ocean floor. To date, an area of over 28 square miles has been trawled, with some areas having been gone over in excess of 20 times. A second pass is being made over the entire area; trawling will continue until wreckage is no longer being recovered.

"Based on the condition of the wreckage from the center forward section of the plane and that surrounding the center wing tank, the investigators are particularly interested in this area and have created mock-ups of this section. Three sets of scaffolding were erected on which this section of plane is being reassembled in order to give the investigators a better picture of what occurred. The fuselage surrounding the center wing tank was on one, the top and sides of the center wing tank on another, and the floor of the center wing tank was on the third.

"It is apparent that an explosion occurred in the center wing tank, but the origin of the explosion and whether it was the initial event or a secondary event is not yet known. To date, with over 90 percent of the plane recovered, there is no physical evidence of a bomb or missile strike.

"The Safety Board and the Federal Bureau of Investigation have called on numerous experts from across the international aviation community, the Department of Defense, and academia to assist in this investigation. Work that is either now underway or will be in the near future include:

- Complete the mock-up of the structure in the vicinity of the center wing tank. Safety Board contractors are completing a mock-up measuring approximately 92 feet, the largest reconstruction in the world.
- Fuel testing — The Safety Board is engaged in laboratory and field testing at Cal Tech to study the ignition and explosive properties of Jet A fuel, and the conduct of large scale tests of fuel-air explosions.
- Acoustic analysis of the cockpit voice recorder — Safety Board investigators are working with experts from NASA and the United Kingdom on additional sound spectrum analysis to develop data against which the events registered on the TWA 800 CVR may be compared.
- Extensive mapping of interior damage patterns — Safety Board investigators will extensively map interior damage patterns, including damage to occupants, seats, carpet, and floorboards.
- Extensive mapping of center wing tank parts and surrounding structure — Safety Board investigators will extensively map the center wing tank and surrounding area, including integrating the cabin interior map.
- Evaluation of potential ignition mechanisms that may have triggered the center wing tank explosion. This will include testing of the fuel line fittings, measuring the static electricity generated by fuel spray, assessment of potential sources of an electrical discharge, and evaluation of the potential for

penetrations of the tank by high speed particles or fragments. "Mr. Chairman, the investigation into the crash of TWA Flight 800 has been unprecedented, and all parties remain committed to finding the cause of this tragic event."

There are several important items of information that should be noted in these two reports to Congress by the NTSB Chair. First, and most importantly, is the change between the September 1996 and March 1997 testimony regarding the explosion of the center wing tank. In September, the obvious explosion in the center wing tank was tacitly assumed to have been the cause of the crash. But in March, the NTSB is obviously questioning whether the explosion of the center wing tank was the cause of the crash or whether that explosion was merely a result of some other "ignition mechanisms," specifically "high speed particles or fragments."

Next, the discussion of evaluation of interior damage patterns, including damage to seating and occupants is consistent with the claims of some theorists, that the occupants' bodies were pierced by missile fragments. This is also indicative of the fact that the 'red stain' fiasco, discussed below, may be having an effect on investigators' priorities, or at least their sensitivity to public concerns.

Lastly, the report that the cockpit voice recorder is undergoing a detailed acoustic analysis by experts from NASA and Great Britain is supportive of the report, discussed later in the book, that the final seconds of the recording indicated a missile impact. (More information from the NTSB on cockpit voice recorders and flight data recorders is included at Appendix D.)

January 22, 1997
Iranian Majlis (Parliament), Tehran, Iran

The Majlis, Iran's legislative body, approved a bill allocating 25 billion Rials ($14.2 million) for purposes of military and covert confrontation of the United States. According to the bill, the money will also be used for making "headway in international organizations and mobilizing world public opinion against America."

This was the second time the same $14.2 million appropriation had been made. The initial appropriation was supposedly made in response to a published report that US House Speaker Newt Gingrich had publicly advocated the US appropriating $20 million to be used in a covert action to bring down the Iranian government.

The Majlis' 1997 legislative action against the US was carried out by a unanimous vote during which massed chants of "death to the United States" were shouted by the members.

On the next day, January 23, 1997, Iran accepted delivery from Russia of its third Kilo-class submarine. That day, President Rafsanjani said in Tehran that Iran would "powerfully respond to any possible US military measures and reveal to the world the real power of Iran."

May 23, 1997
Tehran, Iran

On May 23, 1997, 20 million Iranians voted for Hojjatoleslam Mohammad Khatami, the fifth president of the Islamic Republic of Iran, nearly 70% of the vote. President Khatami's inauguration speech in the parliament after his oath on August 4, 1997 made it clear that the promises of openness and freedom made during his campaign would at least be carried forward in word, and perhaps deed, during his administration. Many observers feel he is positioned to radically change Iranian national policy, especially Iran/US relations.

Holding the holy title of Hojjatoleslam, Mohammad Khatami is an admixture of both the traditional and modern in Iran, educated in the most conservative of Islamic institutions, credentialed as an early supporter of Ayatollah Khomeini, but familiar and knowledgable about the West. He was born in Ardakan, in the central Province of Yazd in 1943 to a religious family. Son of respected Ayatollah Ruhollah Khatami, President Khatami finished his early school years in Yazd. Then, he attended Qom Theology School in 1961. Later, he got his BA in philosophy from Isfahan University, and finished in senior level religious studies at Qom Seminary. Having started his post graduate studies in educational sciences at Tehran University from 1970, he returned to Qom later to pursue courses on *Ijtihad* (practice of religious leadership) at Qom Seminary.

President Khatami was involved in political activities and the anti-Shah campaign by preparing, duplicating and distributing political statements, especially those issued by the Founder of the Islamic Republic, the late Imam Khomeini. He began his political activities at the Association of Muslim Students of Isfahan University, worked closely with Imam Khomeini's late son, Hojjatoleslam Ahmad Khomeini and Martyr Mohammad Montazeri and organized religious and political debates.

Khatami left Iran in those years of western influence and political repression under the Shah and chaired Islamic Center of Hamburg in Germany before the victory of the 1979 Islamic Revolution. Khatami's center in Germany turned into an Islamic campaign center when the late Imam Khomeini went to France. He returned to Iran after the Revolution and represented Ardakan and Meibod constituencies in the first term of Majlis [Parliament] in 1980. He was appointed as the head of Kayhan Institute by the late Imam Khomeini in 1981.

In 1982, he was appointed as the Minister of Culture and Islamic guidance during the premiership of Mirhossein Mousavi. During the 1980-1988 Iran/Iraq war, he served different responsibilities including head of the Joint Command of the Armed Forces and chairman of the War Propaganda Headquarters. After his wartime service, Khatami was again appointed as the Minister of Culture and Islamic guidance by President Akbar Hashemi Rafsanjani in 1989.

Following his resignation in 1992, President Khatami was appointed as cultural advisor to President Rafsanjani and head of Iran's National Library. He is fluent in three foreign languages, English, German and Arabic. He has written a number of books and articles in different fields. He is a family man, he married in 1974 and has two daughters and a son.

In a radical departure from earlier Iranian leadership, Khatami ran a campaign with slogans and promises a European or American electorate might hear, and he even set up an Internet Web site for his campaign for the Iranian Presidency. His Web site, http://www.khatami.com, now offers anyone the opportunity to send Email to Khatami, directly.

The hoped for openings in Iran/US relations and Iran's earlier support for terrorism were discussed in a January 7, 1998 interview with Christiane Amanpour of CNN. Amanpour asked, "Let me ask you some specific issues that concern the people of the United States. As you know, many US experts say that the evidence is overwhelming, that elements of the Iranian authorities, Iranian officials, provide not only political and moral, but financial support to organizations that commit acts of terrorism, and result in the deaths of innocent women and children. If you were presented with proof and with evidence that any kind of Iranian was involved in that kind of financial support or action, what would you do about it?"

President Khatami answered, "You see, this is another example of the sort of problem that exists between us and the United States. They first level unfair and unsubstantiated accusations against you. And, when they propose to hold talks, they say that they want to have a dialogue with you about these very unfounded accusations. They are in fact trying to put the other side on trial.

"Well, let me tell you this. We believe in the holy Koran that says: slaying of one innocent person is tantamount to the slaying of all humanity. How could such a religion, and those who claim to be its followers get involved in the assassination of innocent individuals and the slaughter of innocent human beings. We categorically reject all these allegations.

"Secondly, the logic of history has proven that violence is not the way to achieve a desired end. I personally believe that only those who lack logic resort to violence. Terrorism should be condemned in all its forms and manifestations; assassins must be condemned. Terrorism is useless anyway, and we condemn it categorically. Those who level these charges against us are best advised to provide accurate and objective evidence, which indeed does not exist."

While one cannot really hope for Khatami to openly admit to the types of across-the-board support of terrorism that the Western nations undisputedly assign to earlier Iranian governments, the failure to acknowledge any such activities, as even his predecessor, Rafsanjani, did (indirectly) is disappointing. In the same interview, Khatami mentioned the Iran Air disaster as being one item that still remains a sore point in the minds of Iranians toward the US and as shown above, he further acknowledges the Koran's exhortation on dealing with the slaying of innocent lives which this book begins with. One can only wonder if, in answering Ms. Amanpour's question about Iran's terrorism, Khatami was indirectly giving an excuse for it.

June 17, 1998
Waldorf Astoria Hotel, New York, NY

US Secretary of State Madeleine K. Albright addressed the 1998 Asia Society Dinner. Forewarned that her remarks would be a major policy statement, the world press was also in attendance. Secretary Albright's remarks included what was viewed by many as a pivotal change in US policy towards Iran, a capstone of a process aimed at opening up relations between Iran and the US.

"Last May, Iran's people were given a chance to voice their support for a more open society, and did so. Nearly 70 percent supported the election of Mohammad Khatami as President, providing him with a mandate for change, demanding from the Iranian Government greater freedoms, a more civil society based on the rule of law, and a more moderate foreign policy aimed at ending Iran's estrangement from the international community. At the time, President Clinton welcomed this election, and as a former professor and lifelong student of history, I found the vote remarkable. The depth of the demand for change was obvious. So too was the evident desire of young Iranians and many Iranian women for greater openness and more personal liberty.

"I was most impressed by the size of the mandate. Twenty million Iranians came forward to make themselves heard in the hope that, by so doing, they could effect real change in their government and in their daily lives.

"Since taking office, President Khatami has responded

to the demands of the Iranian people by emphasizing the importance of dialogue among nations and cultures, and by acknowledging the world's growing interdependence. He has said that 'a society intending to reach development cannot succeed without understanding Western civilization.' I would say, in response, that the same can be said with respect to Eastern civilization and Islamic civilization.

"President Khatami has said that the American Government deserves respect because it is a reflection of the great American people. I would say that President Khatami deserves respect because he is the choice of the Iranian people. In his interview with CNN in January, President Khatami called for a dialogue between civilizations, something which President Clinton welcomed because of our strongly held view that there is much common ground between Islam and the West, and much that we can do to enrich each other's societies.

"In past years, Iran's opposition to the Middle East Peace Process and to those willing to negotiate with Israel has been vitriolic and violent. The Islamic Republic still refuses to recognize Israel, and its leaders continue to denounce Israel in inflammatory and unacceptable terms. But last December, Iranian officials welcomed Chairman Arafat to the Islamic Summit in Tehran and said that, although they did not agree with the logic of the peace process, they would not seek to impose their views and would accept what the Palestinians could accept.

"In January, President Khatami publicly denounced terrorism and condemned the killing of innocent Israelis. He argued that terrorism was not only against Islam but also counterproductive to Iran's purposes. Iran, after all, has also been a victim of terrorism.

"If these views are translated into a rejection of

terrorism as a tool of Iranian statecraft, it would do much to dispel the concerns of the international community from Germany to the Persian Gulf, and from Argentina to Algeria.

"There are other signs of change, as well. For example, Iran's record in the war against drugs has greatly improved — at least within its own borders — and it has received high marks from the UN for its treatment of more than two million Iraqi and Afghan refugees. Iran is also participating in diplomatic efforts to bring peace and stability to Afghanistan and is making a welcome effort to improve relations with Saudi Arabia and other neighbors in the Gulf.

"We view these developments with interest, both with regard to the possibility of Iran assuming its rightful place in the world community, and the chance for better bilateral ties. However, these hopes must be balanced against the reality that Iran's support for terrorism has not yet ceased; serious violations of human rights persist; and its efforts to develop long range missiles and to acquire nuclear weapons continue.

"The United States opposes, and will continue to oppose, any country selling or transferring to Iran materials and technologies that could be used to develop long-range missiles or weapons of mass destruction. Similarly, we oppose Iranian efforts to sponsor terror. Accordingly, our economic policies, including with respect to the export pipelines for Caspian oil and gas, remain unchanged.

"But let me be clear. These policies are not, as some Iranians allege, anti-Islamic. Islam is the fastest-growing religious faith in the United States. We respect deeply its moral teachings and its role as a source of inspiration and instruction for hundreds of millions of people around the world. US policy is directed at actions, not peoples or faiths. The standards we would like Iran to observe are not merely

Western, but universal. We fully respect Iran's sovereignty. We understand and respect its fierce desire to maintain its independence. We do not seek to overthrow its government. But, we do ask that Iran live up to its commitments to the international community.

"As in Indonesia, we hope Iran's leaders will carry out the people's mandate for a government that respects and protects the rule of law, both in its internal and external affairs. Certainly, Iranian voters last year were concerned primarily with domestic issues. But, the Iranian people are also conscious of the critical role their country has long played in a region of global importance. What Iran must decide now is how its strength will be projected and to what ends. Much has changed in the almost twenty years Iran has been outside or on the fringes of the international system."

In an interview on NBC-TV's *Meet the Press* with Tim Russert and Andrea Mitchell on June 21, 1998, Secretary of State Albright further explained what she had in mind with Iran and how the traditional role of the Iranian government in terrorism factored into the equation.

MR. RUSSERT: "Let me turn to Iran. You gave a very historic speech this week, suggesting there may be an opportunity or road map to resume some kind of relations with Iran. Only last April, the State Department put out its book on global terrorism – your department. And let me show you and our viewers what this said about the country of Iran: 'It remains the most active state sponsor of terrorism. There's no evidence that Iranian policy has changed, and Iran continues both to provide significant support to terrorist organizations and to assassinate dissidents abroad.' Why would we engage in dialogue with that kind of behavior?"

SECRETARY ALBRIGHT: "Well, first of all, it goes back to the question or the point in your lead-in, which is that there have been some significant changes in Iran. But, let me also make quite clear that Iran still is on the terrorist list, and in my speech, I made very clear that if they were to be a part of the international community, they could not use terrorism as a part of statecraft, and that we are continued [*sic*] to be concerned about that.

"But, I think it is very important – and this is the point that I made in my speech – to respect the Iranian people who elected a new leader about a year ago, President Khatami, who is responding to the desire by a large proportion of the Iranian people for change and for openness. Ayatollah Khomeini had said that they had to be isolated. I think that these people, the new voters, have said that they want to be a part of the world. And, I said that if there was some parallel steps that could be taken over time, we would like to have a road map towards normalization. But, we continue to be concerned about their support for terrorism."

MR. RUSSERT: "Now, the Iranian radio, state-sponsored, has spoken out in response to your speech. Let me show you and our viewers what they had to say: 'In order to restore relations with the US, the US must end support for Iranian opposition guerrilla groups based in Iraq, free frozen Iranian assets and apologize to the Iranian nation for US wrong policies the last 50 years.' Will we end support for opposition groups; will we unfreeze assets; and will we apologize?"

SECRETARY ALBRIGHT: "Well, we're not going to apologize. I made quite clear already that I could [not]– the policies that we had were the policies that were appropriate to the period we understood. I think it's understandable that there was some resentment from the Iranian people, but we need to move forward. They made some statements about regret for the hostage crisis. I think we need to move forward.

"I think that clearly, we have to look at what can be done to make this relationship one that leads towards normalization."

MR. RUSSERT: "We would consider unfreezing assets?"

SECRETARY ALBRIGHT: "I'm not going to comment specifically on what we would consider."

MR. RUSSERT: "Last on this subject, as you know, this morning there's an article in *The New York Times* that the investigation into the Khobar bombing, where 19 Americans were blown up in 1996 in Saudi Arabia – the Iranians are allegedly responsible for that – the investigation has broken down. Must we have accountability by the Iranians for whether or not they were involved in that bombing before we can normalize relations?"

SECRETARY ALBRIGHT: "Well, we have to go forward with the investigation. The FBI is in charge of the investigation; we raise the issue diplomatically. We have to have some conclusion to the investigation. I mean, we can't – it may take a while.

"I think one of the other parts, again, that we need to remember, things don't happen overnight. For instance, the Rashid* rendition, who had been involved in a TWA incident, that took over ten years to get him here. So, these investigations are very complicated. We pursue them; and we will plan to pursue this one."

On June 18th in Madrid, Spain, Iranian Foreign Minister Kamal Kharrazi responded to Secretary Albright and gave the United States a challenge that it must change its "hostile policies" towards Iran before the two countries could hope to normalize relations. "Until the United States shows that it is ready to have an attitude towards Iran that is based on mutual respect and equality, there won't be very many possibilities for relations." Kharrazi said Albright's speech indicated that "Americans are coming to some new understandings." However, Kharrazi went on to say that no major progress in relations was likely "until hostile policies of the United States against Iran are changed and they approach Iran with new attitudes."

Foreign Minister Kharrazi ended with what can only be viewed as an entreaty to the US Government, "Only coming with new words and political words is not enough. I believe words have to be followed by deeds."

Five days later the United States showed how much it wants an easing of tensions between the US and Iran when President Clinton vetoed legislation imposing tough sanctions on firms that sell missile technology to Iran, setting himself up for an all-but-certain override in Congress. Clinton issued a written statement explaining his veto, "This bill would hinder, not help, our overall national interests...making it harder to achieve the goals it is intended to serve, therefore, I am vetoing this bill."

Clinton called the measure "inflexible and indiscriminate," and said it would require the imposition of sanctions "based on an unworkably low standard of evidence."

Congressional Democrats had earlier vowed that if Clinton rejected the bill they would join with the Republicans to override his veto. The legislation passed in both houses of Congress by wide margins, making an override of Clinton's veto near certain.

The bill established three types of sanctions — denial

of munitions licenses, prohibitions of dual use licenses or denial of US foreign aid. The President would have the same power to waive sanctions in matters needed to "protect US national security." Clinton has used the same waiver power to avoid the effects of the Iran sanctions bill passed by the US Senate the evening TWA 800 was shot down.

Thus, Clinton was in the position of having made a gesture to Iran with his own deed of vetoing the anti-Iran legislation, knowing full well that the Congress would override the veto and make the legislation the law.

It was unclear whether the Iranians would accept such hollow 'deeds' as those Foreign Minister Kharrazi demanded. What was clear was the lengths the US administration would go to bring Khatami's new government into rapprochement range of the US. Whether this would have included a policy directive from the highest levels to squelch talk of Iranian complicity in TWA 800, unless absolute certainty could be achieved, is also unclear.

On July 12, 1998, Iran's supreme leader, the Ayatollah Khamenei, with Iranian President Khatami at his side, denounced President Clinton's efforts so far as mere "gimmickry."

The FAA Radar Screens and What They Show

One of the most startling disclosures in the course of the TWA 800 investigation has been the controversial FAA radar tapes. These tapes have been the source of much speculation and a great deal of derision for the federal agencies involved. They have been powerful fodder for the various conspiracy theories, especially the Salinger 'friendly fire' concept, now recanted. They are, of course, a factor in this book's evaluation of the evidence.

From the earliest weeks of the investigation, there were rumors that the federal government had information from the radar screens of the Federal Aviation Administration (FAA) that showed a missile hitting TWA 800. A week after this crash, this rumor spread to reports in such papers as *The Times* of London and the *Boston Globe* that American satellites had definitive proof of a missile strike. The FBI and NTSB routinely denied any report of any sensors picking up anything that helped their investigation.

In mid-March 1997, the speculation regarding the possibility of radar images took a new turn when an aviation and radar consultant, Richard D. Russell, announced that he had copies of an FAA radar tape which showed a missile traveling at a speed of 1,500 to 2,000 miles per hour hitting the 747. Shortly thereafter, copies of frames from the tape of the FAA radar screens were published. Russell stated that he had undertaken to find and make the truth known to the public when, after getting an opportunity to review a debris field document prepared by the FBI/NTSB investigators (see below), he ascertained that the public statements of the federal authorities were not complete or entirely truthful.

It must be noted that paragraph XIII.A of the FBI report (Appendix C) states that the object in the Russell tapes "...*WAS NOT A MISSILE*, since it was positively identified. Object was a Ghost of Jet Express 18 which was at a different location." [*Emphasis as contained in the FBI report.*] Simple statements are rarely convincing, no matter who says them. While ghosting on radar systems is a common, known phenomenon, there are many curious elements in the Russell tapes and especially in light of the NTSB radar data. The authors chose to recount the events surrounding the Russell tapes.

There were indications that these tapes were the same ones complained of in a November 15th memorandum by the NTSB which stated that the FBI had sent sensitive radar data showing a missile converging on the airliner to the White House and FAA before it went to the NTSB, which was, in name, the lead agency for the investigation. Other sources have argued that the FAA radar tapes would not normally be considered 'sensitive' so that must mean that there is other radar data from Department of Defense or satellite sources which also confirms the missile track. In mid-March, Richard Russell made the tapes public, allowing them to be published in *Paris Match* magazine in France, possibly through the Salinger connection, and later by posting on the Internet.

The immediate response was that the tapes were a hoax. Then, the official word changed to that the image was an anomaly, a stray electronic ghost. Then, on March 20, 1997, the FBI and NTSB responded that the blip shown on the tapes was really the Navy's P-3, anti-submarine, patrol aircraft and not a 'friendly fire' missile as the leading proponents of the radar tapes were saying.

At that point, the FBI and NTSB were meshing the two reports, that of a 'friendly fire' missile and the radar tapes together. They vehemently discounted the 'friendly fire' theory by attacking the evidence brought forth to support it, such as system capabilities, the illogic of keeping such a thing secret, and the patent absurdity that the US Navy would run a missile test adjacent to both the busiest air route on earth, one of the busiest sea lanes, and the largest metropolitan area in the country.

By lumping the radar tape evidence together with the 'friendly fire' theorists who were first using it and by an ever changing story of denial that the radar tapes showed anything, the federal authorities seemed to hope that the obvious questions raised by the radar tapes would go away. They were only partially successful in this aim.

We have included in this book nine images from the FAA radar tapes. It appears from these tapes that an object rises up from the ocean (i.e., appears out of nowhere in the radar image, in an area where only the ocean exists) and intersects with the airliner after a twelve second flight. As explained below, the climb rate/speed for a shoulder-fired surface-to-air missile is just above 1,000 feet per second, or the equivalent of a twelve second flight to hit a target flying at 13,000+ feet, as in the case of TWA 800. Thus, the object could be a missile fired from a ship or submarine. It appears seconds before the explosion and is not seen after the explosion.

The radar images included in this book cover the time from 2029:50 to 2034:52 EDT July 17,1996, across the critical moment in time, 2031:12 EDT. They show each of the aircraft we have discussed in this book. The only unidentified blip is that of the 'missile.'

The first image is FAA Radar #1. The concentric rings are the ten-mile distance rings from the FAA Islip Control Center. The time (in Greenwich Mean Time four hours ahead of Eastern Daylight Time) is shown as 0029/50, or 8:29 PM and 50 seconds EDT. The barometer is shown as 29.92 inches of mercury. Under the time, you can see that this is a 'replay.' TWA800 can be seen in the center of the screen, labeled TWA8∅∅. Underneath the label, you can see 'BET' which is an abbreviation for the BETTE intersection on the departure route from JFK eastward. The 37 is the aircraft's speed, 370 knots (nautical miles per hour), or 426 miles per hour. The 'H' stands for 'heavy,' a large, heavy aircraft with strong wake turbulence. The leader line points to a 'C' symbol that is the location of the TWA800 Identify-Friend-Foe (IFF) transponder in the nose of the 747.

Also off FAA Radar #1, you can see TWA 900, just behind TWA 800. It is traveling at 410 knots. There is an air track to the south of TWA800 with the IFF code 2237 showing an altitude of 244 (24,400 feet) and speed of 47 (470 knots). This aircraft is a USAir flight going north to Rhode Island. TWA 800 has been kept at a relatively low altitude to keep it lower than this other flight above it. We have put a circle around the USAir flight to distinguish it as we go through the screens. To the far east of the radar screen (right) is a track that has been identified as the Navy P-3 patrol plane heading southwest from Brunswick, Maine to a Navy operations area to the south. We have put a square symbol around the P-3 to keep track of it. The P-3 is not using its IFF transponder.

The next screen, FAA Radar #2, is at 0030:17 GMT or twenty-seven seconds after the first. The Navy P-3 in the square has traveled on closer to TWA 800. The USAir flight in the circle has moved north. The FAA operator has changed the screen to show no label on the USAir flight (which is not under this operator's control) and the TWA8ØØ track now shows the altitude as 12,900 feet.

Eighteen seconds later, at 0030:35 GMT, in FAA Radar #3, a new blip appears in the middle of the screen. It is marked by us with a triangle. The TWA8ØØ, USAir and P-3 tracks have all flown closer together. In reality, they are at staggered altitudes. The new blip does not have a transponder shown.

The new blip is at about the same spot in the next frame five seconds later, as though either stationary or climbing in the same spot. In this frame, FAA Radar #4 at 0030:40, the three aircraft have all moved slightly together.

In FAA Radar #5 at 0030:45, the new blip has disappeared (it disappeared at 0030:42). TWA 8ØØ is shown at 13,300 feet and is getting within a few miles of the other two aircraft. The mystery blip has stayed on screen for precisely twelve seconds, being hit with a radar beam every four seconds for four hits. The successive hits in the same spot rule out radio wave noise.

2031:12 EDT, (0031:12 GMT), 17.July.1998

Thirty seconds later, in FAA Radar #6 at 0031:16, there are three blips shown together in almost one point, the P-3, the USAir flight and an unknown blip. The TWA 8ØØ track is farther to the east with a transponder altitude of 13,700 feet showing. The third blip near the P-3 and US Air tracks has been speculated as being either the mystery blip having moved farther east toward TWA 800 or a large part of TWA 800 falling away from the transponder which still shows a return to the east. The upper right corner of the FAA screen shows a CA Alert or 'close approach alert' indicating that two tracks have gotten alarmingly close to each other.

The track for TWA 800 then disappears. Seen in FAA Radar #7 some two minutes later, the P-3 has flown on to the south. The USAir has gone north. TWA Flight 900 has passed the point where TWA 800 has now blown into a fireball. A new track is coming down from the north and shows a transponder. Other tracks to the west of the 'C,' the '0901 T' and those nearby seem to be drawing over toward the site of TWA 800's explosion and impact.

In FAA Radar #8, at 0034:02, the track to the north (in our pentagon shape) is shown at 200 feet. The tracks to the west are now almost over the crash site. The P-3 is almost off the screen, but the aspect (radar view) of the P-3 track seems different from the previous five minutes.

In the final FAA screen, FAA Radar #9 at 0034:52, the FAA controller has identified the track to the north as 'Jolly 14,' the Air National Guard rescue helicopter. Five other tracks have all congregated over the crash site.

The last radar image included here is a view of the National Weather Service weather radar a few minutes after TWA 800 exploded. The computer generated outline of Long Island and the coastline clearly shows the location of the blossom of debris which is falling through the sky littering the weather radar that is designed to pick up 'clouds' rather than aircraft. The cloud of minute debris thrown out by TWA

800 shows up clearly at the crash site.

The next question is obviously, 'what does this radar tape show us?' Like many clues in a mystery, what it disproves is almost as valuable as what it hints at.

One of the most important things it shows is that there is no long-range, large, naval missile fired from the USS *Normandy* to the south or from above Long Island to the north. The use of this radar imagery by those who claim it shows a 'friendly fire' incident is nonsensical. It does no such thing. There is no track for a Standard missile coming from over the horizon to the south. The track from the north is a P-3 on a noticed flight. It is not flying at missile speeds, and it continues on after it crosses the path of TWA 800.

So, the question remains as to the mystery blip that shows up for twelve seconds and disappears. Does this blip prove that there was a missile launched from the ocean surface up toward TWA 800? The answer is no, it does not prove that. But, it does nothing to disprove it, and it is one possible explanation, considering the closeness of a SAM's flight time to 13,000+ feet and the duration of the mystery blip. It could also be radar ghosting as indicated in the FBI report. Without a more thorough public examination and analysis of the radar tapes and the information they do or do not contain, this issue can not be resolved. The FBI's 'not a missile' claim can not be substantiated, no more so than the popular missile hypothesis.

There is another explanation of the short-lived blip which, in fairness, must be considered. If you look at FAA Radar #3 and #4 very closely, you will see that the image of the mystery blip between the two moves slightly south, away from TWA 800 rather than toward it, then it disappears. Thirty seconds later the image of TWA 800 itself disappears. As discussed in detail in our section on debris field evidence later, the approximate time between the initial explosive event and the final explosion that destroyed the rear section and wings was estimated at 24 seconds more or less. That initial explosive event may have included the blasting of the forward cargo door and air-conditioner unit outward to the right. At that same time, the forward section was falling down into the ocean. An FAA radar's computer track of a plane does not instantly disappear when the transponder or radar signal is lost. Considering all these factors and the probable destructive sequence of the airplane, the most logical explanation of the short-lived blip is that it was the cargo door, Center Wing Spar (CW504), air-conditioner or some other item blown away from the main body of the plane, or the nose itself, after the initial explosion. This would explain the fact that this is a real radar return, not an echo, that it lasts only seconds, and it appears to move away from the flight path of TWA 800 to the right.

The Damage, the Debris and the Crash Site:
What does it mean?

The debris from the destruction of TWA 800 fell in two elongated streaks running along the flight path some ten miles off shore of Moriches, Long Island. Following the initial mass confusion that seemed to defy analysis, a distinct pattern of the resting place of the aircraft and its passengers in the ocean, and on the ocean floor emerged. This pattern of the debris, along with the damage shown to the aircraft pieces, when viewed as a whole gives a remarkably clear picture of the final seconds of Flight 800.

The flames from the wreck were still burning when the first Coast Guard, Navy and civilian craft arrived on the crash site. Those boats arriving on the scene from New York City and other points to the West noticed that there was debris floating in the water several miles west of what appeared to be the primary crash site where all the fire was. Indeed, the first helicopters and boats had some hope that they might find some survivors since there were so many bodies floating in the open water far to the west of the mass of flames which covered the eastern half of the debris field.

The distribution of parts as they were shed from the aircraft provides important information to the investigators. As indicated in Appendix B, an item identified as CW504 will show up in several different contexts. The item was determined to be a large portion of the center section of the wing's front spar. It was also one of the earliest structural pieces to be separated from the aircraft, and therefore is of considerable significance.

Many of the early boats on the scene started pulling bodies and sometimes wreckage from the water, knowing that the National Transportation Safety Board would want it. The scenes of the then-recent ValueJet disaster in Florida and the massive effort to recover debris were on everyone's mind.

However, this haphazard pulling of debris from the water without clear notation of where it came from was a disservice to the needs of the NTSB. The precise location of the bodies and wreckage was of critical importance to piecing together the cause of the crash. By mid-day on the day after the crash, the NTSB had the Coast Guard and Navy vessels clear the well-meaning civilian boats out and had set up a plotting scheme to track the locations. By the time the bulk of the wreckage and most of the bodies were recovered by the official searchers, the NTSB was able to correctly plot their locations.

Aside from the physical evidence of the condition of the various pieces, their location is the most critical item of information. And, if we are to believe the statements of the NTSB investigators that the physical evidence is inconclusive, then the locations may be our best clues. Indeed, they do give us a perspective of the crash from which we can draw conclusions. (See graphic "Clues from the Debris")

The vast bulk of the debris fell in an area roughly five by seven miles in size lying along the flight path of TWA 800 from west to east about ten miles offshore. Much of this debris was wind blown and the main, heavy wreckage pieces were in a two mile by three mile area. The farthest westerly debris and bodies are conspicuous in their origin on the plane.

The seats, passengers and overhead bins from Rows 17, 18, and 19 are found far to the west of similar debris from the rest of the plane. Also to the far west and to the right from the main debris field is the front right cargo door and the air conditioning unit believed to have been just forward of the wings, below Row 19.

To the east from the Row 17-19 debris and bodies, the investigators found a scattering of bodies, luggage and aircraft parts from the forward section of the aircraft, from Row 17 forward. This part of the debris field includes things which would have been loose in the cabin forward of Row 17 and the nearby passengers. There are no bodies or debris from the aft section prior to a point approximately fifty percent of the way through the debris field.

At that point, there is a broad widening of the debris field clumped, for the first time, to the left of the flight path. In this wide swatch, there are small parts that might have blown clear of the aircraft when a mainfuel tank exploded catastrophically, spreading the central galley, wing area underbelly parts and center seated passengers.

It is important to note that to this point, fifty percent of the way through the crash debris, the vast bulk of the debris and corpses are not burned or charred. From this point on, there are increasingly charred debris clusters, but they are from the rear section of the plane, not the front.

Starting about midway through the debris field, the investigators started to find larger sections of plane wreckage. The major pieces of cockpit were found almost centerline in the debris field. Also found here is the nose gear, first class and business class cabins and cargo bins which would have been in the forward section. While the large heavy parts of the forward section are mostly found centerline in the flight path, the loose debris and many bodies from the forward section are often found off to the right side of the flight path, flung there or blown by the 16 knot winds.

To the east in this debris field, but on a slightly different path, to the left or north, from the cockpit debris, was found the parts of the rear passenger cabin, the wings, two whole engines and parts of another, most of the tail and both the cockpit voice recorder and flight data recorder which were located in the tail section of the plane. Much of this debris and some bodies are charred. This was the area where the flames on the water were viewed by many, arriving minutes after the crash and photographed for television.

After months of searching and clue seeking, the investigators have pieced together a reasonable explanation of what happened, at least physically, to TWA 800. While the location of the debris may not conclusively show a cause for the cataclysm, it can help rule out causes.

It is clear that the forward section of the aircraft was violently severed from the rear, breaking apart at Row 17 or 18 approximately. There is some evidence that some of the bodies from the adjacent seats were mutilated by the force that severed the fuselage. Pierre Salinger, in his Paris press conference to support his theory of 'friendly fire' stated that some bodies in these rows were pierced by a missile. The authors here do not have any independent proof of this.

The location of the bodies and debris from Rows 17-19 on the earliest part of the flight path is clear evidence that the ripping apart of the fuselage at Row 17 was the first disintegration to take place in the catastrophe. The lack of major structural parts of the aircraft at this point is indicative that the ripping apart of the aircraft may not have been caused by an internal

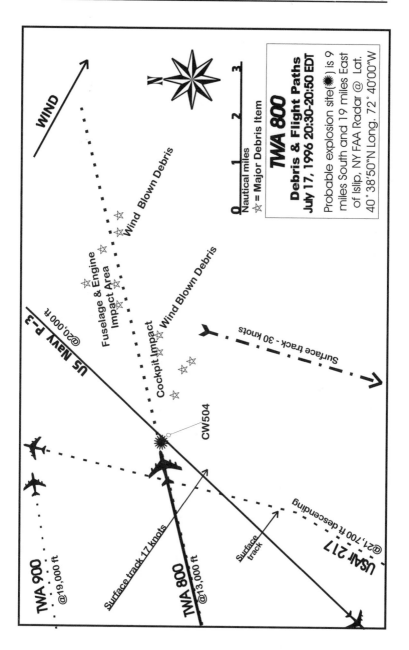

WIND

N

TWA 800
Debris & Flight Paths
July 17, 1996 20:30-20:50 EDT

Probable explosion site(✸) is 9 miles South and 19 miles East of Islip, NY FAA Radar @ Lat. 40°38'50"N Long. 72°40'00"W

Nautical miles
0 1 2 3
☆ = Major Debris Item

US Navy P-3
@20,000 ft

Wind Blown Debris

Fuselage & Engine Impact Area

Wind Blown Debris

Cockpit Impact

Surface track - 30 knots

CW504

TWA 900
@19,000 ft

Surface track 17 knots

TWA 800
@13,000 ft

Surface track

USAir 217
@21,700 ft descending

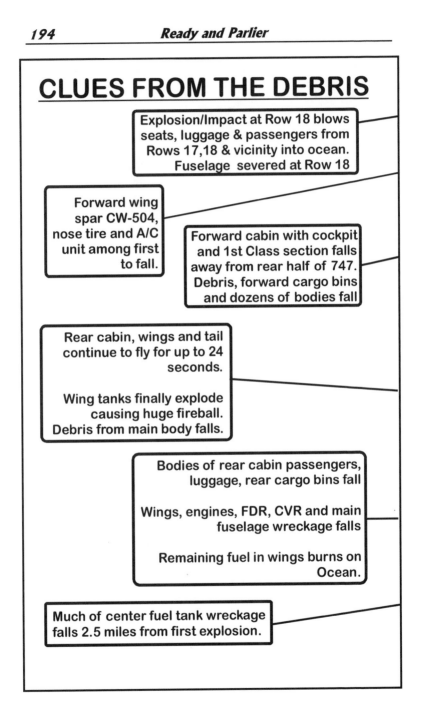

CLUES FROM THE DEBRIS

Explosion/Impact at Row 18 blows seats, luggage & passengers from Rows 17,18 & vicinity into ocean. Fuselage severed at Row 18

Forward wing spar CW-504, nose tire and A/C unit among first to fall.

Forward cabin with cockpit and 1st Class section falls away from rear half of 747. Debris, forward cargo bins and dozens of bodies fall

Rear cabin, wings and tail continue to fly for up to 24 seconds.

Wing tanks finally explode causing huge fireball. Debris from main body falls.

Bodies of rear cabin passengers, luggage, rear cargo bins fall

Wings, engines, FDR, CVR and main fuselage wreckage falls

Remaining fuel in wings burns on Ocean.

Much of center fuel tank wreckage falls 2.5 miles from first explosion.

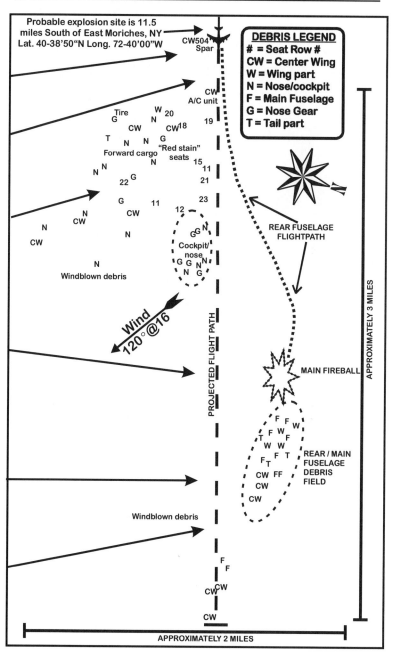

Probable explosion site is 11.5 miles South of East Moriches, NY Lat. 40-38'50"N Long. 72-40'00"W

CW504 Spar

DEBRIS LEGEND
# = Seat Row #
CW = Center Wing
W = Wing part
N = Nose/cockpit
F = Main Fuselage
G = Nose Gear
T = Tail part

CW
A/C unit

Tire
G
W 20
CW
19
CW18

T
N
N
G
Forward cargo
"Red stain" seats
15
N
N
N
N
11
22 G
21
G
11
23
CW
12
REAR FUSELAGE FLIGHTPATH
N
CW
N
G G N
N
Cockpit/nose
CW
G G N N
N G
Windblown debris

Wind 120°@16

PROJECTED FLIGHT PATH

MAIN FIREBALL

F F W
T F W F
W W
F T
F T
CW FF
CW
CW

REAR / MAIN FUSELAGE DEBRIS FIELD

Windblown debris

F
F
CW CW
CW

APPROXIMATELY 3 MILES

APPROXIMATELY 2 MILES

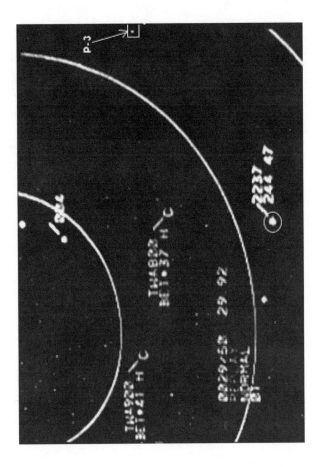

FAA Islip Control Radar Screen #1 - 20:29:50 EDT July 17, 1996. See text for explanation.

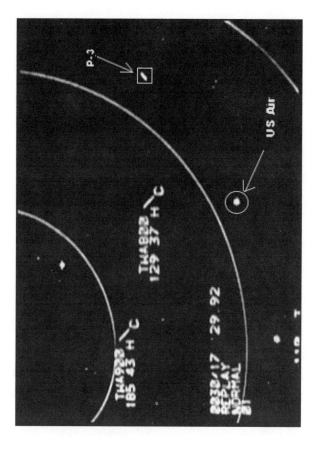

FAA Islip Control Radar Screen #2 - 20:30:17 EDT July 17, 1996. See text for explanation.

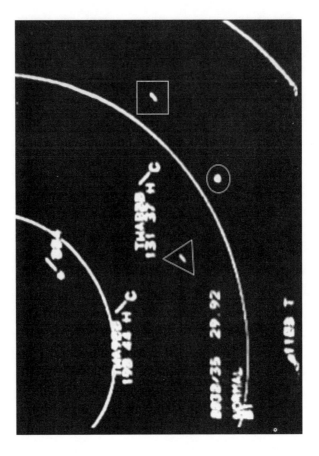

FAA Islip Control Radar Screen #3 - 20:30:35 EDT July 17, 1996. See text for explanation.

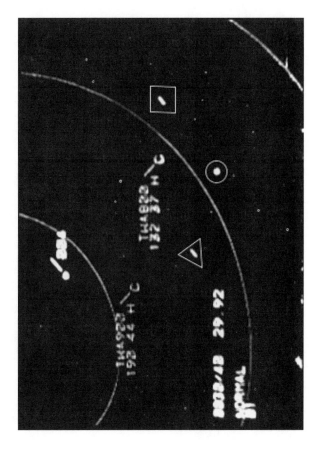

FAA Islip Control Radar Screen #4 - 20:30:40 EDT July 17, 1996. See text for explanation.

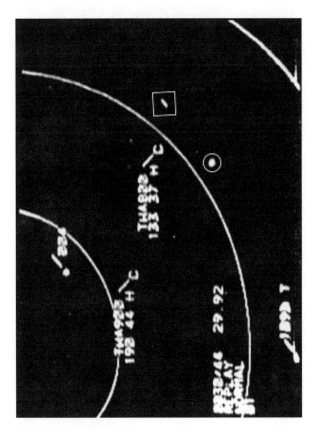

FAA Islip Control Radar Screen #5 - 20:30:44 EDT July 17, 1996. See text for explanation.

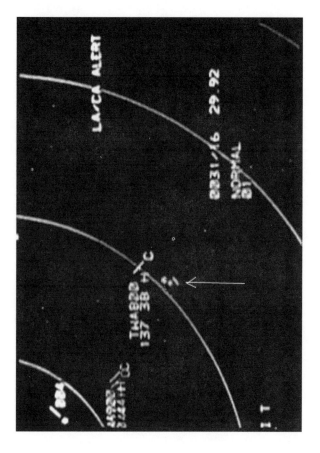

FAA Islip Control Radar Screen #6 - 20:31:16 EDT July 17, 1996. See text for explanation.

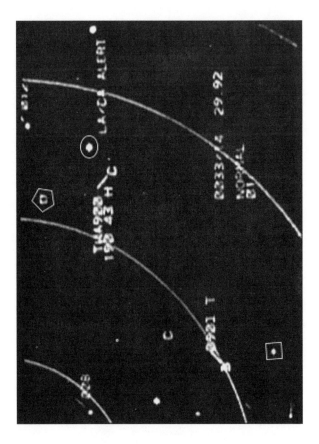

FAA Islip Control Radar Screen #7 - 20:33:14 EDT July 17, 1996. See text for explanation.

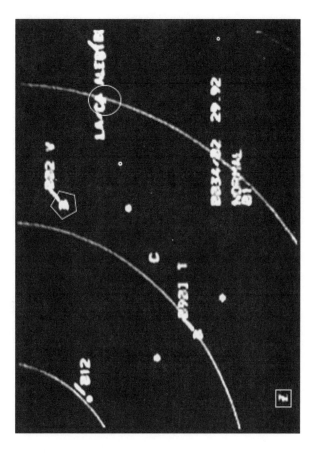

FAA Islip Control Radar Screen #8 - 20:34:02 EDT July 17, 1996. See text for explanation.

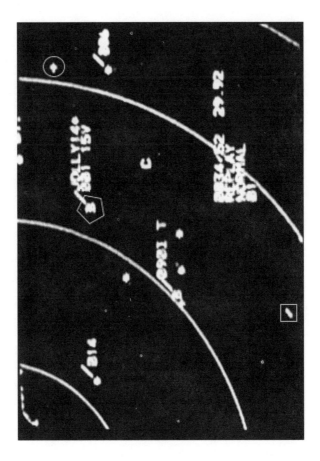

FAA Islip Control Radar Screen #9 - 20:34:52 EDT July
17, 1996. See text for explanation.

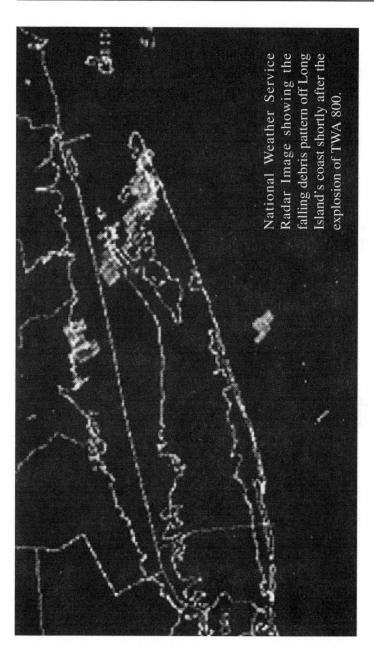

National Weather Service Radar Image showing the falling debris pattern off Long Island's coast shortly after the explosion of TWA 800.

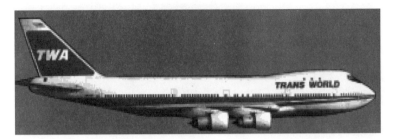

TWA 800 - A Boeing 747-131. First flight August 18, 1971. Curiously, once owned by the Iranian Air Force. TWA 800 using the aircraft number N93119 had been in service with Tran World Airlines since December 16, 1976

Kilo-Class Submarine - The Russian made Kilo-class submarine is used by Iran, which has purchased three, so far. The one pictured is the third. This photo was taken on the transit of the Mediterranean Sea in December 1996. US Navy Photo.

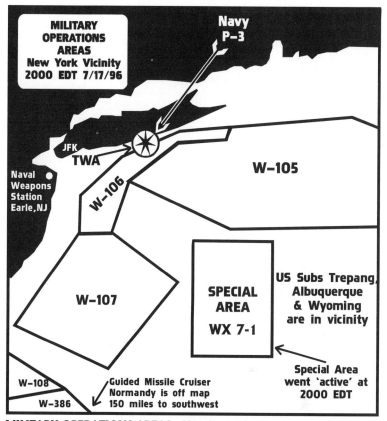

MILITARY OPERATIONS AREAS - New York Vicinity, July 17, 1996

Military Operations Areas are set up to provide safety zones to protect civilian flights and shipping from dangerous military maneuvers and training. There are several areas depicted on published airline route maps as W-108, W-105, etc. Two of these areas were 'active' on the evening when TWA 800 went down.

Additionally, the Navy had declared a 'Special Area' which was off limits to civilian air traffic below 10,000 feet. This area was to be used by a US Navy P-3 anti-submarine warfare aircraft and Navy submarines in the area. The P-3 was on its way from Brunswick, Maine to this area and was 10,000 feet directly above TWA 800 when the airliner went down. The P-3 continued south and carried out its anti-submarine warfare mission after the crash.

The guided missile cruiser USS *Normandy* had onloaded missiles at Naval Weapons Station, Earle, NJ that morning and had moved 150 miles south by 2030 EDT.

AEGIS CRUISER - The USS *NORMANDY*, like its sister ship, the USS *VINCENNES*, has been alleged to have played a part in the TWA 800 story. US Navy Photo.

The launch of a Standard Missile from an AEGIS cruiser is an impressive sight. If, as in the 'friendly fire' theory, a Standard had been launched by the USS *NORMANDY* from Chesapeake Bar to Long Island, it would probably have been viewed by thousands of people. US Navy Photo

explosion that blew the structure of the plane apart. However, it could be explained by an external explosion, as from a missile, which physically blew the forward section away. The location of wing spar piece CW504 early in the debris field and the cargo door and air conditioning unit to the south of the flight path is also supportive of the missile theory — a contact fused missile would have partly penetrated the skin of the plane from the lower quadrant blowing nearby pieces free and away to the right.

The first major structural parts from wings and rear fuselage, and the charring starting at the midway point is indicative of the powerful central explosion which initiated the fireball seen by witnesses. This would explain the wide spread of debris at this point and the first interior debris from the rear section.

The cockpit, first class and business class section and occupants clearly fell in a pattern in the center of the debris field. The forward section seems to have fallen, relatively intact for much of its descent. The spread of bodies and debris at some distance from the corresponding cabin sections might indicate that the forward cabin tumbled spewing debris and passengers as it went down.

The debris from the rear section, some charred, begins to appear thereafter, followed by the heavy portions of the rear section and wings. These heavy sections kept going further than anything else on the aircraft, except lightweight wind blown debris. These heavy items which fell together at the far end of the debris field indicate that the wings and rear fuselage continued on, 'flying' if you will, for some time after the nose section detached. The most important evidence here is that much of the central fuel tank assembly with its telltale indications of internal explosion was found at the far end of the debris field almost two and a half miles from the location of the first Row 17 passengers' body. The center wing spar (CW504) and some other center wing parts closer to the Row 18 point do appear early on in the debris field, but the main center fuel tank is found near the end of the debris field.

The total view which the location of the wreckage gives us is this:

- The nose and forward section ahead of Row 17 was violently blown away from the rear, probably by an external explosion or one near the lower inside skin of the aircraft. The NTSB report suggests that the Center Wing Tank (CWT) explosion was the initiating structural event that separated the nose section. The separation of CW504, the wing spar piece, is possibly the key, and no conclusive evidence has been presented. Thus, the authors proffer an alternative scenario.

- The forward section falls free from the rear. The severed bullet shaped nose section falls steeply into the ocean. The wings, with at least three of the engines producing thrust, and the tail representing the majority of the mass of the airplane carried forward by the plane's mere momentum down the flight path line.

- The rear two-thirds of the fuselage, with the wings and tail still attached, continues to 'fly.' Some witnesses reported seeing the aircraft's running lights still electrified until the later fireball, indicating the generators in the engine nacelles, and the engines may still have been running. It is estimated that the rear section with most of the passengers probably still alive continued on for several seconds.

- At this point (the forty percent point), the central fuel tank explodes, (this sequence is debatable, however it is representative) possibly set off by remnants of the first explosion fires or the still operating, but shredded electrical circuits. This internal explosion starts to break apart the main fuselage and wings. This explosion sets off the first of the fireball explosions witnessed by the private pilots to have occurred at just below 8,500 feet.
- The nose section, relatively unburned, has already fallen to the ocean below as the remainder of the plane farther overhead arcs downward in flames. The final twists of the nose section spinning downward have thrown the loose contents of the nose to the sides.
- The heavy structural parts of the rear section, having now blown apart in the fireball explosions, crashes into the ocean at the far end of the debris field.

There are three possibilities for the cause of the crash of TWA 800 as noted by the FBI and NTSB at virtually every press conference; a terrorist bomb inside, a missile from below or a catastrophic structural/mechanical failure. With the evidence of an internal explosion in the Center Wing fuel Tank (CWT), this latter possibility has been carried as one of the most likely and oft referred to causes of the catastrophe. While the above analysis can only slightly differentiate between the likelihood of a bomb and a missile, it does do serious damage to the likelihood of the central fuel tank explosion being the triggering event of the crash. More properly, it is a significant causal factor/result that produces the eventual disintegration of the aircraft.

The CWT was empty upon leaving New York. It was

the main reserve tank for globe spanning twelve to sixteen hour flights. The eight-hour hop to Paris did not require a full center tank. Designers want weight (fuel) in the wings to partially relieve lift stresses in the wing, thus the center tank is usually the last to be filled.

Jet fuel is of course flammable, but not necessarily explosive. That means that it burns as a liquid. It will flash into a fireball when sprayed into the air and ignited. But only in vapor form when properly mixed with air will it actually explode. It should be noted that a potentially explosive fuel-air vapor exists in every operating fuel system with empty or partially full tanks. Aircraft fuel system designs account for this reality.

The remains of the center fuel tank found on the far eastern end of the debris field show clear signs that it blew up. It was empty and sealed shut. Remaining vapors could have blown up when set off by a spark or some other initiator. It is not likely, but possible. It is designed not to explode, even when empty. Many safeguards are built into every modern aircraft to avoid any internal ignition source. It also could have exploded if pierced by shrapnel. High energy fragments from a missile warhead or the disintegration of an engine turbine, when they impact a metal sheet, produce sufficient heat to turn the metal into a temporary molten state. In addition to a hole, there is usually 'splatter' of the molten metal. This process is quite sufficient to ignite a fuel-air vapor common in any fuel cell. It is important to note that military aircraft utilize a variety of methods, e.g., self-sealing fuel cell liners and nitrogen-inerting systems to minimize the likelihood of any penetration igniting the fuel-air vapor. These methods could be used on commercial aircraft, but would be very expensive in many ways and would be useful in only very low probability events. Would a fuel cell, nitrogen-inerting system have prevented the explosion of the CWT? Possibly, perhaps even probably.

The location of the bulk of the CWT two and a half miles from the first row 17 passenger's body leads to the inevitable conclusion that the explosion of the center fuel tank was secondary to the first event that brought the plane down. We know the nose section severed early on. The center fuel tank is aft of the break in the fuselage between the wings. The nearby wing connections show the force of the explosion. The center fuel tank must have exploded some time after the initial event, otherwise, the rear fuselage and wings would not have still been in one piece. While the explosion of the center fuel tank is the probable cause of the fireball 'explosion' at the 8,500 foot level, it is not likely the cause of the initial breakup of the aircraft at 13,700 feet which blasted the Row 17 passengers out. The implausibility of the CWT causing the initial fuselage break and the eyewitness reports are the principal reasons for the consistent belief of retired Navy commander, William S. Donaldson, that it was a missile warhead explosion that initiated the break-up of TWA 800.

This leads us to the question of what other evidence is available. Obviously, in the course of an investigation, the FBI and NTSB would be remiss if they allowed wholesale perusal of the physical evidence. Their statements have almost universally used the word 'inconclusive,' to the ongoing frustration of reporters and closely concerned citizens. Inconclusive can be easily used at any point up to a clear, concise, irrefutable conclusion.

As early as July 20th, three days after the crash, CNN

reported the finding of bomb residue in the crash debris. At that time, the FBI spokesman, Jim Kallstrom, did not deny the report, but said, "We're not prepared to say anything until we believe it's absolutely true."

At that same time, US Senator Orrin Hatch, after a closed briefing by federal investigators stated, "We're looking at a criminal act. We're looking at somebody who either put a bomb on it or shot a missile, a surface-to-air missile. It's very — almost 100 percent unlikely — that this was a mechanical failure."

Word of a coverup was already circulating. The early rumor was that the FBI knew it was a bomb, but had kept it quiet because of the start of the Olympics or the national political conventions in the coming weeks after the crash. The FBI naturally denied all accusations of a coverup.

While these statements obviously occurred early on in the investigation and should not be held as being definitive of anything, they are important because of the tenor they set for the remainder of the investigation. Just as the initial reaction to the Oklahoma City courthouse bombing had been one of questioning about international terrorists (wrongly so); in the month after the TWA 800 crash, the public and the press were prepared for information which confirmed the eyewitness accounts of a possible missile shot at the plane. The lack of a firm response from the FBI on what the public viewed as an obviously good lead, a missile or bomb, led many to question the purposes of the FBI and NTSB in saying so little. It even led to some discomfiture between the two federal agencies.

This is important in the discussion of evidence because it seems to have been the motivating factor in one of the few major leaks of forensic evidence about the crash, the efforts of James Sanders. An ex-policeman and private investigator, James Sanders was working with the Riverside (CA) *Press-Enterprise* newspaper to publish some rather startling evidence and analysis which was apparently either negligently ignored or curiously covered up by the federal investigators. Like the FAA radar tapes brought forward against the will of the FBI and NTSB, the forensic evidence Sanders brought out shook the public's trust in the FBI's handling of the case.

The important parts of Sanders' evidence are his report of leaked documents from the NTSB that, from his analysis, indicate a missile was the most likely cause of the crash — analysis much like that given above. Sanders openly accused the FBI and NTSB of covering up this knowledge of the probable cause of the crash. He stated at that time he had no idea of why they would do such a thing.

The important forensic evidence gleaned by Sanders involved a 'red stain' found on the seats in the Row 17 adjacent area. When first leaked out, the information about these streaks was dismissed in press conferences as carpet or seat cushion adhesive. Sanders allegedly obtained a sample of the red stain from a TWA pilot working on the investigation with the NTSB, Terry Stacy. In a story first carried in the *Press-Enterprise*, Sanders disclosed that an independent laboratory test showed the 'red stain' samples contained a long list of metallic compounds which are similar to metallic compounds found in solid fuel, rocket motors on missiles. This chemical composition of rocket propellant was confirmed by engineers from both Hughes Aircraft and Morton-Thiokol, makers of military missile motors. The monomeric esters, complex metallic compounds and nitrates identified by a NASA scientist (see below) strongly suggest the possible chemical relationship between the 'red stain' sample and commonly used rocket fuel ingredients.

James Sanders went on, two months later, to write a book about what he saw as an attempt by the US Government to cover up the fact that TWA 800 had been downed by a mishandled US Navy missile test. This theory was further fueled by the disclosure that FAA flight control radars showed a mysterious blip that appeared near the doomed 747 and disappeared just before the explosion.

Sanders, his wife and Terry Stacy would pay for their inquisitiveness, when after the FBI failed to reach any answers on their criminal investigation of TWA 800, the FBI chose to indict the three for stealing the sample and interfering with a Federal investigation. The pilot plea bargained and is testifying for the prosecution, while Mr. and Mrs. Sanders are fighting the charges on malicious prosecution and First Amendment/ Pentagon Papers grounds. The sample itself was returned to FBI custody when CBS News bowed to FBI pressure and returned the sample that they had received from Sanders to, hopefully, bring the issue out. One could wonder, though, if the sample really was just 3M™ glue, why the FBI would not want an independent source like CBS to confirm it.

To this day, even in face of the indictment and a widespread disbelief that the Navy could actually keep a coverup of its downing of TWA 800 secret, James Sanders still believes in the 'friendly fire' theory. He says he is "absolutely certain" a missile downed TWA 800, and he is "pretty sure" it was a US Navy demonstration project of a submarine launched anti-aircraft missile.

Either the FBI laboratory had been enormously

irresponsible in determining the 'rubber' was an adhesive, they had missed the streak across the key three rows of seats entirely, or they were withholding important evidence of a missile they were not ready to admit to.

In response to the 'red stain' issue, the NTSB contacted a NASA scientist they had worked with in chemical analysis of an earlier Federal Express plane crash. They asked this NASA chemist, Charles Bassett, to run a chemical comparison test on the residue evidence disclosed by the Sanders affair.

However, the authors of this book have learned that tests requested by the NTSB of Bassett, rather than answering any major questions, raise serious questions about the handling of this aspect of the investigation by federal investigators.

"They just didn't ask me the right questions. If they had, I could have found them the answers," says the NASA chemist. "They gave me various samples to evaluate; among them was a brand of adhesive, and an unknown 'gunk' material. They never asked me to compare the samples with explosives, and they never asked me to compare the samples to rocket fuel."

Charles Bassett, a chemist at NASA's Kennedy Space Center in Florida, went on to explain that if he had been given representative samples of the explosives or missile fuel that some people fear was used to bring down the TWA flight he could have given an extremely accurate opinion of whether the explosives were present. But, all the National Transportation Safety Board (NTSB) gave him to compare to was a sample of 3M™ Brand glue.

"I told them there was a neoprene present, like the 3M stuff, but I wasn't certain it was 3M™, and I also told them that there was more there, but I wasn't asked to go into that." Bassett's reports, which were included in the NTSB's report disclosed at their Public Hearing into the TWA 800 crash in Baltimore last December, also indicated that various samples include monomeric esters, metallic compounds and nitrates which are believed by some to be indicative of military ordnance. However, despite the direct evidence that the samples given to Bassett to analyze contained far more than simple glue, both the NTSB and the FBI have used those tests to unequivocally identify, as 3M™ glue, the mysterious 'red stain' found on seats closest to the point where the TWA 747 aircraft split in two pieces after a catastrophic explosion.

However, the federal investigators' story that the 'red stain' is just glue is belied by their own chosen scientist. "There were no metals in the reference sample (of glue) the NTSB gave me. The monomeric ester is something other than neoprene glue," says Bassett.

Bassett further says he was never asked to identify the elements and compounds present in the sample nor make any comparisons to explosives or rocket propellant. This is extremely curious considering the reasons the federal investigators had for testing the 'red stain' in the first place. "I was not asked to prove or disprove the presence of explosive chemistry. If they had asked me to identify the sample I would have done things differently. There are ways to tell just about everything on anything, chemically speaking. You give me a charter and the assets, I can give you an answer. But, the NTSB did not ask that."

Of course, Charlie Bassett and his NASA chemical laboratory was not the only laboratory working on the TWA 800 case. The FBI crime laboratory had the task of determining the presence of explosives or any other compounds relevant to a criminal investigation on the various samples gathered by FBI agents, who immediately seized any suspected explosive residue item when discovered by an NTSB investigator.

Unfortunately, the FBI laboratory's Explosive Unit and its chief, James Thurman, were subsequently rocked by a scandal that the evidence for the World Trade Center case, the Oklahoma City bombing case and others had been altered to favor the prosecution. This casts doubt on the reliability of the tests run on explosives during the early, critical days of the TWA investigation.

The FBI report/press release carefully notes that the FBI's conclusions were verified by an 'independent expert' and confirmed that no high explosives were found, without mentioning the scandal. It can only be hoped that this 'independent expert' does not refer to Charlie Bassett, who swears he was never asked about explosives.

As indicated above, the NTSB asked the wrong questions of at least one of the analytic chemists supporting the investigation. The NTSB Public Hearing Exhibits shows the consequence of the erroneous and presumptive question.

The NTSB's Fire and Explosion Group Chairman's Factual Report makes the following conclusion. "The passenger cabin seats were examined for <u>evidence of high explosive</u> damage such as hot particle penetration, metal erosion, and high degree of fragmentation. None of this evidence was noted either above the center wing tank or in other areas of the cabin. Selected seat back panels in rows 17, 19, 24, and 27 were damaged, exposing a brown to reddish-brown colored material. This material was analyzed by infrared spectroscopy. <u>Analysis showed the material to be</u>

consistent with a polychloroprene 3M™ Scotch-Grip™ 1357 High Performance contact adhesive. The report is attached in Appendix III-Tests and Analysis." [Emphasis supplied]

However, the analysis in Appendix III they refer to, is Charlie Bassett's three reports, none of which excludes, or even looks for, explosives. The NTSB, thus, concludes, that the 'red stain' is just contact adhesive, when the chemical report they had asked for was never meant to exclude other possibilities, merely confirm the presence of one substance - neoprene.

Bassett explains, "They (NTSB) asked me to run a FTIR, that's Fourier Transfer Infrared Spectroscopy, on the evidence and a reference sample of contact adhesive, glue. It showed that there was a similar substance present, but not necessarily the one they gave me, 3M™ Brand. But, it was not just glue, there were elements present that were not in the reference sample. There were metals present that were not in the reference sample. The FTIR I ran just confirms the presence of a comparison sample, it does not exclude unknowns, unless you're specifically looking for something. I did find neoprene (like the 3M™ glue) in the sample -- they did not ask me to identify what else was in the sample."

The failure to ask the right question and, perhaps, to fully appreciate the answers given is further complicated by the very substance in question.. As explained by NASA to the world after the Challenger space shuttle disaster, a representative solid rocket fuel consists of ammonium perchlorate (oxidizer, 69.6 % by weight), **aluminum** (fuel, 16 %), iron oxide (a catalyst, 0.4 %), a **polymer** (a binder that holds the mixture together, 12.04 %), and an epoxy curing agent (1.96 %). Neoprene and its close chemical cousins are commonly used polymers. Charles Bassett found unexplained aluminum and other trace metals not found in 3M™ contact adhesive, a neoprene glue. If a neoprene-based rocket fuel was used to down TWA 800, the 'red stain' may be the proof of it, ignored by both NTSB and FBI. Or, if you look at this with a dubious eye, if the 'red stain' was suspected to be rocket fuel residue, the best way to explain it away was to ask an outside expert, like Bassett, if the stain was 'similar' to common neoprene glue, without also asking him to determine what the material was. Whether by negligence, oversight or intent, the correct and complete questions were not asked.

So, the NTSB investigators charged with determining the presence of explosives may have come up with a wrong conclusion by asking the wrong question. In fact, the expert they asked to test their sample found the same kind of metallic compounds that James Sanders had concluded were similar to rocket fuel components, but the NTSB had failed to recognize or acknowledge it, even though listed in their own report's appendix. Lastly, their own expert finds fault with the basic question presented, "If they wanted me to prove or disprove the presence of explosives, they should have asked me. I would have worked differently."

One conclusion that can be drawn from this information about the 'red stain' and its location in the aircraft is obvious. Missile fuel stains on the seats in Row 17, 18, 19 and adjacent areas would be consistent with the impact of a missile just forward of the right wing that then exploded sending its constituent parts outward and through the parts of the fuselage closest to the missile hit.

A missile hit in this area of the plane is also consistent

with the characteristics of both infrared (IR) and laser guided missiles. A laser guided missile would be aimed at the center of mass of the airplane, roughly the wing-fuselage junction. An IR missile would track in from behind toward the heat source, the engines. If an IR missile fired from the probable ocean side of the flight path missed an engine by flying directly through the hot engine exhaust, it could impact the wing or the fuselage forward of or adjacent to the engine nacelle. If an IR missile hit an engine from this same direction it could explode with the warhead's blast forward into the fuselage in about the same area, just forward of the wings, at Row 17. As mentioned before, a missile hitting the lower right fuselage in front of the wings would explain why the cargo door and air conditioner were blown far to the right of the plane. This is why item CW504 is so important. It could be the confirmatory piece of a missile impact.

In addition to the forward wing spar disclosed in the debris analysis Sanders obtained and as discussed in the NTSB report, there have been parts of the number three engine (second from right), an antennae from the wing assembly and wing pieces found in the first half of the debris field far away from the remainder of the wings (other than the spar) and engines in the far eastern portion. This is the engine closest to the probable point of break in the fuselage. It is this scenario that the authors have used in our account of the last minutes aboard TWA 800. Of interest, although the four engines' main assemblies were found in the far northern debris field, there is essentially no discussion of engine debris analysis in the NTSB report. The engine data may also be a key element in the cause determination.

The remainder of the evidence disclosed through Jim

Sanders' efforts is not as startling, although it does seem to be correct. Touted as being a surreptitious release of a January 22, 1997 NTSB analysis by a nine-member panel including manufacturer, airline, and other government and industry experts, the analysis of the debris field reported by Sanders appears to be correct, but it did not substantially add to the information known about TWA 800. This leaked analysis of the debris field is amazingly similar to that reported in the August 12, 1996 issue of *US News and World Report,* and it is not dissimilar to the evidence in the NTSB report. However, the analysis provided by Sanders did go a bit further in showing how the debris field concept might support a missile impact, especially in light of the 'red stain.' The "Sequencing Report," as Sanders' disclosure was called, identified a few previously undisclosed items found in the Western end of the debris field, including a portion of the front wing spar (CW504) and second passenger door. The NTSB responded to the Sanders' reports with a comment that the reports contained "numerous factual and interpretive errors," but they failed to disclose what those errors were, and they did not discount the leaked information.

In mid March 1997, Dr. Bernard Loeb, the NTSB's director of aviation safety, in testifying before the US House of Representatives to get more funding to continue the TWA 800 probe admitted that the evidence available on that date was consistent with the plane being struck by a missile fragment. He did not elaborate, and the House panel did not pursue this line of testimony. Again, if an IR missile had hit the number three engine or nearly hit it, this would be consistent with the 'red stain' near the rupture in the fuselage and the possible engine parts in the first half of the debris field.

The damage to the aircraft, the debris field and the other evidence gathered by the investigators is not complete, even with the NTSB's December report and in the words of one confidential source inside the federal team, "there are no big pieces screaming missile, but there are many little pieces crying for attention." The problem many members of the public and the press are having is that the convenient oversight, apparently intentional understatement of available evidence by the authorities and the myopic ignorance of obvious possibilities is leading to a sense of distrust for what is disclosed and the assurances that everything is being done.

The FBI has said that the evidence of PETN and RDX explosive found in the plane (see below) are mere traces left over from a police dog training session months before. They say that there is no other evidence of explosives. Then, it is leaked that there is a mysterious red stain. The FBI says it is adhesive. Then it is announced by third parties that it is really missile fuel. The FBI seizes the red stain samples under federal court subpoena. The FBI says there is no sensory evidence of a missile. Then, FAA videotapes are made public which a reasonable person can see are suspicious. The FBI seizes the radar tapes under federal subpoena. It does not take too much of this process to lead even the moderately concerned citizen to question what is going on with the investigation of TWA 800.

Sanders, his wife, Elizabeth, and a TWA pilot assigned to the investigation were indicted and charged with crimes surrounding the acquisition of the samples. The FBI press release regarding the Sanders/Stacy case is provided in Appendix C. As alleged in the press release: "The tests were conducted [on the stolen material] and provided no conclusive evidence of the presence of solid rocket fuel." The word 'conclusive' is the key word. Most likely, the tests did not prove or disprove the presence of solid rocket fuel. At best, it established the existence of a material consistent with solid rocket propellant. It is improbable any definitive markers could be identified that would establish irrefutably that the substance was solid rocket propellant, thus the phrase, 'no conclusive evidence.'

Surface-to-Air (SAM) Missiles vs.TWA 800

There has been much speculation concerning the possibility (or probability) of TWA 800 being hit with a Surface-to-Air Missile. Much of this speculation has included not a small amount of misinformation and often that misinformation was conveniently focused to support one theory or the other about how TWA 800 came down.

There have been many newspaper and magazine articles and at least one book published which offer the 'friendly fire' argument that the US Navy brought TWA 800 down with a missile test gone wrong. Well-meaning, but blithely ignorant, journalists and public figures have looked at military operations areas (Op Areas) on the map and noticed the several military flights in the area at the time of the crash and have put together scenarios showing:

- That a cruise missile or other missile was launched from the north over Long Island which hit TWA 800 on its way to the Op Areas to the south.
- That the US Navy P-3 flying almost directly overhead of TWA 800 was doing some missile test, either itself or supporting one of the submarines or a surface ship one hundred eighty miles south.
- That the surface ship, USS *Normandy*, located in Chesapeake Bay launched a brand new, Standard, fleet, Anti-Ballistic Missile over the horizon toward New York

and Long Island, and it hit TWA 800 180 miles away.

- One of the submarines the Navy had in the region, now identified as the attack submarines USS _Albuquerque_ and USS _Trepang_ and the ballistic missile submarine USS _Wyoming_, launched some missile which hit TWA 800.

When the proponents of the 'friendly fire' theory, including Pierre Salinger (who has since recanted his accusation and apologized to the Navy), came forth, they were immediately met with denial and considerable derision on the part of federal investigators and the military. This denial was pointed to as a coverup. "How could the Navy be so sure? There had been accidents before."

The proponents of the 'friendly fire' theory pointed to the type of damage, the debris evidence, and the unlikelihood of mechanical damage causing such a catastrophic explosion. The 'conspiracy and coverup' theorists played up the 'red stains' on the seats, the 'missile' photo over Long Island and the eye witnesses who had reported the missile hit, only minutes after the crash.

While the authors agree that the bulk of the evidence that has been publicly admitted so far would indicate a missile hit is the most likely candidate, we vehemently disagree with the hypothesis that an errant US Navy missile is the culprit. Such a theory is illogical and so nearly impossible as to be easily discarded. The likelihood of silencing 300 sailors on a cruiser, 150 sailors on a submarine or 10 crewmembers of a Navy patrol plane in the light of such a horrific disaster is beyond comprehension.

First, as to the 'cruise missile' over Long Island theory, the woman who took the photographs was, according to news reports, facing north at the time of the photo. The photograph is so blurry that nothing can really be made of it. After computer enhancement, some can speculate that it looks like a Harpoon or Tomahawk missile, but with enough computer gyrations almost anything can be enhanced to look like anything. Further, both Harpoon and Tomahawk are ground hugging missiles that would never reach the 13,000-foot level of TWA 800. Furthermore, they are very large objects that would do substantial structural damage to any aircraft regardless of any warhead involvement. There is no such evidence.

As to the P-3C Orion aircraft above TWA 800, much sport was made of the Navy spokesman's comment that the Orion does not carry missiles, and then a much publicized PR photo of the Orion with a full ordnance load including cruise missiles was shown. Yes, the Orion does carry, in wartime or scheduled exercises, Harpoon anti-ship cruise missiles among many other weapons. As a very capable platform, it could be modified to hang many types of ordnance under its wings including Air-to-Air Missiles.

The USS *Normandy* is of the same class as the AEGIS cruisers who are testing the new Standard Type IV Fleet ABM in the Pacific. And, apparently, the USS *Normandy* did onload weapons, possibly missiles, at Navy Weapons Station, Earle, New Jersey, in the New York harbor area only ten hours before the TWA 800 event. The Fleet ABM missile type has only been fired twice, to the authors' knowledge, and both times were on fully instrumented missile ranges. Although the Standard Type IV ABM has greatly increased range and speed, it does not have a range of nearly two hundred miles. Published reports indicate that the new Standard missile's maximum range is less than eighty miles. The middle of Chesapeake Bay is not the place to launch a SAM test and metropolitan New York is not a good down-range target area for one. If a Standard had been tested, whatever range was utilized, the area would have been closed to all traffic, at all altitudes for far in excess of the maximum range of the missile. That is why the prior firings were in the mid-Pacific. An AEGIS cruiser cannot fire a Standard missile 'by mistake.' As discussed in regards to the USS *Vincennes*, the launch requires the coordinated efforts of several people in several different locations onboard ship, the Tactical Action Officer or Commanding Officer, the Weapons Console Officer and the fire control radar crew. Further, once fired, the missile is utterly dependent on the shipboard systems for guidance, its semi-active radar could not find an airliner 180 miles away unless someone, or something (the AEGIS computer), was telling it what to hit. The launch of a Standard missile is a loud, brilliant event that would be unmistakable by even a casual observer. Lastly, a Standard is also a rather large missile traveling at very fast speeds and would do substantial damage to a commercial airliner regardless of whether the warhead exploded.

The subsurface to air missile concept, that a US submarine fired something that hit the 747, is the most speculative of all. There is not even any good reason to believe that any submarine has this operational capability. Further, if such a missile were being tested it would have been on an instrumented missile range, not adjacent to the busiest commercial air route on earth. The cruise and ballistic missiles on US submarines are not anti-aircraft missiles; the 747 would have to fly into the flight path of one to get hit.

Any of the larger weapons, Harpoon, Tomahawk or Standard, or any missiles or other weapons in their categories, would leave considerably more evidence of a collision, impact or detonation by virtue of their size and mass alone. Likewise, their debris would be obvious, considering their size, compared to a small, shoulder-fired, SAM.

Even, if we ignore the impossibility of any of these military platforms shooting down the 747, the possibility of carrying off the coverup is ridiculous. First, a Standard missile launching is a modestly spectacular event, especially in pre-dusk lighting. Unlike a shoulder-fired SAM, like the Stinger, Mistral, Grail or RBS-70/90, which are meant to be as unobtrusive as possible to protect the infantryman firing it, a naval SAM is a full-fledged missile. A Standard missile launched from Chesapeake Bay toward New York shortly after sundown would have been witnessed by several million people, not just 244 on the coast around Moriches, Long Island. The same can be said for a ballistic missile or cruise missile in boost phase from a submarine, only more so. Further, a Standard missile launched from that distance would have been in a coast phase at the end of its flight with its motor spent, it would not have been seen as a 'flare-like' light rising from the water. From a 'witness' standpoint alone, the idea of a US Navy platform shooting TWA 800 is ludicrous.

As much as conspiracy theorists, in general, love to accuse a bureaucracy of covering up notorious events, a bureaucracy, by its nature, is a poor keeper of secrets. A bureaucracy in an open political system could never truly keep a secret that involved such elements. While it might be possible to keep critical national security information compartmented within an intelligence or military command structure (for either the US or Iran), keeping a horrendous foul-up quiet is impossible. From a novice deckhand to the politically astute insider, there would be enormous pressure and much opportunity to 'squeal.'

Furthermore, the Navy keeps all weapons tracked by serial number. While everyone doubts the efficiency of any 'government' system, the accountability system for military weapons simply would not allow an intermediate commander who 'screwed up' to keep this from seniors. The Navy, and the FBI, has announced that an independent audit of all potential weapons has disclosed no missing weapons. Other than the natural proclivities of conspiracy theorists to doubt everything anyone in authority says, there is no rational reason to believe that there is any coverup of any 'friendly fire.'

The irrationality of a 'friendly fire' coverup does not, however, mean that there might not be a coverup of another sort involved with TWA 800. While there would be no reason for anyone within the military but not directly involved to keep a 'friendly fire' event secret, there would certainly be neither reason nor justification for an investigator from the FBI or NTSB to remain mum. However, if from the outset, it was determined that the crash had been the work of a foreign power, such as Iran, and it was made an item of critical national security interest to keep it quiet until action was complete, there would be every reason for everyone, military at all levels, FBI, NTSB, government officials and witnesses who were taken aside and lectured on what was at stake, to keep quiet until the Commander-in-Chief was satisfied with the evidence and took appropriate action. This is discussed in more detail later.

So, if TWA 800 was brought down by a missile and it is unlikely to be an American missile, then what missile brought it down, whose was it and why? Obviously, the bulk of this book goes to explain the authors' opinion of who might be the perpetrators, why they might do it and how they got in a position to fire on TWA 800. However, integral to this scenario is the ability for the Iranians' missile to hit and destroy a 747 at more than 13,000 feet in altitude.

Throughout the period since the TWA 800 crash there has been discussion of whether a SAM fired from the ground was capable of bringing the plane down. There have been many would-be experts in the press and especially on the Internet who have theorized one way or the other. The key information for the reader to understand on this issue is that throughout the investigation, while there have been periods where one cause or another has been in ascendancy, there has never been any denial by any senior American spokesperson, neither FBI, NTSB, nor military, that a SAM could have brought down the plane. This is significant, and correct.

At every stage of the investigation, the most that anyone in authority would say is that "a missile has not been ruled out." Even when they were pointing to the possibility of mechanical failure or fuel tank rupture, when pressed to exclude a missile hit, they refused to do so. At the very end, when 'suspending' their investigation, the FBI did not categorically deny the possibility of a missile, they simply said they had no evidence, one way or the other.

There are several types of small missiles that could have brought a 747 down from this altitude. Many of the reports in the press that certain types of missiles, such as the

Stinger which was given by the United States to Afghan guerillas, were physically incapable of hitting TWA 800 are incorrect. The 'experts' making these conclusions were quite often simply reading specifications from published journals or repeating others' mistakes. The hills around Kabul are littered with the wrecks of Soviet aircraft whose pilots made similar errors.

The oft-quoted specifications on weapons systems are the <u>unclassified design</u> specifications of the weapon. The 'unclassified' specification is that which the nation of manufacture tells everyone about the weapon. You do not want to tell your enemy, or your customer's enemy, what your full capabilities are. An example of this is the M1 Abrams Main Battle Tank that was announced to have a modest top speed of 35 miles per hour until a rogue soldier took one for a joy ride at virtually freeway speeds. The other word, 'design,' is equally important to understanding weapons specifications. A 'design' specification is that at which the weapon is designed to have a certain level of effectiveness, say a 50% kill ratio. Thus, a missile with a maximum unclassified design altitude of 12,000 feet will go higher. It is meant to. Everyone, confidentially, knows this. They just do not advertise it as such. Likewise, it will certainly go farther than its specifications say, it just will not be as certain of a tactical kill at greater range.

Further, the maximum ranges and altitudes for Surface-to-Air Missiles are a combination of both distances. A missile fired straight up will have more height capability than its maximum listing. However, going straight up uses up a missile's energy faster, and it may not be as powerful in its kinetic striking power. For example, a Bofors RBS-70

SAM has a maximum range of 5 kilometers and a maximum altitude of 3,000 meters. That means, in this case, that it has a 30% chance of a target kill at 3,000 meters altitude and 5,000 meters range. It can actually hit lower targets at greater range and higher targets at closer range.

Another significant consideration in deciding if a SAM could take out a 747 is the fact that the 'kill' probabilities that set the maximum range and altitude are for tactical targets, that is, a maneuvering combat aircraft in a combat environment. A fighter-bomber or an attack helicopter on a combat mission is an immensely different target than a lumbering jumbo-jet climbing in a clear sky. The term 'sitting duck' is not altogether inappropriate.

Fifteen countries make various designs of Surface-to-Air Missiles, maybe more. Iran probably has the capability, on the world's arms market, to come into possession of virtually any of these. Iran itself has a growing armaments industry. Indeed, the US Congress is currently considering legislation to sanction companies who assist Iran in their missile development industry and the President vetoed a first attempt thereto on June 23, 1998. Iran followed with the first operational test of an intermediate range ballistic missile in mid-July 1998. A country with an active program for building nuclear reactors, maybe atomic weapons, and ballistic missiles could certainly try its hand at a shoulder fired SAM. However, to limit speculation to some degree, we have limited our consideration of what missile Iran or any other perpetrator might have used against TWA 800 to three choices that are representative of the field. These are:

• The Swedish RBS-70/90. This is man portable and

adaptable to a variety of configurations. This system is believed to be in use by the Revolutionary Guards. Considering the 747's damage the RBS-90's 1+ kilogram shaped charge is less likely than the RBS-70's fragmentation warhead. It is about four feet in length. It uses a laser targeting system. An observer points a laser source at the target plane and the missile follows the laser light in. This is feasible for the huge 747 with running lights on in the early dusk. Design altitude 4,000 meters/ 13,000 feet at 6 kilometers.

- The Russian SA-7B Strela 2M/Grail or SA14 Gremlin. These have been sold to numerous foreign countries. They are probably in the Iranian arsenal. The 2-kilogram warhead could rip the 747 apart. They use the heat signature of the aircraft to home in. While they would most likely track into an engine, on a multiple engine aircraft they could track between the exhausts to explode on contact with the fuselage or wing. Probable design altitude 4,300 meters/14,000 feet at 5.6 kilometers for the SA-7B and 5,000/16,000 for the SA-14.

- The US-made FIM-92 Stinger. This is the SAM that the US gave to Afghan guerillas to use against the Soviets. The main group of Afghan Muslims is now aligned with Tehran. It should be assumed that Iran has Stingers. This missile is similar in operation to the SA-14. It homes on heat signature and has a contact fuse with a 3-kilogram warhead. The published design specs are 4,800 meters/ 15,500 feet altitude at 5.5 kilometers.

Portable SAM Comparison Chart

Country Missile Name	Type	Max Distance	Max Altitude	Warhead	Length
Sweden RBS-70/90	Laser/ Aimed	5/7 km	4,000 m	1+ kg shaped charge	1.32m
Russia SA-7B Grail	Infrared	5.6 km	4,300 m	2 kg Fragment (?)	1.35m
Russia SA-14 Gremlin	Infrared	6 km	5,000 m	2 kg (?) HE/Shaped	1.30m
United States FIM-92	Infrared/ UV	5.5 km	4,800 m	3 kg Shaped	1.52m

Thus, even without that much of a stretch, the 'unclassified design' specifications gives this consideration, the likely weapons are generally capable of a kill at the 4,200 meter (13,700 foot) altitude the FAA radar tapes listed TWA 800 at when it went down.

The next consideration is whether the warhead of the size of these SAM missiles could bring down a huge 747. To answer this question, we need only go to the other infamous terrorist bombing of a 747, the Pan Am 103 jet over Lockerbie, Scotland. In that case, the explosive was a bomb believed hidden inside a piece of consumer electronics, certainly smaller than the 1+ to 3 kilogram warheads here. These weapons were designed to bring down armored combat aircraft, much less vulnerable than airliners. In addition, the aircraft fuselage was pressurized, and its airspeed was nearly 370 knots, significant static pressure differential and considerable dynamic pressure. There is little doubt that any of these weapons could have brought down TWA 800. As the NTSB clearly establishes, the detonation of the fuel-air vapor in the essentially empty center wing fuel tank was the catastrophic event that ultimately initiated the events of structural failure that brought down the airliner. A single fragment from a missile warhead or secondary fragmentation from the disintegration of an engine turbine penetrating the skin of the fuel tank would provide the necessary ignition mechanism. It would take only one small fragment, that would not leave much evidence, to provide the initiator.

Therefore, if we have concluded that a portable SAM was capable of downing TWA 800, what evidence do we have that a SAM was actually used. Naturally, our consideration of this question is limited by the paucity of evidence thus far released by the FBI and NTSB. However, certain substantial evidence that has leaked out gives strong indications that a SAM might be involved.

Early on in the investigation, word leaked out that the chemical compounds PETN and RDX were found in the aircraft. As early as July 20th, three days after the crash, the chief FBI investigator, Assistant Director Kallstrom was answering questions about these two explosive compounds. By early September, the presence of these two explosives was explained by the fact that the plane had been used as a training location for a St. Louis, Missouri team of explosive sniffing dogs. No explosive had been set off in the plane, it had simply been placed in the plane to be found. When questioned about how minute fragments of the sample explosive, not just odor, could remain for weeks in a plane being used constantly and still be detectable after a violent mid-air explosion ripped the metal of the plane apart and submerged it in seawater for weeks, the FBI investigators simply responded that the tests were 'extremely accurate.' PETN and RDX are used in military munitions. The shaped charge portion of the Stinger is an RDX relative.

There has been much reporting in the press about the 'red stained' seats immediately forward of the wings. The 'red stain' substance was found on fifteen seats between rows 17 and 19, the seats just behind the point where the cabin tore apart (See "Clues from the Debris" graphic). When first reported, the federal investigators dismissed this stain as adhesive used for seat cushions or carpet. James Kallstrom said, "There is a red residue trail, but it has no connection to a missile. There's a logical explanation, but I'm not going to get into it." This red material was obtained by private investigator and ex-policeman, James Sanders, and discussed earlier.

As discussed at length in this book, the FAA radar tapes show a short 12-second track leading from the open ocean toward TWA 800. At an initial speed of 580 meters per second, the climb time for the aforementioned SAMs to an altitude of 13,700 feet is precisely 12 seconds.

On March 14, 1997, Kallstrom said that the FBI had ruled out that the US Navy or other government asset had fired on TWA 800, but he said that the FBI is not ruling out the idea of a missile. The NTSB issued an interim memo in

January 1997 that said that the seats and passengers in Rows 17 to 19 that were thrown into the water first were closest to the 'initial event' that destroyed the aircraft. The theory that the fuel tank exploded causing the crash, as discussed in the section on plane debris, is belied by the fact that the bulk of the fuel tanks fragments were found 12,000 feet further on in the doomed plane's flight path, its downward arc, than the debris and bodies from rows 17 to 19. An explosion from a missile hit or bomb somewhere at row 18 or so is the only plausible explanation for this evidence.

The final and perhaps strongest evidence that a missile impacted TWA 800 is the eyewitnesses. Press reports tallied the number of people who saw the flare-like light rising to meet the plane at 154. The FBI, early on, admitted that it had 34 'credible' reports of something rising from the water, heading for the plane. In the November FBI press release, a number of eyewitnesses of 244 was given. Some of the witnesses were pilots and ex-servicemen who knew the looks of a missile launch. Some of those who reported the 'missile' immediately after the crash, ceased their discussions of it after meeting with federal authorities.

In the days immediately after the crash, there were numerous press reports of federal agents interviewing boat rental workers, fishermen, and other boaters about possible witnesses of boat launched missiles. In one case, a fisherman reported being asked about any sighting of a long metal tube, like a launcher. And, as seen in the FBI report (Appendix C), they have apparently totally discounted many credible witnesses, and closed the door to any public debate regarding the witnesses.

The federal authorities investigating the crash of TWA

800 have consistently refused to rule out the use of a missile. At the same time, they have consistently stymied serious discussion of this possibility. Of course, there are many reasons why, if they believed the attack was by a foreign power, but as yet unproven so, that they would not want to officially speculate on that suspicion.

Would Iran Shoot Down TWA 800?

Does answering the question of whether Iran would shoot down TWA 800 put the authors in the position of rationalizing an irrational act? No, it does not, for several reasons.

What may seem irrational from a Western perspective may be rational from the perspective of the planners of such an attack. The mullahs in Iran and the Iranian leadership have greatly different standards of conduct, ethics and accountability than do their Western counterparts.

We need only look at the exhortations of the radical Islamic clerics to encourage such acts as suicide bombing and their apparent success in recruiting operatives to see that the rules of the game as played by Iran are not the West's rules. The combination of ancient religious fervor with modern military capabilities makes for a powerful force to be reckoned with. Urging caution in the face of such a combination is one of the purposes of this book.

What kind of commitment can allow a 19 year old youth to drive a truck full of explosives into a building in Lebanon, Israel or New York and set himself off in an explosion? Well, in part, it can be the same patriotic determination that allows any warrior to risk death to achieve victory for his cause. We need only look to the American airmen who risked their lives in Dhahran to warn their comrades to see that such intensity of commitment is not unique to the radical cause. History is replete with stories of those willing to give their lives for a cause. If, to this basic courage you add the heart felt belief that the action you are taking is the manifest will of God, then you have a capability to take almost any act.

Next, you have to consider that much of the leadership in Iran is of a like mind to the young suicide bomber. In a rather unique theocracy, the Islamic Republic of Iran is led by both clerics and civilians who presumably believe that their national cause, their basic laws and their destiny is directed and protected by God himself. The Word of God, as disclosed 1300 odd years ago to Mohammed in the Holy Koran is the central theme of their political as well as social system. We have included in Appendix E, F and G a detailed analysis of the political and religious system in Iran to give the reader some idea of the really unique set of values and priorities that drive the Iranian Nation. While recent changes in the Presidency of Iran may lead to an opening of dialog with the US, it should be recognized that the underlying political and religious foundations of the Iranian state have not significantly changed. Twenty million people may have voted for a new President, but it must be recognized that Khatami is, in reality, the second in command to the Ayatollah who sits as the Leader of the Revolution and that the bureaucratic and military cadre of the government have not changed. Equally worrisome, is the fact that in recent interviews President Khatami has denied the existence of Iranian state-sponsored terrorism, such as Hizbollah International, and, thus, is probably not ready to invoke any changes to this instrumentality of Iranian power.

In this book, we have touched upon several justifications the Iranians might have for taking violent action against American interests — the Iran Air disaster and the religious connection therein — the ongoing enmity of the two governments on the international scene — the hostility of Iran with Israel, a country seen by Iran as protected by America — the numerous other Mid-East states which are allied with the US interests but which are at odds with the fundamentalist Shiite policies of Iran — and, the lists goes on and on. But, there is one particular theme running all through these reasons — the commitment of Iran's leadership for Iran to assume what they see as a holy role in achieving a movement toward an Islamic Revolution world-wide. In this literally holy task, they see America as the primary stumbling block to their success, thus, America as the 'Great Satan.'

To understand the extent to which the leaders of Iran will go beyond normal international law to carry out their *jihad*'s and *fatwa*'s, not to mention their protection of national security, it is necessary to take a hard look at their track record. After the listing of TWA 800 victims below, there is a listing in Appendix A of those persons attacked by Iranian operatives within the borders of foreign countries. Besides these deaths, there have been numerous lesser instances of Iranian state security personnel being responsible for violent acts overseas. To this can be added the hundreds of instances of death and violence carried out by Iranian supported terrorists. This level of violence far exceeds the espionage episodes of the Cold War. These violent covert operations can only be compared to the actions of the nations at war in World War II in its level of violence and disregard for international and national law.

In fairness to the truth, Iran is a nation under siege.

There are numerous subversive organizations that would like to generate unrest within Iran and bring about the Islamic Republic regime's downfall. These range from old royalist supporters of the Shah, to the *Mujahideen Khalq* front to the Kurdish and Baluchistani minority and the communist front groups. There has been ongoing military action taking place against Iran in almost all neighboring countries. Iran has responded to these actions in its neighbors' domain with a similar list of atrocities. These regional acts of violence were largely excluded from the Appendix A list.

In conclusion, in Iran we can see three factors that not only would allow them to do something like the TWA 800 downing but actually makes them the most likely culprit. Iran has a national religious ethic that justifies actions that the West would normally reject in time of peace. Iran sees the United States as its opponent, indeed its arch-enemy, and is publicly committed to confrontation with America. And, Iran has a long record of disregard for the norms of international law when it comes to carrying out its policy objectives by means of violent acts in foreign countries. In its attempts to take the lead in opposing the United States amongst its Islamic brethren, there seems little doubt that the radicals in control of Iran's policy making apparatus, or perhaps its intelligence apparatus acting independently of national leaders, would consider the course of action outlined here.

Why is the American Government acting like it is?

Throughout the investigation of the downing of TWA 800, the federal authorities involved have had to deflect questions regarding why they were so ploddingly unwilling to give full credence to the many witnesses who say they saw something shoot up at the airliner. They have responded that no evidence of a conclusive nature has been found. As discussed elsewhere, 'conclusive' evidence may be an unavailable luxury in this case. Evidence need not be 'conclusive' in order to be indicative of the truth.

Coming as it did a month after the Khobar Barracks bombing and in the years after both Oklahoma City bombing and the NY World Trade Center blast, there was a natural inclination to suspect terrorist foul play in the TWA crash. With the early eyewitness accounts, it appeared that TWA 800 had joined its Pan Am relative in the annals of terrorist attacks.

Then, in the months following the crash, there were the numerous conspiracy theories, the most prominent that the downing of TWA 800 was an act by the US Navy when a test missile went awry. There was also a theory that the Clinton Administration had kept the cover on a foreign bomb plot for a variety of reasons; first, to protect the Olympic games the month following the incident from foreign repercussions and then to assure Clinton's victory in the fall election without any taint of failure by the federal government. There were numerous accusations of mismanagement, bureaucratic in-fighting and coverup, some of which we have addressed in this book.

As these conspiracy and foul-up accusations came in, they sometimes brought with them an iota or smidgeon of new information which often added credence to the suspicions that a terrorist act had taken place.

Why then has there been this almost ardent refusal of most federal authorities to even mouth the suspicion of so many in the press and in the public who saw the supposed 'fingerprints?' Why have they been so determined to simply repeat the three possible causes, bomb, missile and malfunction, and state that there was nothing conclusive?

The first answer is obvious, but not wholly ingratiating of the public and press. It is that both the FBI and the NTSB are investigation professionals who are trained and required to keep an open mind about all possibilities until an obvious 'smoking gun' is found. There is clearly precedent for this excuse in the numerous investigations in which the federal authorities steadfastly refused to give any type of interim answer until a final report was due.

The next answer is that the federal authorities did not want any speculation by the investigators to set off the feeding frenzy of suspicion of foreign terrorists that occurred after Oklahoma City. In the hours and days after the Oklahoma City bombing, the press was racing to check the docket list of the federal court in the building to see what foreign nationals had been before the court, and what other matters could explain the 'terrorist' bombing. There was a collective embarrassment by all concerned when the ultimately accused perpetrators were home grown.

However, there is a third answer that the authors believe requires further explanation and analysis here. This answer is that if United States had reason to believe, but short of certain or 'conclusive' proof, that a foreign power had been responsible for the downing of TWA 800 that it would not be in the national interest for any federal official to make any public comment on that suspicion until the proof was certain and the Commander-in-Chief decided what action to take, militarily or otherwise.

This answer presupposes a conclusion that Iran or some other country did it, but since that conclusion is one of the premises of this book, we will skip to the analysis of why this answer is logical, and what it means to the investigation.

If any federal official gave any voice whatsoever to the concept that TWA 800 was brought down by a missile, there would be an unstoppable groundswell of demand to know who did it. Thus, even if there were conclusive information in crash wreckage that a SAM or a terrorist bomb brought down the plane it would be foolhardy of federal officials to announce it. Oklahoma City's rush to judgment would occur all over again only with justification. In the case of the Pan Am Lockerbie bombing, it is the opinion of authorities that the early announcements of factual evidence that eventually led to identification of the suspects also gave those suspects notice in time to allow them to flee to Libya. Therefore, during the course of the investigation the federal authorities in TWA 800 are naturally reticent to disclose anything.

If any federal official were to announce his or her opinion as to the country of origin or the state which supported the downing of TWA 800 it would be tantamount to accusing that foreign country of an act of war. Remember Press Secretary Mike Curry's words at the White House on the day after TWA 800 went down that "no official with half a brain" would do such a thing.

There is a clear double standard involved in diplomacy and international relations. The system requires it. All nations have hidden agendas that conflict with their public pronouncements and positions. Newt Gingrich made headlines in November 1995 when he gave public vent to his wish to have the US confidential intelligence budget to bring the Iranian regime down allocated more money. Iran was thus not hesitant to publicly announce its similar budget to thwart the United States. There are undoubtedly American operations taking place under CIA or other agency direction to cause harm or damage to the Iranian Government's interests. They are kept secret and when carried out, the operatives attempt to cover the trail to them. If Iran would ever have proof of these affairs, whether espionage or military, it would probably announce it or take action to seek retribution therefor. So too would the US in a like situation.

This brings us to the last reason why federal authorities would probably never speculate if they thought a foreign power, such as Iran, had downed TWA 800. Given the clear precedent of American retaliation against Libya and Iraq, it would be highly unlikely that the United States would announce the conclusive proof of this act in a press conference by an FBI spokesperson rather than by a salvo of Tomahawk missiles from the US Navy ships in the Arabian Sea.

Given all of this reasoning as to why there should not be speculation about Iranian complicity in the downing of

TWA 800, the obvious question is "Why are you writing about it then?" The answer is also obvious — there is a profound difference between the suppositions of private persons in a work such as this and an official of the federal government even hinting at his or her agreement or consideration of the same suppositions. We have not, in this book, disclosed anything that reaches the level of national security information. We have merely retrieved, coalesced, analyzed and reported on a matter which we believe plausible, and which we see has not been given full consideration by the world public.

What we have done in this book is nothing more than what a prosecuting attorney does at trial. We have presented a theory of the case that we believe plausible and supported by the facts that are known. However, in this prosecution allegory, we, the prosecutors, have not had the benefit of all the evidence in the hands of the investigators. We have made due with what was available.

The prosecuting attorney in court, when presenting this theory of the case to the jury, has several duties. He must describe the crime. He is asked to present evidence on several factors — intent, identity, possibility, motivation, modus operandi, and the corpus delicti. The prosecutor has to present this evidence at two stages. First, he has to prove enough of the case to get into trial. He has to prove probable cause. In doing so, that attorney can weave facts and evidence into a story, or theory of the case, which shows a judge that the crime was likely to have been committed in the manner presented. Later, to achieve a conviction the prosecutor must prove the entire body of evidence beyond a reasonable doubt.

What we have done in this book is to provide the

readers, as judges, the theory of a case that says that Iran is probably the cause of the downing of TWA 800. We have shown their intent, their motivation, their modus operandi in their past acts and history of terrorist operations, the corpus delicti is obvious and we have shown one strategy (there are others) which would have allowed them to carry out the operation against TWA 800. You, the reader, are the judge of this probable cause. However, we obviously have not presented a case for Iran's guilt beyond a reasonable doubt. The evidence for this has not been disclosed, or is not yet found. In the end, the judge of the reasonable doubt issue will be the President of the United States. When his investigators give him the proof beyond a reasonable doubt, we are certain the world and Iran will hear of his decision.

The NTSB and FBI Interim Summary Reports

It is difficult to discuss the topic of the TWA 800 tragedy without directly addressing the performance of the NTSB & FBI. As stated earlier, the authors believe both principal Federal agencies have performed their duties vigorously, thoroughly and extensively. As you will see, the authors believe both agencies have operated under the pressure of other influences beyond their control for reasons that we can only surmise.

An indicator of those pressures is the controversy regarding the eyewitnesses to the incident.

Eyewitness Evidence

The NTSB's Witness Group Factual Report, Exhibit 4A, as indicated in Appendix B, is noticeably 'not available.' The FBI's Interim Summary Report (Appendix C) indicates 244 eyewitness interviews were accomplished, and yet no conclusion could be reached, when conclusions, however terse, are provided for just about everything else. The paucity of eyewitness data in any form should attract considerable attention.

On Wednesday, December 10, 1997, the *New York Times News Service* issued an article titled, Boeing Rethinks

Design After TWA Crash. The quarter page article discusses the title content regarding the possible actions Boeing might take in light of the prevailing theory that a short circuit in the fuel pump in the CWT initiated the tragic event.

The last paragraph of that article reads,"Last week, in meetings with the NTSB and in a letter to NTSB Chairman James Hall, the FBI said that it wanted no public discussion or publication of the interviews conducted with witnesses to the crash, no presentation of the video simulation of the crash created for the FBI by the CIA, and no reference to the search for residue of explosives on the wreckage."

Furthermore, an *Aviation Week & Space Technology* article published December 15, 1997 was much more direct in the inquiry regarding the FBI prohibition on discussion of witness information. "NTSB efforts to elicit potentially vital information from witnesses to the flight and crash of TWA Flight 800 were stymied for months by FBI agents who blocked any attempts to interview the witnesses, according to a copy of a safety board report obtained by Aviation Week & Space Technology. The witnesses included mechanics, ramp service personnel and gate agents who worked on Flight 800 immediately prior to its takeoff on its final flight, as well as 96 other witnesses who claimed to have seen a streak of light rise from the surface prior to the 747-131's crash.

"On July 21, 1996, the report states, Assistant US Attorney Valerie Caproni informed Magladry and Norm Weimeyer, head of the Flight 800 probe's operations group, 'that no interviews were to be conducted by the NTSB.'

"Safety board investigators could review FBI-supplied documents on the witnesses, 'provided no notes were taken and no copies were made.'

"The next day, FBI and NTSB officials reached an agreement that safety board officials could conduct interviews 'under the direction and in the company of the FBI, and all information would be kept private with no notes taken.' The report said that there were 458 witness interviews provided by the FBI. Of those, 183 reported seeing a streak of light, and 102 provided information on the origin of the streak. The report stated that six witnesses said the streak originated in the sky, and 96 said it rose from the surface.

"It is not clear whether the accounts of the 96 witnesses were included in the 244 analyzed by the CIA for the FBI. The analysts concluded that the witnesses did not see a missile strike flight 800."

As late as January 9, 1998, the Riverside, California, *Press-Enterprise* reported on the continuing efforts of retired Navy commander, William S. Donaldson, who believes based on the witness information available from other sources that a missile warhead exploded in front of the aircraft severing the nose section from the remainder of the fuselage.

With so many people seeing portions of the disastrous events from various locations, it is extremely odd that the witness information would be excluded from such a high visibility investigation. Eyewitness evidence, while often not entirely accurate or precise, nor indicative of the cause of accidents, usually provides crucial clues to the investigators that lead to the cause factors. According to the *Aviation Week* article, the NTSB investigators were eventually given access to the eyewitnesses.

In a letter response to US Congressman James A. Trafficant, dated January 21, 1998, the FBI responded to written questions submitted by a letter from Trafficant's office to then Assistant Director in Charge James K. Kallstrom, dated October 1, 1997. Of particular intesest is the FBI's response to Question 13.

QUESTION: "If the FBI determines, based upon an exhaustive review of the available evidence, that the crash of TWA Flight 800 was not the result of a criminal act, will the FBI share with the committee all the information and evidence it collected to reach such a conclusion?"

ANSWER: "As was noted by then Assistant Director Kallstrom at his press conference in November, 1997, there is a possibility, admittedly remote, that new evidence could be discovered in the course of the continuing National Transportation Safety Board (NTSB) accident inquiry, from intelligence sources or wreckage that heretofore has not been found that could cause the FBI to renew its investigation to the cause of this crash. Therefore, the FBI is not prepared to share all the information and evidence it has collected. The FBI will continue to answer specific questions directed to the FBI by the committee as are authorized by Chairman Duncan."

First, the FBI did not answer the question. There is no indication they intend to ever share or disclose eyewitness information relative to TWA 800. Second, the FBI still has a reasonable doubt about closing their criminal investigation, and yet, they do not appear to be overly eager to assist the NTSB in determining the cause. They appear to be perfectly content to let the investigation remain as...cause unknown. Lastly, and, perhaps, most importantly, they are willing to give such an obtuse non-answer to a senior member of Congress.

The Tischler Hypotheses

In the March 1998 issue of *Aerospace America*, the periodical publication of the American Institute of Aeronautics and Astronautics, Adelbert O. Tischler, a renown engineer and scientist, rocket propulsion specialist, and former director of propulsion at NASA responsible for the development of the Saturn rocket engines, published a Viewpoint article titled: <u>What Happened to Flight 800</u>. Tischler uses his experience and intellect to articulate several other potential mechanical hypotheses as to plausible causes for ignition of the CWT fuel-air vapors.

He begins by recounting the flight conditions prior to the incident and a broad description of the 747's fuel system. He then goes on to present several hypotheses as to how a non-penetrating ignition source could be introduced into the CWT.

The first hypotheis he presents involves the action of the scavenge pump in a run-dry or intermittent run-dry condition where energy imparted by the pump is transformed into heat. There are conceivable local ambient conditions that could result in the trapped fuel-air vapor to reach an auto-ignition threshold. Once the flash was introduced into the CWT, an explosion would clearly result.

The second hypothesis involves a complex interaction between a fuel transfer pump, various fuel line check valves and the resonant or near resonant energy transfer. The proper conditions are achievable, but encompass an important thermal balance between heat generation and dissipation.

Tischler concludes, "Using only what is already known, we have assembled concepts for the Flight 800 accident that are not mysterious, are based on established science, and are plausible.

"There is no way for me to prove that these concepts explain the accident, nor was that my primary intent. My intent was to stimulate scientific examination of a phenomenon that must be explained.

"Until detailed calculations are made, with strict adherence to characteristics of the aircraft and its operating conditions, to determine whether these hypotheses provide quantitative results that support the accident observations, the hypotheses must be regarded as personal conjecture. Should results coincide with reality, however, I would propose further confirmation by experiment."

Tischler's article is intriguing in that, as he states, there are plausible alternative conditions that could produce the CWT explosion. As he states, it is impossible to prove or disprove without additional information and experimentation. As such, the authors consider presentation of this information as critical to the furtherance of the primary objective — to absolutely determine the cause factors and take appropriate actions. While Tischler's hypotheses do not support the missile or terrorist theories, they must be addressed in a balanced, logically, methodical examination. In essence, no stones should be left unturned.

The Scarry Hypothesis

In an Associated Press story dated July 13, 1998, another possible hypothesis was presented. Harvard University

English Professor Elaine Scarry suggested, in an article first published in the April 1998 issue of *New York Review of Books*, a scholarly magazine, and subsequently in an exchange of letters with NTSB Chairman Jim Hall published in the July 16th issue, that electromagnetic radiation from a High Intensity Radiated Field (HIRF) source may have induced sufficient current in several adjacent wires to produce an arc — possibly a spark within the CWT.

HIRF is a broad term that identifies a well-known phenomenon associated with electromagnetic radiation like radio and radar. There are many known effects depending upon the frequency and power of the emissions, range from the emitter, and protection on the aircraft. Without getting into a lengthy discussion of HIRF, let it suffice to say, a HIRF induced initiator is possible. Different frequencies of electromagnetic energy produce different effects depending upon the circumstances and the immediate environment. The field strength at any point decreases by the square of the distance from the emitter, thus proximity becomes a very important factor. Lastly, there are a variety of means to protect circuits from HIRF effects, e.g., a metal, electrically grounded fuselage, shielded wiring, electromagnetic shields, among others.

Scarry asked several questions and drew specific attention to the erratic fuel flow indication on the No.4 engine. Erratic instrument indications are some of the first indicators of ElectroMagnetic Interference (EMI). All civil aircraft are tested for EMI during the certification process. Military aircraft are hardened and extensively tested for HIRF vulnerability. As Scarry accurately notes, civil aircraft are also vulnerable to HIRF. A modicum of protection is provided in commercial aircraft, but they are not hardened like military aircraft. The general rule for civil aviation is avoidance.

Commercial airways are routed to circumnavigate known emitters by substantial distances and are demonstrated safe at specified ranges. Furthermore, high power emitters are generally surrounded by restricted areas that are well marked on navigation maps. As noted earlier, power level decreases rapidly. To produce observable effects and especially arcing between insulated wires, a considerable amount of power would need to be generated to produce local effects in imbedded insulated wires, in an aluminum fuselage at 13,000 feet. Or, a very directed, 'focused' beam or pulse would be required to affect an aircraft.

The interesting aspect of Scarry's hypothesis is, it does begin to explain the erratic fuel flow indication. Depending upon the field strength at the aircraft, erratic indications by only one instrument is quite plausible at relatively low local field strengths. It is also possible to produce a local HIRF with sufficient strength to cause arcing between adjacent, lightly shielded or insulated wires as would be common on commercial aircraft. A field sufficiently powerful to cause arcing would generally cause substantial other indications like completely shutting down an engine, erratic flight control inputs in electronically augmented systems. HIRF affects anything electronic whether on the ground or airborne. The military has considerable documentation of HIRF phenomena in a broad variety of aircraft and conditions. Also, the military uses a broad spectrum of electromagnetic emitters for a host of operational reasons. Frequency, power and range are the key parameters.

The closest military entity we know of to TWA 800

was the Navy P-3 anti-submarine hunter aircraft overhead the ill-fated 747. Did that P-3 have some special, non-standard, high powered radar or other electromagnetic emitter? If the P-3 was involved, there must have been other observable effects on the ground and in the air. Did other pilots see erratic instrument indications?

This hypothesis, like the others, does not account for the eyewitness observations, but it is worth serious consideration and investigation, as apparently the NTSB is conducting according to the AP article.

National Transportation Safety Board

The NTSB report is excerpted in Appendix B. It is presented in the classic engineering investigatory style — collect all the facts you can, build a picture of the evidence, examine each critical element in minute detail, continue the iterative process of answering questions as they develop until a conclusion is reached. In this particular case, no conclusion has been reached.

It should also be noted that the reporting style of the NTSB has evolved over time and has proven to be an enormously important factor in solving mysterious aircraft accidents. They chronicle the investigation for posterity, i.e., this was what was done; but, more importantly, they establish the basis for subsequent examination given additional information about the accident from any source or from other accidents. It also opens to public scrutiny the details of an accident.

As presented earlier, there is no disagreement or debate about the sequence of events from the explosion of the

Center Wing fuel Tank (CWT). As is normally the case, the NTSB has meticulously reconstructed the sequence of events from that point on through the remainder of action.

What is missing, however, is what ignited the explosive fuel-air vapor in the CWT? As summarized in excerpts from the NTSB report (Appendix B), the cause remains unknown. Many questions remain.

First and foremost, what happened prior to the detonation of normal, fuel-air mixture in the CWT? What was found on part CW504, the center section of the wing front spar?

Why does the FDR plot for certain parameters continue past the calculated loss of power to the FDR at 2031.12.27 EDT? (see Appendix D) If the data to the right of the END OF DATA notation is the overwrite data from some flight condition 30 operating minutes previous, why is the plot mislabeled with time 2031:20? And why were the investigators not equally as meticulous in their analysis of and did not specifically address that portion of the published data? If the overwrite condition is valid, which is possible, they should have clearly addressed that aspect in the analysis; it is not intuitive to anyone beyond the investigators themselves.

For the most part, the NTSB report is a model in engineering investigatory documentation. What is most significant is what is missing from the documentation:

- The witness statements.

- While there are numerous comments sprinkled throughout the NTSB report about the absence of evidence, indications of explosives, missile impact or warhead detonation, there is no presentation of what was done to substantiate such statements. With the early concern, it is unusual that specific analysis needed to look for such evidence was not required.

- The FBI report acknowledges 1,400 penetrations while the NTSB report shows only 196 penetrations? The *Aviation Week* article states that 1,500 penetrations were found with only 200 found in the reconstucted portions of the aircraft. Where are the others? How significant were they?

- Exhibit 15D: CW504 Splatter report is missing. CW504 is a large portion of the center section of the wing's front spar and was one of the earliest structural pieces to separate from the aircraft. Splatter is a term often used in reference to the tell-tale cooled remains of molten metal from high energy impacts that usually occur when bullets or other fragments penetrate metal sheets.

- The engine debris analysis is missing. Engine reconstruction is an essential element of aircraft accident investigation. The engine state, as determined by forensic examination of debris, is often crucial in sequence determination, among other tasks.

There are other notatable elements of the NTSB report missing, however the FBI prohibitions make criticism of the NTSB very difficult. Normally, accident reports cover the full range of evidence collected by the investigators. They try to document their work for posterity, but more importantly, they provide essential elements of information to stimulate any other reader to question, search, add, modify or whatever the information with one paramount purpose — determine the cause of the accident so that it can be prevented in the future. While there is beneficial knowledge coming from this investigation, the amount and type of data missing from the report makes this process nearly impossible. The result draws suspicion. Why is this crucial data missing? What forces could possibly outweigh the NTSB in suppressing such information?

Federal Bureau of Investigation

The FBI Interim report is presented in Appendix C is most notable by its paucity of any substantive information regarding the investigation. For the FBI, there is always the conflict between disclosure versus the rules of evidence to ensure proper prosecution should an investigation be marked as criminal. The FBI began the TWA 800 investigation as a criminal investigation and initially took the role as the primary agency because of that concern for the collection and protection of evidence that might be utilized in a felony prosecution. This factor would not be materially different than the protection of national security intelligence assets. There are methods to protect information and sources regardless of whether there are rules of evidence or national intelligence assets involved, and yet confide in interested people regarding the methods and content of an investigation. The contrast between the NTSB and the FBI reports is dramatic.

As can be seen in Appendix C, the FBI report is replete with simple, terse statements 'NO EVIDENCE FOUND.' If there was no evidence found, why hasn't the FBI presented their exhaustive work to the world as the NTSB has done? If there is no reason to protect rules of evidence or national security assets, why haven't they shared their exhaustive work to help those of us who remain concerned about the implications of this tragedy?

As indicated in paragraph VII.F of the FBI report (Appendix C), "Investigators reviewed nine missile attacks on aircraft during a fourteen year period. Those attacks occurred in the former Soviet Union, Afghanistan and Africa. The purpose of this review was to identify potential missiles utilized and launch sites. Forensic evidence from those aircraft were not available for comparison to Flight 800, therefore prompting our own testing."

The need for confirmatory testing regarding the characteristics of impact damage as a result of a missile strike is logical and appropriate considering the lack of standards, indicators, tell-tales, et cetera, relative to damage to aircraft designed for commercial transportation. There is a plethora of information or evidence regarding missile and warhead damage to military aircraft, however the generally hardened structure of military aircraft would not directly translate to a very large, jumbo, airliner. There is one exceptional example for a commercial aircraft, Iran Air 655, however a similar retrieval operation to TWA 800 would be required and the Government of Iran would not likely look favorably on such an operation. So, where are the results of the confirmatory testing? And, how do they compare to the damage found on the remnants of TWA 800?

The FBI report, while laudable as an attempt to address public concerns, fails to present a credible accounting, especially in light of the purported 'exhaustive' investigation. At least the NTSB presented the methodology, results and conclusions for most of their work. It is the elements of the investigation restricted to only the FBI that lead people to question the veracity of FBI statements. In addition, the obvious, extraordinary and somewhat unprecented, efforts of the FBI to exclude certain potentially significant elements of information leads many to ask "what is the FBI hiding?" And why?

If there are concerns for rules of evidence in support of a potential criminal prosecution or even national security, there are methods to 'scrub' sensitive data to preclude disclosure of sources or sensitive methods. Stonewalling has been proven, time and again, not to be a successful approach.

What is the FBI trying to protect?

Boeing Company's Airworthiness Directives

The Boeing Company has taken the high road in dealing with any possible suspicion regarding the safety of the fuel systems on their aircraft. With established or threatened litigation stemming from the TWA 800 tragedy, Boeing has taken substantial legal risk in order to ensure the safety of their aircraft. They have erred on the side of public safety rather than legal protection. Their actions are commendable. With the investigation of TWA 800 still on-going, any dialogue relative to this event would be incomplete without reference to Boeing's pre-emptive Airworthiness Directive (AD) action.

Boeing acknowledged the common aerospace industry standard recognizing the existence of a potentially explosive fuel-air mixture in empty fuel tanks and the design of precluding an ignition sources in or near any fuel tank or cell. The design for the fuel tanks on the 747 have been documented to meet all design standards. In essence, there is substantial protection through redundancy, multiple levels of failure and careful design avoidance. There is no reason to question the design. Just as there is no perfect security, there is no perfect safety. Design intent by definition is to provide sufficient safety given an enormous array of conflicting constraints. Design and regulatory authorities constantly strive for the greatest practical safety given the engineering limitations of the day. For example, puncture resistant or self-sealing fuel tanks were not practical for aircraft 80 years ago; the liner material would have taken up too much volume and weighed too much for aircraft of the day. The levels of safety provided in any modern commercial transport aircraft are substantially higher than in many other forms of transportation.

And yet, Boeing decided to take additional measures to pre-emptively improve fuel tank safety beyond the industry standards. On May 22, 1998, Boeing issued three AD's.

The first service bulletin was applicable to all 747 airplanes and based on a Boeing recommendation from May 1997. The AD initiated an inspection to gather data on the in-service condition of 747 fuel tanks including the CWT, and determine appropriate follow-up activity, if necessary, to ensure the continued airworthiness of the airplane. The inspection included checking the integrity of wiring and grounding straps, a visual inspection of pumps and fuel lines and fittings, and electrical bonding checks on all equipment. As of May, 1998, 213 in-service airplanes had been inspected with no significant problems found.

The second service bulletin will include instructions for the replacement of all fuel probe terminal blocks on older airplanes, and instructions to ensure proper routing of Fuel Quantity Indicating System (FQIS) wires. In addition, it also provides for inspection of FQIS wiring for copper or silver-sulfide build-up that might affect safety. Again, as of May 1998, no detrimental conditions had been found.

The third service bulletin involves the installation of a flame arrestor at the open end of the scavenge-pump inlet tube. Testing by various agencies has not found a condition that would generate an ignition source. However, Boeing felt the installation of a flame arrestor would provide an additional level of safety. No fuel-vapor ignition in the inlet tube has been reported on any in-service airplanes.

With so many continuing genuine concerns regarding the missile hypothesis, it is imperative that one or more of the cognizant federal agencies present the accumulated body of data regarding the eyewitness statements, and the investigatory methods, results and conclusions surrounding the missile and explosives examinations. Until such time, we must continue to pursue all logical avenues to determine the cause of this tragedy, and if appropriate, bring the perpetrators to justice. Without a full and open dialogue regarding the various missile hypotheses, the speculation, suspicion and intrigue will continue. There are simply too many loose ends that can not be tied up without such a public exchange of all information involving this event.

Conclusion

The authors' case of probable cause has been presented. There is sufficient reason to believe a terrorist act, quite probably perpetrated by the Government of Iran and/or its co-conspirators, was committed upon TWA 800. Numerous unanswered questions have also been presented that should lead to the public inquiry into the cause of the TWA 800 tragedy. This has been one of the most thoroughly investigated aircraft mishaps in history and yet the public remains unconvinced by the evidence offered so far. If a crime was committed, the criminals, no matter what their rationale or justification, must be punished.

There will be readers who will disagree -- some quite vehemently -- with the hypothesis presented in this book. The investigators have presented an exhaustive case that appears to ignore many crucial elements of fact. Some aspects of the investigation have been denied to the public in the light of such an enormous public display, thus raising suspicions — why? The authors can offer no further evidence to support the terrorist missile hypothesis; however, until the anomalies, gaps and incomplete investigation are addressed, answered and presented to the public, the terrorist missile hypothesis remains the most plausible. As stated earlier, it is not the only plausible scenario, but it is the most likely since it ties together all the public facts. In the end, if it looks like a duck, smells like a duck, waddles like a duck, quacks like a duck, then it probably is a duck.

The authors, likewise, recognize the implications and consequences of the terrorist missile hypothesis. We are not advocating any rash, precipitous or confrontational actions against the Government of Iran. We are simply seeking a full and complete disclosure, as well as proper and complete investigatory work, to find the true cause, and if the cause is criminal as we propose, then justice should be rendered swiftly and strongly to the perpetrators.

TWA Flight 800

July 17, 1996

Aikens-Bellamy, Sandra
Aikey, Jessica
Alex, Christian
Alexander, Matthew
Allen, Lamar
Allen, Ashton
Amlund, Svein
Anderson, Jay
Anderson, Patricia
Anderson, Seana
Babb, David
Baszczewski, Daniel
Beatty, Charles
Becker, Michelle
Bellazoug, Myriam
Benjamin, Arthur
Benjamin, Joan
Berthe, Line
Bluestone, Nicholas
Bohlin, Michelle
Bossuyt, Luc
Bouhs, Leonie

Bower, Jordan
Braman, Rosie
Breistroff, Michel
Brooks, Ruth
Buttaroni, Mirko
Caillaud, Anthony
Caillaud, Daniel
Callas, Dan J
Campbell, Richard G.
Carven, Jay
Carven, Paula
Cayrol, Jacques
Chaillou, Jenny
Chanson, Ludovic
Charbonnier, Jacques
Charbonnier, Constance
Chemtob, Monique
Christopher, Janet
Coiner, Constance
Coiner, Anna Duarte
Cox, Monica
Crandell, Pamela

Creamades, Daniel
Dadi, Marcel
D' Alessandro, Anna
Darley, Francois
Deboisredon, Cybele
Delange, Sylvain
Delouvrier, Judith
Dhuimieres, Dominiques
Dickey, Deborah
Dickey, Douglas
DiLuccio, Debra Collins
D'Iorio, Christine Bailey
D'Iorio, Pietro
Dodge, Warren
Dupont,Guy
Dwyer, Larkin
Edwards, Daryl
Ellison, Marie
Ersoz, Clara
Ersoz, Namik
Eshleman, Dougas A.
Estival, Alexandre
Feeney, Deirdre
Feeney, Vera
Ferrat (first name unavailable)
Foster, Rod
Foulon, Didier
Fry, Carol
Furlano, Rosaria
Gabor
Gaetke

Gaetke, Stephanie
Gallagher, Claire
Galland, Jean Paul
Gasq, C.
Unnamed passenger flying with C. Gasq
Gough, Capt. Donald
Graham, Steven
Gray, Charles Hank
Greene, Renee
Griffith, Donna
Griffith, Joanne
Grimm, Julia
Grivet, Cyril
Gustin, Anne
Hammer, Beverly
Hammer, Tracy
Hansen, Lars Groenbakken
Harkness, Eric
Harris, Lawrence
Haurani, Dr. Ghassan
Haurani, Nina
Hazelton, Sandra
Hettler, Rance
Hill, Susan
Hocharo, Jeanpierre
Hogan, David
Holst, Virginia
Holst, Eric
Hull, James
Hurd, James III

Ingenhuett, Lonnie
Jacquemot, Benoit
Jensen, Susanne
Johns, Courtney
Johnsen, Arlene E.
Johnson, E.
Johnson, Jed
Johnson, L.
Jones, Romana
Karschner, Amanda
Kevorkian, Capt. Ralph G.
Krick, Oliver
Krikhan, Margot
Krukar, Andrew
Kwan, Barbara
Kwiat, Patricia
Kwiat, Kimberly
Labys, Jane
Lacailledesse, Antoine
LaForge, Alain
Lamour, Yvon
Lang, Ray
Leim, Ana
Lockhart, Maureen
Loffredo, Elaine
Loudenslager, Jody
Lohan, Britta
Loo, Patricia
Lucien, Dalila
Luevano, Elias
Lychner, Katie

Lychner, Pam
Lychner, Shannon
Manchuelle, Francois
Maresq, Etienne
Maresq, Nicolas
Martin, Betty Ruth
Mazzola, Salvator
McPherson, Pamela
Meade, Sandra
Melotin, Grace
Mercurio, Giuseppe
Merieux, Rodolphe
Meshulam, Avishaim
Michel, Pascal
Miller, Amy
Miller, Elizabeth
Miller, Gideon
Miller, Joan
Miller, Kyle
Miller, Robert
Murta, Angela
Nelson, A.
Unnamed passenger flying
with A. Nelson
Nibert, Cheryl
Notes, Gadi
O'Hara, Caitlin
O'Hara, Janet
O'Hara, John
Olsen, Rebecca Jane
Omiccioli, Monica

Orman, Alan
Ostachiewicz, Elsie
Unnamed passenger flying
with Elsie Ostachiewicz
Paquet, Huguette
Paquet, Ingrid
Pares, Serge
Penzer, Judy
Percy, Marion
Price, Dennis
Price, Peggy
Privette, Glenda
Puhlmann, Rico
Puichaud, Elizabeth
Remy, Jacqueline
Rhein, Kirk Jr.
Rhoads, Marit E.
Rhoads, Scott
Richey, Brent
Richter, Annelyse
Richter, Noemie
Rio, Celine
Rogers, Kimberly
Rojany, Yon
Romangna, Barbara
Rose, Katrina
Rupert, Judith
Schuldt, Mike
Scott, Barbara
Scott, Joseph
Scott, Michael
Shorter, Anna Maria

Siebert, Brenna
Siebert, Chrisha
Silverman, Candace
Silverman, Etta
Silverman, Eugene
Silverman, Jamie
Simmons, Olivia
Skjold, K.
Snyder, Capt. Steven
Story, William R.
Straus, Carine
Teang, Lydie
Teang, Rachana
Thiery, Josette
Tofani, Mauro
Torche, Melinda
Uzupis, Larissa
Vanepps, Lois
Verhaeghe, Rick L.
Warren, Lani
Watson, Jacqueline
Watson, Jill
Weatherby, Thomas
Weaver, Monica
Windmiller, Ruben
Wolfson, Eleanor
Wolfson, Wendy
Wolters, Bonnie
Yee, Judith
Zara, Jean
Ziemkiewicz, Jill F.

APPENDICES

A. Timeline and a Partial List of Victims of Terrorist Acts by Iranian Operatives or Persons Controlled by Iran Outside of Iran under the Current Regime
B. NTSB Report
C. FBI Report
D. Cockpit Voice Recorder and Flight Data Recorder
E. Background On The Political And Religious Situation in Iran
F. Leadership in the Islamic Republic and the Hierarchy of Shi'a Islam
G. Religion and the Dilemmas of Power in Iran

APPENDIX A

Timeline and a Partial List of Victims of Terrorist Acts by Iranian Operatives or Persons Controlled by Iran Outside of Iran under the Current Regime

World events involving major terrorist actions[sponsor]:

November 4, 1979	US Embassy - Iran hostages [Iran]
October 23, 1983	Beirut barracks bombing [Iran]
December 4, 1984	Kuwaiti airliner hijacking [Iran]
June 13, 1985	TWA 847 hijacking, Beirut [Iran]
October 7, 1985	*Achille Lauro* hijacking [Iran]
October 10, 1985	In-flight interception of hijackers
December 27, 1985	Rome & Vienna airport bombings [Libya]
April 5, 1986	Berlin, La Belle discotheque bombing [Libya]
April 14, 1986	US Bombing, retaliation on Libya
April 17, 1986	Hizbollah kills 3 hostages in retaliation for Libyan raid [Iran]
May 17, 1987	Attack on USS *Stark* [Iraq]
July 3, 1988	**IranAir 655**
December 21, 1988	PanAm 103 [Libya/Iran]
February 14, 1989	Khomeini condemns Rushdie
August 2, 1990	Invasion of Kuwait [Iraq]
February 26, 1993	World Trade Center bombing [Iran]
June 25, 1996	Khobar Barracks Bombing [Iran]
July 17, 1996	**TWA 800 [Iran?]**
August 7, 1998	US Embassy bombings - E. Africa [Hizbollah Int'l / Usama bin Ladin?]

Partial List of Other Terrorist Acts by
Iranian Government Operatives

The following list was compiled by an Iranian opposition group. It is believed to be correct by the authors. This list does not include those deaths, including assassinations, inside Iran or involving persons actively engaged in para-military operations against Iran in neighboring countries nor does it include hundreds of Hizbollah and Hamas terrorist acts which were funded, supported or supplied by Iran. The purpose of this list is to show that the Islamic Republic of Iran does not hesitate to take hostile acts in foreign jurisdictions.

Reza Mazlouman, 5/28/96, Paris, France, Assasinated. Former Minister under the Shah.

Abdul-Ali Muradi, 2/20/96, Istanbul, Turkey Assasinated. Supporter of the People's Mujahedin Organization of Iran.

Zahra Rajabi, 2/20/96, Istanbul Turkey, Member of the National Council of Resistance. Assasinated in Turkey while on a mission to aid Iranian Refugees.

Majid-Reza & Ibrahimi 10/30/93, Baghdad, Iraq Assasinated in a Baghdad Store

Behran Azadfer, 8/28/93, Ankara, Turkey, Assassinated by 3 Iranian operatives.

Mohammad Hassan Arbab, 6/6/93, Karachi, Pakistan Assassinated by 4 Iranian operatives

Mohammad Hossein Naghdi, 3/16/93, Rome, Italy Representative of the National Council of Resistance of Iran in Italy. Killed by two terrorists on a motorcycle in broad daylight

Abbas Golizadeh, 12/26/92, Istanbul, Turkey, Shah's ex-bodyguard. Kidnapped. Fate unknown.

Mohammad Sadeq & five others, Sharafkandi,9/17/92, Germany, Leader of the Kurdistan Democratic Party of Iran, machinegun fire

Gholam Ghahremani 8/3/92 Dubai, Supporter of Mojahedin seeking political asylum. Kidnapped from his residence and transferred to Evin Prison in Tehran.

Nareh Rafi'zadeh, 3/26/92, New Jersey, U.S.A. Wife and sister-in-law of intelligence agents under the Shah. Assassinated

Abolhassan Banisadr 12/6/91, Versaille, France Khomeini's first president. Attempted assassination, commandos fled when French security agents opened fire.

Shahpour Bakhtiar &, his secretary, 8/6/91, Paris, France, The Shah's last Prime Minister. Bakhtiar's throat was slit and his aide stabbed to death at Bakhtiar's home

Abdolrahman Boroumand, 4/18/91, Paris, France Aide to Bakhtiar. Stabbed to death in the street in Paris.

Sirous Elahi, 10/23/90, Paris France, Member of Derafsh Kaviani organization. Shot and killed at his residence in Paris.

Gholam Reza Nakha'I, 1/10/90, Turkey, Iranian political refugee. Killed in his hotel room with a severe blow to the head.

Effat Qazi, 9/6/90, Sweden, Killed when she opened a letter bomb

Ali Kashefpour, 7/15/90, Turkey, Kidnapped. His tortured body was later found in a roadside ditch.

Prof. Kazem Rajavi, 4/24/90, Geneva, Switzerland Leader of the Iranian Resistance. Shot to death in his by at least 13 terrorists with Iranian service passports.

Hadj Balouch Khan, 2/16/90, Taftan, Pakistan, Royalist. Assassinated by an Iranian Guards commando squad in Taftan.

Hossein Keshavarz, 9/14/89, Karachi, Pakistan, Machinegun fire gravely wounded, paralyzed in both legs.

Bahman Rashidzadeh & Javadi Youssef, 8/26/89, Cyprus, Members of Komeleh, Javadi was shot and killed in the street. Rashidzadeh wounded.

Abdol Rahman Qassemlou, 7/13/89, Vienna Austria Leader of the Kurdistan Democratic Party of Iran, Abdullah Qaderi-Azar, Fadel Mala, and Mahmoud Rassoul, his aides. Shot dead in Vienna while meeting secretly with representatives of Rafsanjani. A Guards commander oversaw the murders.

Ata'ollah Bayahmadi, 6/4/89, Dubai, Ex-military intelligence colonel under the Shah. Assassinated in his hotel room.

Iranian refugees, 12/3/88, Karachi, Pakistan, Iranian refugees waiting outside the UNHCR office in Karachi attacked. One person killed, 5 wounded.

Javad Ha'eri, 12/1/87 Istanbul, Turkey, Dissident . Stabbed to death by two men at this home in Istanbul.

Behrouz Bagheri, 11/28/87, Paris France, Former Air Force commander, bomb planted in his Paris store.

Iranian refugees, 10/31/87, Quetta, Pakistan B o m b planted in a hotel in Quetta. Police arrested Guards Corps members. One Iranian killed, another wounded.

Abolhassan and Mostafa Abrari Mojtahedzadeh, 10/11/87 Istanbul, Turkey, Kidnapped in Istanbul by Iranian embassy personnel. Abrari escaped his captors. The police discovered Mojtahedzadeh in the trunk of an <u>Iranian embassy</u>

car with diplomatic plates near the Iran-Turkey border.

Ali and Noureddin Nabavi Tavakoli, 10/3/87, London, United Kingdom, Father and son, royalists, Shot in the back of the head in the living room of their London home.

AhmadTalebi 9/10/87, Geneva, Switzerland, Fighter pilot,. Assassinated on the street in Geneva by two armed men.

Mohammad Hassan Mansouri, 7/25/87 Istanbul, Turkey, Anti-Khomeini dissident, and another person, Assassinated

Alireza Hassanpour Sharifzadeh & Faramarz Aqa'i 7/8/87 Karachi, Pakistan, RPG rockets and submachine gun attack. Sharifzadeh and Aqa'i killed & 33 wounded. 9 Iranian Guards arrested

Amir-Hossein Amir-Parviz 7/8/87,United Kingdom Affiliate of Shah's last Prime Minister,Bakhtiar, Severely injured in a car bomb

Hamidreza Chitgar, 5/19/87, Vienna,Austria, First Secretary of the Workers Party. Assassinated.

Ali Akbar Mohammadi, 1/16/87, Germany, Former pilot for Rafsanjani. Assassinated in the street by two men.

Vali Mohammad, 11/12/86, Pakistan, Former Marine officer Shot five times and killed.

Ahmadhamed Monfared, 10/24/86, Turkey, former Army colonel Assassinated by 2 men armed with silencer-equipped pistols.

Ahmad Madani, 1/1/86, Paris, France, Former Defense Minister and governor under the Shah, poisoned.

Moradi, 12/23/85, Istanbul, Turkey, Ex-colonel in the Shah's Army Assassinated in Istanbul.

Mir Monavat, 9/28/85 Karachi, Pakistan, Majlis

deputy from Baluchistan under the Shah, Murdered at his home in Karachi by 3 armed men.

Behrouz Shahvardilou1/6/85 Istanbul,   Turkey, Police colonel under the Shah Assassinated in Istanbul.

Gholam-Ali Oveissi, 2/7/84, Paris, France, Former commander of the Shah's Army, and his brother, an ex-general, Assassinated in the street in Paris.

Shahrokh Missaqi, 1/14/82, Manilla, Philippines, Supporter of the People's Feda'ii Stabbed and killed in Manilla.

Ali-Akbar Tabataba'i, 7/23/80, Washington, DC, Diplomat under the Shah. Shot and killed at his suburban Washington home.

Shahpour Bakhtiar, 7/18/80, Paris, France, Shah's last Prime Minister A five-man hit squad tried to shoot its way into his Paris home. A policeman and a neighbor were killed, three policemen wounded.

Shahriar Shafiq, 12/8/79, Paris, France, Former officer in the Shah's Army Assassinated in front of his Paris home.

APPENDIX B

NATIONAL TRANSPORTATION SAFETY BOARD
December 12, 1997
REPORT

Authors' Note: The NTSB report of exhibits for the public hearings contains substantial technical data as well as other investigatory narrative that makes it too voluminous to reproduce within the limitations of this book. The following is an index listing of the sub-reports published in support of the public hearings as contained on a CD-ROM distributed on behalf of the NTSB. Furthermore, conclusion or summary extracts have been provided as relevant material, where appropriate. Authors' notes are added in [*italics*].

B-747-131, N93119
From: NTSB CD-ROM: TWA Flight 800, July 17.1996, Accident Invesigation: Factual Reports as of November 28, 1997 (DCA-96-MA-070)

As of November 27, 1997, the following items were scheduled to be presented at the public hearing in Baltimore, Maryland, December 8-12, 1997. All exhibits are subject to revision. Some items were not available at the time of printing, as indicated; new exhibits may be introduced later. See the NTSB web site at **http://www.ntsb.gov** for the latest information.

Public Hearing Exhibit List
TABLE OF CONTENTS [Docket Number: SA-516]
Exhibit Number

11P: Airworthiness Directive List

11Q: Airworthiness Directive (AD) 90-25-05

12A: Group Chairman's Factual Report Of Investigation Cockpit Voice Recorder **(available 12/8/97,** *not included on CD, but subsequently downloaded from http://www.ntsb.gov***)**

12B: Sound Spectrum Group Chairman's Factual Report

13A: Aircraft Performance Group Chairman's Factual Report

15A: Metallurgist's Factual Report: Front Spar Lower Chord Fracture Area; CW504 Fatigue

15B: Metallurgist's Factual Report: Examination of Small Holes

15C: Metallurgist's Factual Report: Section 41/42 Joint, Forward Cargo Door

15D: CW504 Splatter **(not available)**

17A: Reconstruction Group Chairman's Factual Report

17D: Reconstruction Slides **(also available as JPG)**

18A: Metallurgy/Structures Sequencing Group Chairman's Report

18B: Supporting Documentation for Overall Breakup Sequence (Drawings)

18C: Nose Landing Gear Doors Sequence

19A: Medical/Forensic Group Chairman's Factual Report Of Investigation

20A: Fire & Explosion Group Chairman's Factual Report

20B: Appendix II: Soot/Fracture Diagrams

20C: Appendix III: Tests and Analysis

20D: Jet A Explosion Experiments: Laboratory Testing

20E: Jet A Explosions: Field Test Plan 1/4 Scale
Experiments
20F: Explosion of Aviation Kerosene (Jet A) Vapors
20G: Jet A Flight Test Samples
20H: Jet A Vapor Pressure **(not available)**
20I: Chemical Analysis of Residue
22A: Trajectory Study
22B: Trajectory Study Supporting Material
22C: Main Wreckage Flight Path Study
23A: Flight Test Group Chairman's Factual Report Of
Investigation
23B: Flight Test Plan
23C: FAA Comments on Flight Test Plan
23D: Component Drawings
23E: Test Item Requirements List (TIRL) Instrument
Locations Flight Test Schedule
23F: Flight Test Results: TWA 800 Emulation Flight

EXTRACTS

2A: Operational Factors Group Chairman's Factual Report
   Takeoff was planned, and occurred, on runway 22R
which is 10,500 feet in length and has a slope of 0.00 degrees.
Based on a temperature of 71 degrees Fahrenheit (22 degrees
Celsius) and a flap setting of 10 degrees, takeoff speeds were
calculated as a V1 (takeoff decision speed) of 113 knots, a Vr
(takeoff rotation speed) of 146 knots, and a V2 (takeoff safety
speed) of 153 knots. Engine pressure ratio (EPR) settings were
1.330 standard and 1.455 maximum.
Takeoff fuel = 176,600 lbs.
Gross takeoff weight (ATOW 708,300) = 590,441 lbs.
Taxi weight = 594,941 lbs.
Maximum certified gross weight = 734,000 lbs.

Captain Steven Snyder. DOB 11/21/38. Captain Snyder was serving as a check airman and was the pilot in command. He was occupying the right seat and was filling the role of first officer on this flight.

Captain Ralph Kevorkian. DOB 10/18/37. Captain Kevorkian was occupying the left seat and was receiving his second "initial operating experience" training flight as part of his qualification as a captain on the Boeing 747 type aircraft. He was filling the role of captain on this flight.

Richard Campbell. DOB 7/2/33. Based on company procedures and CVR voice recognition, Mr. Campbell was occupying the jump seat across from the engineer panel. He was a check engineer conducting training of a "new hire" flight engineer.

Oliver Krick. DOB 7/10/71. Mr. Crick was a "new hire" with TWA and had no previous experience as a flight engineer. He was on his sixth leg of initial operating experience as a flight engineer on the Boeing 747 and had no previous flight engineer experience.

During the investigation, the crew who brought the aircraft to JFK from Athens was interviewed. They said they experienced no operational abnormalities during the flight from Athens and in answer to a specific question concerning the center fuel tank, the flight engineer said he had no fuel migration back into the tank after he had used all the useable fuel in the tank and the scavenge pump worked normally. He said there was about 300 pounds residual fuel in the tank.

Normal operation of the air conditioning packs on the ground in accordance with TWA procedures is two of the three packs. According to information gathered during the investigation, two packs were operated on the ground at JFK.

On this ground operation, the packs were being operated by the APU. Investigation provided information that three packs were in operation at the time the accident.

6A: Airplane Interior Documentation Group's Factual Report
    The aircraft impacted into the Atlantic Ocean at 72:37.46W, 40:39.52N off the coast of Long Island approximately 12 miles east of Center Moriches, New York. *[This report documents in broad terms the condition of recovered interior items without making any determinant findings.]*

7A: Structures Group Chairman's Factual Report
    The FBI Evidence Response Team executed an evidence identification program, which placed a recovery date and recovery shipment ("lot") number on each piece that entered the hangar at Calverton, Long Island, New York. This program marked every piece that was recovered. Often, the lot number can be traced to a single debris field. Occasionally, lots were mixed (red and/or green and/or yellow), thus making it impossible to associate a specific debris field with a particular lot number.

[Items were recovered and tagged with a color to identify the general locations. Red = Area 3; Yellow = Area 2; Green = Area 1; Blue = floating on the surface; Orange = areas other than Areas 1, 2 or 3 during the trawling operation; White = area of recovery cannot be determined]

    The wing landing gears and engines (covered in other summaries) were not connected to the recovered wing debris. The vast majority of the left wing pieces and all of the right wing pieces were found in the Green debris field. Some small pieces of the left wing were found in the Red and Orange areas. The right wing sustained fire and soot damage on the exterior of the upper and lower skin surfaces. The left wing lower surface showed sooting and some fire damage, generally between engines #1 and #2. The sooting and fire damage are covered extensively in the Fire and Explosion Group's Report. Most pieces of the leading and trailing edge flaps, ailerons, and spoilers were found in the Green debris area, however, some pieces were found floating and were not associated with a debris field.

The left wing was more severely fragmented and the lower panel had a more pronounced spanwise curl than the right wing.

Most pieces of the leading and trailing edge flaps, ailerons, and spoilers were found in the Green debris area; however, some pieces were found floating and were not associated with a debris field. These pieces showed general impact damage. Many portions of the trailing edge flaps, ailerons, and spoilers and some portions of the leading edge flaps showed fire and/or soot damage.

Most of the right-hand wing trailing edge flaps were identified/recovered. The inboard flaps separated into large pieces and show little or no fire or soot damage. There is evidence of severe impact damage, including damage to the honeycomb and associated skin. The entire outboard flap sections were recovered and identified, except for a very small area (RW26 to RW32).

9A: Systems Group Chairman's Factual Report Of Investigation

Evidence of fire was found in the center wing fuel tank (CWT) and in a fuel tank located outboard of engine 4 on the right wing, known as 4 Reserve (4R). The evidence included blackened structure, melted wiring and aluminum materials, burned composite materials from the areas of the fuel tanks. Outward bulging or deformation of the CWT upper and lower surfaces was found. Systems Group members participated in the recovery of debris from the ocean and components from the interior of the CWT were in the first wreckage found along the path of flight. Material from tank 4R and the tip of the wing from beyond that fuel tank were found more than a mile down track from the initial debris.

Evidence was found that numerous electrically powered devices stopped at about the same time. The electrically driven altimeters of the Captain and First Officer were found to display 13,820 and 13,800 feet, respectively. Wiring schematics showed the two altimeters to be powered by separate sources on different wings. The Air Traffic Control Group reported that the final secondary radar return was from approximately the same time (0031.08 EDT) and altitude. The recordings of the flight data recorder (FDR) and cockpit voice recorder (CVR) were reported by those groups to have ceased within a quarter second of each other. Although the clocks had run beyond the short interval in which the previous items had stopped, the Captain's clock was found at a display of 0031.30 and the First Officer's clock was found displaying 0031.20. Each clock is set independently. The clocks are powered from the airplane battery located in the cockpit.

The Safety Board and FAA asked Boeing to provide information to show possible ignition sources of a B-747 CWT from faults in the airplane. In a letter of November 12, 1996, Boeing provided information to "...demonstrate all conceivable faults and fault combinations whose occurrence could provide an ignition source...." The document provided a reference for investigating possible failure combinations that could lead to explosive conditions. Boeing wrote that no single failures were found and that "All of the conceivable failure scenarios required between two to four failures for the event to occur." The electrical and mechanical events considered by Boeing included sources in the electrical supply and distribution systems, FQIS [fuel quantity indicating system], fuel transfer pumps, the refueling panel, lightning, wheel well system defects, static electricity, and other topics. The Boeing response contained two illustrated blocks that led to the "CONDITIONS FOR EXPLOSIVE EVENT..." and the first was that an ignition source could be introduced into the CWT. Many of the Systems Group activities were spent investigating potential ignition sources. The results of those activities are contained within this factual report. The second block illustrated by Boeing described an assumption that a proper fuel/air mixture existed in the CWT to support an explosion.

Boeing listed three potential ignition sources in the letter of November 12, 1996. These were CWT internal mechanical faults that could result in ignition, introduction of an external ignition source, and "multiple electrically generated system faults." No evidence of a mechanical fault that led to ignition in the CWT of N93119 was identified by the Systems Group.

Most members of the Systems Group were shown numerous examples and photographs of bomb and missile damage, although no formal training was given. The Systems Group Chairman had previously completed the post-blast investigation course taught by the Federal Bureau of Investigation (FBI) at the FBI Academy. Several group members had military experience with explosives. Law enforcement agents with experience in explosive devices were always available and if any damage were found that differed from surrounding materials, the group members were told to report it, immediately. No evidence of an explosive device was found in the systems of the accident airplane. The B-747 flight tests of July 1997, were used as an opportunity to perform basic EMI tests. Measurements were made of voltage and current induced on FQIS wires that led from the cockpit to the CWT. During the ground portion of the EMI testing, various personal electronic devices (PEDs) were actuated and carried along the length of the FQIS wire routing between the cockpit and the floor of the main deck (passenger cabin). The PEDs included an electric shaver, personal computer, and amateur radio (2.5 watt output) broadcasts. Aircraft electrical systems were also actuated, including lights, radios, and electric actuators. Following ground tests, voltage and current were also measured during a flight test. Dr. Dan Bower of the NTSB Research and Engineering Division documented the flight tests. Less energy was found induced into the CWT FQIS wiring by the PEDs or by airplane systems on the ground than by aircraft systems operated during the flight.

No evidence of arcing was found on wires or fuel probes from the B-747 fuel probes or compensators.

No evidence of arcing to FQIS wires was found.

Boeing issued a service bulletin (SB 747-28-2205) on June 27, 1997 and a Notice of Status Change (NSC) for this SB on September 25, 1997. The SB contains 100 pages of instructions to describe fuel tank inspection procedures for B-747 operators. All but one of nine tasks listed for accomplishment are visual inspections and none call for removal of wiring from fuel probes or the compensator. Removal of wiring to examine the back side was necessary to find damage during the accident investigation.

The review also found the scavenge pump successfully completed explosion proof testing by; (1) never causing an explosion in an explosive atmosphere, and (2) by containing multiple explosions intentionally set-off within the motor and preventing it from propagating to a surrounding explosive atmosphere. Since the group became aware of instances in which the cooling tubes had been broken or missing, a series of tests were conducted in October 1997, to determine whether the pump motor housing would continue to contain explosions with only the check valve. Samples of a new pump and one from service were tested. In each case, the explosions were contained in the housing and the explosive atmosphere surrounding the test pumps did not ignite.

The cockpit voice recording from TWA 800 reportedly indicated that there had been an anomaly with the fuel flow indicator from engine number four. There was no direct physical evidence of an internal electrical failure relative to erratic or erroneous fuel flow indications.

9B: Contracted Laboratory Documentation *(partial)*
[*various supporting component evaluation reports*]

9C: Attachments to Systems Group Chairman's Factual Report
[*various related, supporting, technical papers including fuel system & electrical system drawings/schematics; also communications between Boeing & NTSB regaring FQIS & CWT related systems*]

9D: Accidents, Incidents, and Safety Recommendations
[*recommendation from the NTSB to the FAA for development of fuel tank, nitrogen-inerting systems, and added insulation for heat generating systems. Of interest, an accident report of an Imperial Iranian Air Force B747-131 in-flight separation of the left wing on 9.May.1976 as a result of a*

lightning strike & subsequent fuel tank explosion. Also, a Phillipine Air Lines B737-300 incident on the ground at Manila, on 11.May.1990, the ignition of the fuel-air vapor in CWT, from an unknown ignition source. Also, a Navy C-130 in 1972 involved in the explosion of the No.1 fuel tank in the left wing shortly after takeoff; the fuel quantity indicating system was found to be the source of ignition. And, various other accidents involving fuel system explosions or fires.]

9E: Photographs

[*selected B747 fuel system photographs*]

10A: Flight Data Recorder (FDR) Group Chairman's
 Factual Report

[*data traces of the FDR recording up to the end of recording. It is interesting to note that the FDR continued to record selected parameters after the primary event at 0031:12 GMT.*]
20:31:12.27 (loss of power to FDR) calculated by various correlation methods.

11A: Maintenance Group Chairman's Factual Report

During the maintenance review process, the records confirm that TWA had accomplished mandatory directives, maintained mandatory scheduled maintenance, and maintained a continuous airworthiness maintenance program that incorporates the maintenance alert computer systems (which compiles the flying time and cycles on each aircraft daily, and is the basis for compilation of all time/cycle records maintained on the aircraft, engines, APU, modules and units). The aircraft maintenance planning system tracks and controls aircraft logbook, non-routine, follow-up and call-out requirements for maintenance operations.

Registration Number = N93119

Year Manufactured = July 1971

Serial Number = 20083
Put Into Service at TWA = 10/27/71
Aircraft Total Time: 93,303 Hours
Aircraft Total Cycles: 16,869 Cycles
[*includes maintenance gripes on the aircraft & corrective action taken*]
11B: Periodic Service
[*servicing record of TWA JFK Inbound Flight No.881 on 7/17/96*]
11E: Center Wing Tank Routine Work Cards
[*maintenance record of work done on CWT, 6.Oct.92*]
11F: Check Valve Work Cards
[*maintenance record of work done on APU check valve, 9.Oct.92*]
11P: Airworthiness Directive List
[*Airworthiness Directives issued and compliance dates*]
11Q: Airworthiness Directive (AD) 90-25-05
[*subject AD issued for all Model 747 series aircraft to control corrosion*]
12A: Group Chairman's Factual Report Of Investigation Cockpit Voice Recorder
[*includes both internal cockpit communications and radio communications*]

The recording starts at 1959:40 EDT and continues uninterrupted until 2031:12 EDT when electrical power was removed from the unit.

[*mechanical sound at 2030:42, an unintelligible word at 2031:03, and sounds similar to recording tape damage noise at 2031:05, may be significant*]
12B: Sound Spectrum Group Chairman's Factual Report

The recording was examined to document any unusual

or abnormal occurrences. During the development of the transcript of the recording, the CVR group identified two segments of the recording that needed further examination. Both of these segments were contained in the last several seconds of the recording. One of these segments was approximately 0.73 seconds from the end of the recording. An abnormality was identified as a change in the background 400 Hz aircraft's electrical system hum as recorded by the CVR. The second segment that was identified was the last few tenths of a second of the recording. The recording appeared to terminate very abruptly with a very loud sound. This termination did not appear to be preceded by any event or events on the recording. Both of these areas were the subject of further examination.

At time 0.73 seconds before the end of the recording and again at 0.68 seconds before the end, the normal 400 Hz signal with its associated harmonics changed. This change consists primarily of a lack of the upper harmonics of the 400 Hz. During these two different areas the signal contains only the 400 Hz component, no added harmonics. It can be seen that the disturbance is identifiable only on the Captain's radio track of the CVR.

To further our understanding of how the cockpit voice recorder responds during in-flight explosions and break-ups several CVR recordings were obtained for comparison purposes. These comparison recordings were plotted in a similar way as the accident recording. Chart 8 depicts the 4 CVR channels obtained from the Pan Am Lockerbee accident involving a Boeing 747-100 aircraft. Chart 9 depicts the CVR record of the in-flight accident of a Air India Boeing 747-100. Chart 10 depicts the CVR information obtained from a

United Boeing 747-100 in-flight loss of the forward cargo door. Chart 11 depicts the CVR record obtained from a center wing fuel tank explosion onboard a Philippine Airlines Boeing 737-400 aircraft that was being pushed back from the gate.

In addition to using accident recordings the Safety Board conducted several controlled experiments to document how the cockpit voice recorder system as installed on a Boeing 747 aircraft responds to various types of explosive events. [*no conclusions were presented regarding the CVR spectral analysis*]

13A: Aircraft Performance Group Chairman's Factual Report

Radar data for the accident airplane and the surrounding area were obtained from the Federal Aviation Administration (FAA), Department of Defense (NAVY and NORAD), and Sikorsky. These are all of the known sources of radar data for the area where TWA Flight 800 crashed, with a total of 9 radars located in 5 states (Pennsylvania, New Jersey, New York, Connecticut, Massachusetts).

The radar data review showed the following vehicle and/or object tracks within 10 nautical miles of TWA 800 just prior to the time of the accident (local time 20:30:30-20:31:13):

1.   A Navy P-3 anti-submarine airplane less than 3 nautical miles south-southwest and approximately 6,300 feet above TWA 800 (P-3 altitude data is based on P-3 flight crew interview), moving southwest at over 250 knots ground speed.

2.   USAir Flight 217 approximately 3 nautical miles south-southwest and approximately 8,000 feet above TWA 800, moving north.

3.   TWA Flight 900 approximately 9 nautical miles west and approximately 5,300 feet above TWA 800, moving east-

northeast.

4.   An unidentified track less than 3 nautical miles south-southeast moving south-southwest at just over 30 knots ground speed, consistent with the speed of a boat.

5.   An unidentified track approximately 5 nautical miles west moving east-southeast at approximately 15 knots ground speed, consistent with the speed of a boat.

6.   An unidentified track approximately 5 nautical miles west-northwest moving south-southwest at approximately 12 knots ground speed, consistent with the speed of a boat.

7.   An unidentified track approximately 6 nautical miles northwest moving southeast at approximately 20 knots ground speed, consistent with the speed of a boat.

No sequence of radar returns intersected TWA 800's position at any point in time, nor were there any radar returns consistent with a missile or other projectile traveling towards TWA 800. There was one sequence of 8 primary radar returns from the NYTRACON ISP radar which were studied further. These 8 radar returns, which started at 2030:15 and ended at 2031:30 (18 seconds after TWA 800's last secondary return), appeared to show a target moving at over 400 knots ground speed on a southeasterly heading (156-157 degrees magnetic) away from TWA 800's position. This target track never came closer than 6 nautical miles to TWA 800 and remained on a straight track away from TWA 800 without turning towards TWA 800.

[radar data shows an unusual flattening of the last climb segment for 10 seconds at precisely 2030:42, the mechanical sound recorded on the CVR, then the radar track returns to a normal climb rate until the end]

15A: Metallurgist's Factual Report: Front Spar Lower Chord

Fracture Area; CW504 Fatigue

[detailed examination of a segment of the front spar. No conclusions]

15B: Metallurgist's Factual Report: Examination of Small Holes

Various holes in the airplane structure were documented and examined to determine if they had indications of being created as a result of penetration by a high velocity fragment. At the request of the Safety Board, Boeing generated a series of holes (through penetrations) and impacts in test plates, and the features associated with these holes were used to define the characteristics of higher and lower velocity penetrations. These definition were then applied to the holes in the accident airplane.

The pieces of the airplane were examined by the structures group; a total of 196 holes were identified. All but 25 of the 196 holes were therefore initially determined not to have characteristics indicative of a higher velocity hole.

Similar examinations of the other holes in the structure indicated that most of these were also classified as lower velocity holes. However, two holes in the horizontal pressure deck above the wing landing gear bay (in pieces LF137 and RF60) contained some features of both lower velocity holes and higher velocity holes, making a field determination of the velocity characterization difficult. These two holes were each about 3/16 inch in diameter and were very similar in appearance with the following features:

1.   Lack of overall deformation in the sheet around the hole.

2.   No splashback.

3.   Chipped out metal on the lower surface of the sheet on one side of the hole.

4.   Smooth hole wall, generally perpendicular to the surface with some exit deformation on the lower surface. The hole in piece LF137 was located in the pressure deck at STA1457 and LBL110. The chipped out metal on the lower surface and the exit deformation associated with this hole indicate penetration from a fragment moving downward and slightly aft. The hole in piece RF60 was located in the pressure deck at STA1452 and LBL62. The chipped out metal on the lower surface and the exit deformation associated with this hole indicate penetration from a fragment moving downward and slightly inboard. The lack of overall deformation in the sheet around these two holes suggests higher velocity holes, but the lack of splashback suggests lower velocity holes.

15C:Metallurgist's Factual Report: Section 41/42 Joint, Forward Cargo Door

Overall examination of the forward portion of the airplane showed that sections 41 and 42 contained uniform crushing damage that extended from S39L across the bottom of the fuselage and up above the right side main cabin window belt to S14R. This crushing damage is consistent with the intact forward portion of the airplane (including section 41 and 42) impacting the water with a right wing low attitude. The lower lobe forward cargo door was in the crush area.

17A: Reconstruction Group Chairman's Factual Report

[*details the reconstruction effort along with the piece map for the bottom of the fuselage under the CWT and front & rear fairings.*]

17D: Reconstruction Slides

[*photographs of reconstruction sequence & various angles of completed structure*]

18A: Metallurgy/Structures Sequencing Group Chairman's Report

In the WCS [*wing center section*], the earliest

identified event involved an overpressure.

The Group strove to fit a proposed scenario to all relevant observations in a given area. In some cases there was more than one identified possibility for a particular feature. In some cases, the Group had to accept that some feature(s) either could not be explained by the proposed scenario or might even be in conflict with the proposed scenario. A case in point of an apparent conflict is the recovery location of front spar piece CW504 in the earliest part of the red area. An example of a feature which was not explained in the breakup sequence is the localized recrystallization of portions of the rear spar cited in an NTSB Metallurgical Report.

The recovery operation is still underway but is probably within a few percent of being complete. There is still some significant missing structure in the key wing center section and fuselage red zone areas. It is therefore possible that new scenarios (sequences) may emerge as new information is acquired whether it be from newly identified parts or simply a new interpretation of current information. The Metallurgy and Structures Sequencing Group was not able to precisely locate the initiation of the center wing tank overpressure event and the Group's activities did not include addressing potential causes of the overpressure. At the present time in concluding its efforts, the Group did reach a consensus that the facts and data on the whole support the sequence documented herein.

[detailed sketches of the recovered piece & their associate are provided as well as observation regarding sooting of pieces]

18B: Supporting Documentation for Overall Breakup

Sequence (Drawings)

[*detailed structural analysis supporting the break-up sequence*]

18C: Nose Landing Gear Doors Sequence

The nose landing gear doors were of particular interest because they were tagged as "Red" zone pieces with diver tags.

The left aft door contained heavy damage consistent with being attached to other structure at water impact. In contrast, the three other doors contained much less damage, indicating that they separated from the other structure before water impact. Recovery positions in the red zone, as indicated by the tags on the door pieces, indicated that the two forward doors and the right rear door separated from the airplane early in the sequence of the breakup of the airplane.

Five different general categories of possible failure sequence initiation and propagation were considered by the Group:

a)   Initial door deployment and/or failure precipitated by an independent event preceding and unrelated to anything currently identified and documented in the structural breakup sequence.

b)   Initial door deployment and/or failure as a direct result of the earliest event currently documented in the structural breakup sequence; failure of the CWT due to a fuel-air explosion.

c)   Initial door deployment and/or failure as a result of separation of the forward body which may have followed the initial CWT fuel-air explosion by several seconds.

d)   Initial door deployment and/or failure propagation following separation of the forward body but still at close to the same altitude and speed.

e)   Door failure associated with water impact of the forward body in the yellow area.

The Group tried to approach the exercise by identifying all possible scenarios potentially consistent with the initial nose gear door evidence. This provided a path for a more focused search for specific evidence to support or refute any given scenario. No direct evidence could be found to either confirm or refute the first two scenarios (sections 5.1 and 5.2). However the absence of any direct evidence supporting their existence probably indicates a relatively low likelihood of occurrence. The third scenario (section 5.3) related to door deployment due to systems disruptions/failures is very plausible given the documented nature of the airplane breakup sequence. The fourth scenario (section 5.4) related to door overload/failure due to aerodynamic loading effects is also plausible. Confirmation of the door actuator lock status will be a key step toward concluding which of the third or fourth scenarios is in fact the most likely overall scenario. The final scenario (section 5.5), door failure on water impact, has been essentially ruled out.

19A: Medical/Forensic Group Chairman's Factual Report Of Investigation
[defined forensic process & generalized results]
20A: Fire & Explosion Group Chairman's Factual Report

Pieces of the tank [*CWT*] that were found in the first debris field below the flight path of TWA 800 show little if any fire or soot damage. These include the majority of the parts from the front spar and spanwise beam #3, and the manufacturing access panel from spanwise beam #2. No other pieces of spanwise beam #2 were found in the first debris field.

The passenger cabin seats were examined for evidence of high explosive damage such as hot particle penetration, metal erosion, and high degree of fragmentation. None of this evidence was noted either above the center wing tank or in other areas of the cabin. Selected seat back panels in rows 17, 19, 24, and 27 were damaged, exposing a brown to reddish brown colored material. This material was analyzed by infrared spectroscopy. Analysis showed the material to be consistent with a polychloroprene 3M Scotch-Grip™ 1357 High Performance contact adhesive. The report is attached in Appendix III-Tests and Analysis.

No evidence of a bomb, missile, or high order explosive damage was found on any of the pieces of wreckage that have been examined. In areas of the bottom and top skins of the center wing where small pieces are missing there is no evidence on the surrounding hardware, including aircraft skin and cabin flooring, of a missile entry and damage or damage from a bomb. In addition, there was no evidence observed of projectile penetration of the aircraft structure below the center wing tank. Evidence of a fuel vapor explosion (over-pressurization) in the center wing tank was noted on the front spar, spanwise beam number 3, parts from spanwise beam 2, the bottom and top tank pieces. Based on the fire damage and soot deposits, a fire occurred after the explosion in this tank. An ignition source for this explosion, has not as yet been identified. No evidence of electrical arcing or other mechanical failure signature has been noted on the hardware.

[*also contains detailed catalogue of recovered parts*]
20B: Appendix II: Soot/Fracture Diagrams

[*detailed sketches of fire damage on exterior & interior as well as wing; punctures on left wing*]

20C: Appendix III: Tests and Analysis

[*specific samples submitted to spectral testing*]

20D: Jet A Explosion Experiments: Laboratory Testing

This report describes a series of experiments and analyses on the flammability of Jet A (aviation kerosene) in air. This is a progress report on ongoing work.

The source of ignition in the TWA 800 explosion is not the focus of the present study although future experiments are planned on determining ignition energy for spark-type ignition sources in Jet A air mixtures.

Conclusions:

Key findings of our study are:

1.   Flammability limits of Jet A are uncertain.

2.   The composition of Jet A is poorly known.

3.   Most Jet A vapor pressure data are really unreliable correlations.

4.   Jet A vapor pressure can be modeled with a binary mixture.

5.   Previous studies on Jet A have not examined the effect of fuel loading (mass of fuel per ullage volume) on ammability and explosion peak pressure.

6.   The ash point of Jet A is 10 to 15° C higher than the flammability limit temperature as determined by actual explosion testing.

7.   It is not suffcient to know the vapor pressure but the vapor composition must also be known in order to predict flammability from pressure and temperature conditions.

8.   The fuel vapor in the ullage of the TWA 800 CWT was flammable at the time of the explosion and the estimated

peak pressures are suffciently high that structural failure is a credible consequence of flame propagation within the tank ullage. However, the magnitude of the peak pressure and the pressure-time history within the CWT cannot be predicted with any certainty given the present data.

<u>20E</u>: Jet A Explosions: Field Test Plan 1/4 Scale Experiments

The primary objective of the investigation is to determine the location and source of ignition in the CWT.

[*this section contains the proposed test plan, no results*]

<u>20F</u>: Explosion of Aviation Kerosene (Jet A) Vapors

[*vapor ignition testing at CalTech*]

[*summary results*]

• vapor composition very different than bulk liquid
• vapor pressure alone not useful without vapor composition
• multicomponent fuels do not have unique vapor pressure
• mass loading $M=V$ affects composition
• flash point is not a useful characterization of explosion hazard

<u>20G</u>: Jet A Flight Test Samples

The fuel to air mass ratios for the fuel vapors measured in this study fall within the flammable range for all samples at the 10,000' and 14,000' levels. The taxi samples are near the lower flammability limit. The single highest fuel to air ratio found was for flight 2, the TWA 800 simulation flight, at 14,000'. These results show that even after over 60 hours of operations (from time of fueling), the fuel can easily reach the flammable range at the altitude which the accident aircraft exploded.

While these studies are the first to investigate samples taken directly from the CWT of an in use 747 aircraft and analyze them for hydrocarbon vapors, they represent only a very small set of data to begin to draw conclusions about jet fuel behavior. Still, these results are very promising in how well they relate to other research results such as those from CIT's vapor pressure experiments, and in the ability of these results to clearly show some of the mixing and venting behavior of the CWT.

At the same time, several recommendations emerge:
- Protocol for this type of study should include collection of liquid fuel samples and speciation of those samples to relate fuel vapors to the liquid composition.
- Physical vapor pressure measurements at temperatures bracketing those seen in the tank should be conducted.
- If these experiments are repeated, an inert tracer gas should be used to confirm the sample collection from and mixing and venting of the CWT.

20I: Chemical Analysis of Residue
[*FBI laboratory chemical analysis report*]
22A: Trajectory Study

The wreckage distribution shows that parts were initially shed from the area just forward of the wing. This was followed by the separation of the forward fuselage. This study concentrated on items in the red field, the first ground search area along the flight path. This corresponded to items shed between the initial event and the separation of the forward fuselage.

As will be seen, the trajectory study shows that the red zone pieces departed the aircraft in the first few seconds after the initial event.

Implicit in trajectory analysis is the assumption that the wreckage items fell in a ballistic manner, without a stable lift vector. In this particular analysis, wreckage items were assumed to have the final FDR velocity as their initial velocity. These assumptions may not be valid for wreckage items CW504 and RF35. These parts are addressed separately in following sections.

Wreckage item CW504 is a flat irregularly shaped portion of the front spar on the far left side of the center tank. As with RF35, the location this item was found would, assuming that CW504 departed the aircraft with the same initial velocity as the other wreckage items and behaved in a ballistic manner, require that CW504 depart the aircraft at a point on the course line well prior to the last transponder radar hit. Since the structural breakup of the front spar would most likely have disrupted electrical power to the transponder, the initial event is believed to have occurred after the last transponder radar contact. It is possible that item CW504 departed the aircraft with significant angular momentum.

22B: Trajectory Study Supporting Material
[*supporting plots & calculations for trajectory analysis*]
22C: Main Wreckage Flight Path Study
[*macro-trajectory analysis through estimates of weight, CG & Inertia changes due to loss of forward fuselage*]

CLOCK TIME	ELAPSED TIME	EVENT
8:31:12	743.77	Initial Event
8:31:13.4	747.0	Nose deparure
8:31:51.4	785.0	Wing tip failure immediately followed left wing failure

[*plot shows through simulation that the engines may have been running to 767 & 771 elapsed time depending on motion sequence; variety of trajectory simulation plots*]

23A: Flight Test Group Chairman's Factual Report Of Investigation:

In support of the investigation into the TWA Flight

800 accident, a series of nine flight tests were performed to obtain time/temperature histories within a 747-100 series airplane. The tests followed specific preflight, taxi, takeoff, and climb flight profiles. Data was collected from center wing tank (CWT) surface temperatures, CWT air temperatures, and pressure within the several bays of the CWT and the wing tip surge tanks. Also obtained were the air temperature time history of the environmental control system (ECS) air conditioning pack bay beneath the CWT, air conditioning pack component surface temperatures, and vibration measurements, CWT ullage vapor samples, and some electromagnetic interference data.

23B: Flight Test Plan
[*elements of test plan & schedule*]
23C: FAA Comments on Flight Test Plan
[*as it states*]
23D: Component Drawings
[*pneumatic systems, CWT, and air conditioning packs*]
23E:Test Item Requirements List (TIRL) Instrument Locations
Flight Test Schedule
[*aircraft equipment & instrumentation listing + selected location sketches*]
23F: Flight Test Results: TWA 800 Emulation Flight
[*flight test plots of CWT temperature profiles during TWA 800 simulation flights*]

APPENDIX C

PRESS RELEASES AND STATEMENTS
FEDERAL BUREAU OF INVESIGATION

November 18, 1997
INTERIM SUMMARY REPORT

[Authors' Note: Extracted from the Website/URL of the Federal Bureau of Investigation: http://www.fbi.gov _Italics_ have been added for emphasis.]

FBI PRESS CONFERENCE - TWA FLIGHT 800
For Immediate Release
Date: November 18, 1997
FBI - NEW YORK OFFICE - PRESS RELEASE

      Yesterday was the 16-month anniversary of the TWA 800 tragedy. From the very beginning, the FBI and the other members of the law enforcement team worked closely with the National Transportation Safety Board (NTSB) seeking to determine what happened to Flight 800. The FBI and the law enforcement team became involved in the investigation because initial reports were that a TWA Flight was "in the water," that there had been a large explosion and fireball, that all communications from the plane were normal and no distress calls were issued, and the reports of numerous eyewitnesses seeing "flarelike objects" and other events in the sky. If there was ever a chance, whether it was 10% or 90%, that this catastrophe was criminal, it was critical that the proper investigation take place immediately. The mission of the law enforcement team was to determine whether a criminal act was responsible for this disaster.

The time has arrived to report to the American people the results of our efforts.

Following 16 months of unprecedented investigative effort which extended from the shores of Long Island to several countries abroad - an investigation where hundreds of investigators conducted thousands of interviews - an investigation which was confronted with the obstacle of having the most critical pieces of evidence laying in 130 feet of water at the bottom of the Atlantic Ocean, we must report that...NO EVIDENCE HAS BEEN FOUND WHICH WOULD INDICATE THAT A CRIMINAL ACT WAS THE CAUSE OF THE TRAGEDY OF TWA FLIGHT 800.

We do know one thing, however. The law enforcement team has done everything humanly possible - has pursued every lead - and has left no stone unturned.

I would like to take a few minutes to outline, in some detail, our investigation.

I. TWA 800 EXPLOSION

TWA 800 was on the tarmac at JFKIA for approximately 3 hours and 48 minutes prior to departure. The outside temperature was approximately 81°. The flight arrived from Athens at 4:31 p.m. and lifted off the ground at 8:19 p.m. At approximately 8:31 p.m. the flight experienced a mid-air explosion.

II. RESPONSE TO EVENT

A. FBI RESOURCES:

INITIAL RESPONSE TO SCENE: Hundreds of Agents

COMMAND CENTERS ESTABLISHED:

- New York Office

- US Coast Guard East Moriches
- Westhampton Fire Department and
Later -> Grumman - Calverton, Long Island
B. FEDERAL/LOCAL LAW ENFORCEMENT
RESOURCES: Response to the tragedy of Flight 800.

All Federal Agencies of the Task Force responded:
ATF, NTSB, FAA, Secret Service, US State Department, Naval
Criminal Investigative Service, US Park Police, INS and from
Local Law Enforcement: Port Authority PD, Suffolk County
PD, Suffolk County Park Police, Nassau County PD, New
York City PD, NY State Police and local town police.
C. OTHER AGENCIES
1. NY Fire Department and local Volunteer Fire Department
2. Red Cross
3. Suffolk County Medical Examiner
4. Clergy
III. RECOVERY EFFORTS - VICTIMS/AIRCRAFT
1st 3 Days: Massive on the water recovery of bodies/plane
parts
Dive Efforts: 4600 dives
Search Area: 40 square miles
Trawling Operation: 75 square miles
A. RECOVERY OF VICTIMS: 230 victims recovered and
positively identified.
B. RECOVERY OF AIRCRAFT: 96% of aircraft recovered.
Approximately 1 million pieces
C. RECOVERY OF PERSONAL EFFECTS: 39,600 items
RECOVERED.
IV. AIRPORT INVESTIGATION - JFK AIRPORT - TWA 800
A. 186 interviews were conducted with all individuals who
had access to TWA Flight 800. All met with negative results.
1. Security Personnel   2. Mechanics and Fuelers

3. Luggage/Cargo Handlers   4. Caterers/Food Service
5. Cleaners   6. Customer Service
7. Ogden Food Service
8. Outside Contractors - i.e., in-flight movie, special catering, linen, dry cleaning

B. PASSENGER/BAGGAGE RECONCILIATION: All passenger flight coupons were matched to the passenger manifest. All checked baggage was accounted for prior to departure.

C. CARGO RECONCILIATION: All cargo was identified from point of origin until placement on Flight 800. All shippers were identified as legitimate.

D. FAA/AIR TRAFFIC CONTROLLERS:
- Air traffic controllers interviewed.
- Radar tapes duplicated and analyzed.
- Air Traffic Controller transcripts obtained and reviewed.
- Analysis determined no unusual activity.

V. AIRPORT INVESTIGATION - ATHENS GREECE -
TWA FLIGHT 881

452 interviews were conducted with all individuals who had access to TWA Flight 881, information requesting unusual person(s), events, objects, met with negative results.

We acknowledge and greatly appreciate the cooperation and assistance afforded by the government of Greece and their police agencies.

A. PASSENGER INTERVIEWS - 349
B. CREW INTERVIEWS - 17
C. AIRPORT PERSONNEL - 86
1. Security Personnel
2. Mechanics
3. Luggage/Cargo Loaders
4. Caterers/Food Service

5. Customer Service Employees

6. Fuelers

7. Outside Contractors - i.e., duty free merchandise, in-flight movies, linen, dry cleaning, etc.

D. PASSENGER/BAGGAGE RECONCILIATION: All passenger flight coupons were matched to the passenger manifest. All passenger baggage was identified.

E. CARGO RECONCILIATION: The authenticity of all cargo and shippers was verified. No cargo from Flight 881 was placed on TWA Flight 800.

VI. BOMB INVESTIGATION

A. VICTIM FAMILY INTERVIEWS:236 victim family members from the USA, France, Italy, Sweden and Norway were interviewed. The results of all interviews met with negative results regarding possible sabotage, conspiracy to bomb or criminal acts. 5 victim families refused to be interviewed.

B. PREVIOUS AIRCRAFT BOMBINGS: Investigators reviewed ten previous airline bombings covering a period of fourteen years. The purpose of this review was to identify vulnerable areas for the placement of explosive devices and modus operandi of individuals involved in bombings.

C. REVIEW OF COCKPIT VOICE RECORDER: The cockpit voice recorder tape contains 31:47 (thirty-one minutes and forty-seven seconds) of cockpit crew/ATC conversation. This tape starts while the aircraft is positioned at the gate prior to takeoff and ends at the time of the explosion. The CVR review disclosed no evidence of a criminal act.

D. INVESTIGATION OF CLAIMS OF RESPONSIBILITY: All claims of responsibility were without credibility.

E. COMMERCIAL HISTORY OF AIRCRAFT: The 25 year

old Boeing aircraft was sold to Iran in 1975. Iran never took physical possession. The aircraft never left hangar in the United States and was never touched by Iranian personnel. The aircraft was returned to the TWA fleet.

F. MILITARY HISTORY OF THE AIRCRAFT: Military records reflect that the aircraft was utilized for troop transport on April 1-2, 1996. 8 Explosive Ordinance Disposal (EOD) personnel were onboard. Records reflect that all troops were issued new uniforms and gear. Little potential for explosive residue transfer.

G. TRAINING CONDUCTED ON AIRCRAFT: On June 10, 1996, the St. Louis Airport Police Department conducted canine explosives training aboard the victim aircraft. The residue collected after the explosion of Flight 800 was consistent with the explosives utilized during the exercise.

Overseas law enforcement agencies routinely conduct canine training utilizing explosives with little or no documentation.

VII. MISSILE INVESTIGATION

A. WITNESS EVENT INTERVIEWS/PLOTTING: 244 eyewitness accounts were analyzed. Witnesses' observations and their location in relation to the event were recorded, plotted and mathematically analyzed.

B. ROADSIDE CHECKPOINTS: Roadside checkpoints were established in the vicinity of East Moriches to identify potential witnesses to the event or suspicious persons or activity. Investigation met with negative results.

C. CANVASS OF MARINAS: Tri-state area marinas were canvassed for any witnesses or suspicious activities related to the explosion. Investigation met with negative results.

D. POLICE DEPARTMENTS UNUSUAL EVENT/

PERSONS COMPLAINTS: Police Departments provided all 911 telephone calls and person's complaints reporting suspicious behavior/cars/boats in all precincts bordering waterways and JFK Airport for a period of two months prior to the event. Investigation met with negative results.

Twenty-nine 911 calls received by Suffolk County Police were investigated and met with negative results.

E. REPORTED STOLEN/ABANDONED BOATS: Reported stolen or abandoned boats in the tri-state area were identified and held for forensic examination. This investigation was met with negative results.

F. PREVIOUS ROCKET ATTACKS: Investigators reviewed nine missile attacks on aircraft during a fourteen year period. Those attacks occurred in the former Soviet Union, Afghanistan and Africa. The purpose of this review was to identify potential missiles utilized and launch sites. Forensic evidence from those aircraft were not available for comparison to Flight 800, therefore prompting our own testing.

G. REVIEW OF VESSEL TRAVEL THROUGH NEW YORK HARBOR: During the 24-Hour Period: 371 vessels identified area of Long Island One Month Period: 20,000 records area New York Harbor Investigation met with negative results.

H. INVESTIGATION OF SUFFOLK COUNTY BRIDGE OPENINGS: 20,000 records obtained for every vessel that passed under three Suffolk County drawbridges for 3 months prior to the crash and 2 weeks after the crash. Investigation met with negative results.

I. RADAR ANALYSIS: Radar data was collected, reviewed and analyzed by the FAA and an independent radar consultant who examined radar tapes and determined that what was depicted on the screen was NORMAL AIR TRAFFIC and *NOT A MISSILE*.

Sources of Radar Tapes: 9 FAA locations: Islip, JFK, Newark, White Plains, Stewart's Field, Riverhead New York, Trevose PA, North Truro MA, Cummington MA.

3 Other Radar sources: Sikorsky Aircraft, National Oceanic and Atmospheric Administration - Boston and New York

VIII. CALVERTON INVESTIGATION

A. EVIDENCE COLLECTION: Law Enforcement Team personnel supervised evidence collection and transportation from the crash site to the Calverton facility, always mindful of contamination and chain of custody.

B. EVIDENCE REVIEW AND ANALYSIS: All evidence received at the Calverton facility was initially examined by certified bomb techs, metallurgists, and chemists for explosive damage with negative results. Subsequent intensive testing/ examination of pieces exhibiting any unusual characteristics was conducted by law enforcement, military, and independent experts and was met with negative results.

    The following agencies/personnel provided additional expertise:

1. US Naval Air Warfare Center Weapons Division, China Lake, California

2. US Army Aeromedical Research Lab Fort Rucker, Alabama

3. US Air Force, Wright Patterson AFB, Aircraft Accident Investigation Office, Dayton, Ohio

4. Armed Forces Institute of Pathology Bethesda, Maryland

5. Defense Intelligence Agency, Missile and Space Intelligence Center, Redstone Arsenal, Alabama

6. Picatinny Arsenal

7. Hughes Missile Systems, Hughes Aircraft Company

8. Independent Radar Consultant

9. Contract Metallurgist

10. Department of Energy Laboratories Brookhaven National Lab, Sandia National Lab

C. AIRCRAFT RECONSTRUCTION EFFORT: FBI/NTSB projects resulted in extensive reconstruction of areas of the aircraft deemed to be vulnerable to a missile and/or explosive device.

The reconstruction project included the following:

1. Main 92' Forward Fuselage

2. Aft Cargo Bay

3. Left and Right Wing Spars (front and rear)

4. Cabin Interior

5. Cargo Containers

6. Underbelly Fairing

7. Power Cable Routing

8. Left and Right Leading Edge Wing Structure

9. Nose Wheel Well and Surrounding Structure

10. Top Skin-Left Wing

11. Cabin Interior Carpet/Flooring over the Center Wing Fuel Tank

12. Flight Data Recorder (FDR)/Cockpit Voice Recorder (CVR) Wire Routing

13. Center Wing Fuel Tank Section

D. DAMAGE ANALYSIS

Combined metallurgical and engineering review of aircraft debris (reconstructed and non-reconstructed) IDENTIFIED *OVER 1400 PENETRATIONS* and 259 AREAS OF MISSING FUSELAGE MATERIAL that WERE CLOSELY EVALUATED.

An alternate light examination (blacklight) of all

aircraft wreckage for the purpose of identifying latent material deposits was conducted with ***negative results.***

All wreckage was also inspected by industry experts for any evidence of drone aircraft impact with negative results.

E. RECOVERY ANALYSIS
       The logged recovery location of all debris from the wings and the cabin structure was verified.

F. FORENSIC BOMB/MISSILE ANALYSIS CONDUCTED AT CALVERTON
       Over ONE MILLION PIECES of aircraft debris VISUALLY INSPECTED by bomb technicians and laboratory personnel. This screening process included taking over 2,000 CHEMICAL SWABBINGS, x-raying all seat cushions and utilizing explosive detection canines on site.

       Examination and analysis at DAVIS MONTHAM AIR FORCE BASE at Tucson, Arizona with STATIC DETONATIONS of man pads in pressurized and non-pressurized aircraft fuselage produced DAMAGE which was NOT SIMILAR to any WRECKAGE observed AT CALVERTON. ALL WRECKAGE was REVIEWED.

       Inspection of missile damaged aircraft at the NAVAL AIR WARFARE CENTER (CHINA LAKE) revealed NO SIMILARITIES to the wreckage AT CALVERTON. ALL WRECKAGE was REVIEWED.

G. LABORATORY ANALYSIS
MAN HOURS 5000   EXAMINERS 12
RESIDUE EXAMINATIONS 3000
FBI/ATF LABORATORY CONCLUSION: *NO EVIDENCE - HIGH EXPLOSIVE DAMAGE. NO EVIDENCE - EXPLOSION OF A MISSILE WARHEAD. NO EVIDENCE - MISSILE IMPACT*

INDEPENDENT EXPERTS CONCLUSIONS: *NO EVIDENCE - HIGH EXPLOSIVE DAMAGE. NO EVIDENCE - EXPLOSION OF A MISSILE WARHEAD. NO EVIDENCE - MISSILE IMPACT*
METALLURGICAL EXAMINERS CONCLUSIONS:
DAMAGE CONSISTENT WITH:
- OVER PRESSURIZATION of the CENTER FUEL TANK;
- BREAK UP of the aircraft;
- FIRE;
- IMPACT of the aircraft into the ocean.
IX. MILITARY INVESTIGATION - FRIENDLY FIRE
A. SIGNED CERTIFICATIONS RECEIVED FROM EACH CHAIN OF COMMAND
- All military assets within 200 Nautical Miles.
- Documentation of all training exercises.
- Accounting of all armaments capable of reaching Flight 800.
B. INTERVIEWS AND INSPECTIONS: The crew of the following vessels/aircraft were interviewed and their ships inspected, due to their immediate vicinity to the crash site. Investigation determined the crafts were either out of range, unarmed or did not have the vertical launch capability of reaching Flight 800.
USS *NORMANDY* - US NAVY CRUISER
USS *TREPANG* - US NAVY SUBMARINE
USS *ALBUQUERQUE* - US NAVY SUBMARINE
USS *WYOMING* - US NAVY SUBMARINE
US NAVY P-3 ORION
NY AIR NATIONAL GUARD HH-60 HELICOPTER
NY AIR NATIONAL GUARD C-130 AIRCRAFT
NY AIR NATIONAL GUARD CC-10
CALIFORNIA AIR NATIONAL GUARD C-141 (TRANSITING AIR SPACE)

X. CRIMINAL ACT / NON-TERRORIST Investigation was not limited strictly to terrorist motives. All avenues of potential criminality were explored with negative results.

XI. PUBLIC RESPONSE: Over 3000 leads were generated through the establishment of the FBI 800 lines, Internet and US Mail.

XII. DEPTH OF THE INVESTIGATION: There were a total of over 7000 INTERVIEWS CONDUCTED in this investigation.

XIII. ISSUES

A. RUSSELL TAPE (Richard Russell) SALINGER'S MISSILE

The SPLITT (GHOSTING) from the Russell tape IS FROM JET EXPRESS 18. Analysis by experts determined that the *OBJECT WAS NOT A MISSILE*, since it was positively identified. Object was a Ghost of Jet Express 18 which was at a different location.

B. THE LINDA KABOT PHOTO

The photo taken by Kabot depicts a bearing of north/northeast. TWA Flight 800 was south/southwest almost directly behind her. Photograph analyzed by CIA National Imagery and Mapping Administration (NIMA) advised that:

1. THERE IS OBJECT IN PHOTO

2. OBJECT IS NOT A MISSILE

3. OBJECT APPEARS TO BE AN AIRCRAFT

Not possible to ID aircraft because:

- Not possible to determine distance of object from camera.

- Exact time of photo unknown. (time frame only is known)

- Insufficient detail in photo to determine type of aircraft.

4. OBJECT IS NOT A DRONE

- No drone exercises conducted near Long Island July 17, 1996

C. HEIDI KRIEGER PHOTOGRAPH (STREAK IN SKY)
Negative was sent to FBIHQ for analysis, which determined that there was DEBRIS ON THE FILM SURFACE.

D. SEAT CUSHION RESIDUE (Reported in Riverside California Press)
The residue appeared red and flaky and was subjected to microscopic and chemical examination. The analysis determined the items were consistent with a chlorinated polymeric material, commonly used as CONTACT ADHESIVE. The red material is *NOT ROCKET FUEL OR RESIDUE OF ROCKET FUEL.*

E. U.S. NAVY ACTIVITY IN W. 105-106-107 - AREAS CLOSEST TO THE SHORES OF LONG ISLAND
The warning areas mutually co-exist with commercial air traffic and were open for COMMERCIAL USE ON JULY 17, 1996. There were NO MISSILE FIRINGS FOR TWO YEARS prior to July 17, 1996, in the Whiskey 105-106-107 areas. Military Search and Rescue Exercise conducted July 17, 1996. NO WEAPONS UTILIZED. NO WEAPONS ON BOARD. NO TRAINING EXERCISES UTILIZING ANY WEAPONS were conducted in those areas on JULY 17, 1996.

There are designated live firing areas within the whiskey areas. Artillery and small caliber weapons fire are authorized in these areas. The closest area of this type is 86 miles east of the crash site. There was no Navy firing on July 17, 1996 in that area.

"I believe promoting the Navy-missile theory was a big mistake. I believe that the evidence is not sufficient to blame the Navy, and I wish to move away from that and all areas of conspiracy inquiry forever." (Ian Goddard's E-mail to the New York Office dated 11/6/97 5:40 AM)

XV. STATEMENT BEFORE VIDEO

The video you are about to see is just an analysis of what the witnesses observed. Despite the fact that our investigation had not uncovered any forensic evidence or intelligence information that Flight 800 was the victim of a criminal act, we were still left with the statements of the eyewitnesses who reported seeing events in the sky. We looked throughout the government to find the people with the best expertise and ability to analyze all the known data about Flight 800 in conjunction with the eyewitness reports seeking to answer the questions - what did the eyewitnesses see? We found the talent we were looking for in the CIA. I want to thank the CIA and its Director, George Tenant, for the brilliant and professional product and for all their cooperation and assistance in this investigation.

XV. VIDEO PRESENTATION

[Actual video was viewed at press conference on 11/18/97.]

XVI. STATEMENT REGARDING THE VIDEO

Of the 244 eyewitness reports examined in detail, the vast majority are consistent with the analysis presented here today. As in any event involving eyewitness reports, there remain a few that cannot be fully explained.

XVII. FINAL STATEMENT

The video you just viewed was only a part of our overall investigation. It is essential that the public and media fully understand that the FBI's disengagement at this time from the TWA Investigation is based solely on the overwhelming absence of evidence indicating a crime, and the lack of any leads that could bear on the issue.

CLOSING REMARKS

-The investigation I just described to you was done primarily by the men and women of the Terrorism Task Force here in

New York augmented by many FBI Agents from other segments of this office and the United States and by investigators from law enforcement agencies not officially part of the Joint Terrorist Task Force.

-They are all professionals and take pride in the thoroughness of their investigations.

-Aside from the families of the victims of TWA 800, no other group of people was more eager to find an answer.

-As the law enforcement team steps from this investigation, I want to emphasize that we will maintain our lines of communication with the NTSB - we will maintain our ability to gear up our criminal investigation should any information ever come to light which would indicate that a criminal act was committed.

****

The FBI, Jim Sanders & the 'Red Stain'

[Authors' Note: Jim Sanders is the author of **The Downing of TWA Flight 800**. He was a contributor to the missile theory based on the laboratory analysis of the 'red stain' material inappropriately removed from the investigation hangar at Calverton, NY. Sanders stands by his interpretation of the laboratory results, in that, the 'red stain' material is similar to and consistent with common solid rocket propellants.

It should be noted that the FBI's statement that there is 'no conclusive evidence of the presence of solid rocket fuel' is most probably correct, albeit somewhat misleading. Namely, there is probably no marker elements that irrefutably identifies the material as rocket propellant. Likewise, the FBI can probably not disprove Sanders claim either.]

FBI PRESS RELEASE
For Immediate Release
Date: December 5, 1997
FBI - NEW YORK OFFICE - PRESS RELEASE

JAMES K. KALLSTROM, Assistant Director in Charge of the New York FBI Office, and ZACHARY W. CARTER, United States Attorney for the Eastern District of New York, announced today the filing of two (2) court documents in connection with the ongoing criminal investigation into the theft of wreckage of TWA Flight 800 which crashed off the coast of Long Island on July 17, 1996.

Both documents are filed in United States District Court in the Eastern District of New York. One document is a Misdemeanor Information which charges TERRELL STACY, a TWA pilot involved in the investigation of the crash of TWA Flight 800, with intentionally taking pieces of the wreckage from the hangar in Calverton, Long Island.

The second document is a criminal complaint which charges both JAMES SANDERS and his wife, ELIZABETH SANDERS with intentionally removing, concealing and withholding parts of the recovered wreckage from TWA Flight 800.

According to the criminal complaint, Terrell Stacey, the TWA pilot who was involved in the investigation of the crash, was interviewed by FBI Agents in June, 1997 regarding his knowledge of the theft of certain portions of the TWA 800 wreckage. Stacey told the FBI that he had been contacted by ELIZABETH SANDERS, a fellow TWA employee. ELIZABETH SANDERS told Stacey that she wanted him to assist her husband JAMES SANDERS in investigating the theory that a missile was responsible for the crash of the airplane.

Stacey told the FBI that he had a series of telephone conversations and meetings with JAMES SANDERS. At one such meeting, Stacey gave to SANDERS documents from the National Transportation Safety Board investigation of the TWA 800 crash. Stacey later provided to SANDERS pieces of seat fabric from the Calverton hangar.

The criminal complaint outlines efforts by JAMES SANDERS to have laboratory tests done on portions of the TWA 800 wreckage which he unlawfully possessed. An individual employed at the laboratory has informed the FBI that SANDERS emphasized his desire for the tests to identify the presence of solid rocket propellant. The tests were conducted and provided no conclusive evidence of the presence of solid rocket fuel. These results were communicated to SANDERS.

According to the criminal complaint, despite the laboratory test results, JAMES SANDERS misrepresented those results in media reports for which he was a source.

Mr. KALLSTROM stated, "This criminal investigation is far from over. These defendants are charged with not only committing a serious crime, they have also increased the pain already inflicted on the victims' families. This investigation will continue in an effort to identify any other individuals who may have played a role in this scheme."

If convicted, both JAMES and ELIZABETH SANDERS face ten (10) years in jail. STACEY faces one (1) year in jail, if convicted.

****

FBI Statement
Foreign Terrorists in America:
Five Years after the World Trade Center

Statement of Dale Watson, Chief, International Terrorism Section, National Security Division, FBI, before the United States Senate Judiciary Committee Subcommittee on Technology, Terrorism, and Government Information,

Washington, DC
February 24, 1998

Good morning, Chairman Kyl and members of the subcommittee. I am pleased to participate in this panel as we assess the international terrorist threat confronting the United States five years after the bombing of the World Trade Center. For many of us in this room, the threat of international terrorism was literally brought home by the World Trade Center bombing on February 26, 1993. Much has changed in the world since that event. In many ways, the world has become even more dangerous for Americans. But in the aftermath of the World Trade Center bombing and the attack on the Murrah Federal Building in Oklahoma City, the United States government has adopted measures to enhance its response to terrorism. These efforts have helped to restore a sense of the security Americans felt before the attack on the World Trade Center. Although we should not allow ourselves to be lulled into a false sense of security or underestimate the nature of the threat that confronts us, I believe it is important to note that in the five years since the Trade Center bombing, no significant act of foreign-directed terrorism has occurred on American soil.

This morning, I would like to very briefly discuss some

things we have learned in the past five years. Then, I will elaborate on the international terrorist threat currently confronting the United States. I will close by discussing the FBI's response to this threat, and steps that could be taken to further enhance our response to the challenges international terrorism pose to the United States.

Lessons Learned

We have learned several important lessons since the World Trade Center bombing. I'll focus here on three broad trends we have identified.

One of these is that loosely affiliated groups of like-minded extremists — like the one assembled by Ramzi Yousef for the plot against the World Trade Center — pose a real and significant threat to our security and a particular challenge to law enforcement. These transnational groups often form on a temporary, ad hoc basis. Their memberships are generally unknown to law enforcement. These groups are not always beholden to, or dependant on, traditional state sponsors, such as Iraq, Iran, or Sudan for support. They are free to operate on their own terms and exploit the mobility that technology and a fluid command structure offers.

However, this flexibility and self-reliance can be a double-edged sword. After his capture in 1995, Ramzi Yousef conceded to investigators that a lack of funding forced his group's hand in plotting the destruction of the World Trade Center. Running short of money, the plotters could not assemble a bomb as large as they had originally intended. The timing of the attack was also rushed by a lack of finances. Incredibly, the plotters' desire to recoup the deposit fee for the rental truck used to transport the bomb helped lead investigators to them. As I will discuss in a moment, efforts to disrupt the fund-raising operations of organizations that finance terrorism may prove especially disruptive to the activities of these loosely affiliated terrorist groups.

During the past five years, we also have found that an increasing number of terrorist organizations possess a command of technology and have the expertise to use it for fund-raising, recruiting, and even operational planning. Several organizations with significant terrorist components maintain a regular presence on the Internet. For example, Hamas, Hizballah, and at least one Latin American group maintain their own home pages that include propaganda material and recruiting information.

During the trial of Shaykh Omar Abdel Rahman, on charges relating to the foiled plots to assassinate the president of Egypt and bomb major landmarks throughout New York, supporters used the Internet to solicit funds for his defense. These and more operational uses of technology, that I am not at liberty to comment upon here, clearly demonstrate that today's terrorists feel comfortable using advanced technology to support their destructive ambitions.

The misuse of technology underscores the wide range of tools and capabilities available to modern terrorists. The exploits of Ramzi Yousef, from the time he executed the World Trade Center bombing in February 1993 until his capture in Pakistan in February 1995, illustrate the integral role technology plays in international terrorism and the role it can play in assisting investigators to track down terrorists.

Within days of the explosion at the World Trade Center that left six innocent victims dead and approximately one thousand wounded, Ramzi Yousef made his way to Pakistan. Eventually, he and several associates moved on to the

Philippines and rented a unit at the Dona Josefa apartment complex in Manila, which they used as a safehouse and an improvised bomb factory. On December 11, 1994, Yousef placed a small explosive on a Philippines airliner en route to Tokyo via Cebu. A Japanese businessman was killed when the device exploded under his seat. Subsequent investigation determined that the plotters had used the device to test a new bomb design. As we later discovered, Yousef was planning to place more powerful devices on US airliners.

While mixing chemicals at the Dona Josefa apartment on January 7, 1995, a fire broke out forcing Yousef and two co- conspirators, Abdel Hakim Murad and Wali Khan, to flee into the street. Concerned that he had left his laptop computer in the apartment, Yousef sent Murad back into the unit to retrieve it. Philippine Police arrested Abdel Hakim Murad and were able to recover the computer intact. Wali Khan was arrested days later. Yousef successfully fled the Philippines and ultimately madehis way back to Pakistan.

By decrypting Yousef's computer files, investigators uncovered the details of a plot to destroy numerous US air carriers in a simultaneous operation. Codenamed "BOJINKA," the plot involved using a timing device made from an altered Databank watch. Flight schedules and a decrypted letter found on the computer indicated that five participants were to simultaneously plant devices on flights to the United States. After the bombings, four of the participants were to return to Karachi, Pakistan. The fifth was to return to Doha, Qatar.

Meanwhile, back in Pakistan, Yousef's luck finally was running out. A plot to kidnap and kill US diplomats and foreign officials in Pakistan was foiled by a cooperating witness who revealed the plan to US Embassy personnel. On

February 7, 1995, the FBI arrested Yousef in Islamabad and rendered him back to the United States.

Approximately two months later, Abdel Hakim Murad was rendered from the Philippines after his arrest at the Dona Josefa apartments. In December, Wali Khan also was rendered to the United States. Eventually, Khan and Murad were convicted and sentenced to life in prison for their participation in the plot to bomb US airliners. Yousef has now been convicted of both the plot to bomb airliners and for masterminding the bombing of the World Trade Center.

If we doubt the level of commitment that drives rogue terrorists to strike at their perceived enemies, just weeks ago Ramzi Yousef provided a glimpse into the mind set of a terrorist. When sentenced to life in federal prison without possibility of parole, Yousef boasted of his destructive exploits saying, "Yes, I am a terrorist and proud of it."

As this case illustrates, the threat of international terrorism demands continued vigilance. Today's terrorists have learned from the successes and mistakes of terrorists that went before them. The terrorists of tomorrow will have an even more dizzying array of weapons and technologies available to them.

One of the more challenging aspects of this threat stems from the third aspect of modern international terrorism I would like to discuss. That is the interrelated nature of certain terrorist incidents. As recent events have shown, this "web of terrorism" perpetuates violence upon violence and poses a particular challenge to nations like the United States that take a firm stand against terrorism. There is an indication that the November 1997 attack on foreign tourists in Luxor, Egypt, was apparently an example of this type of interwoven violence. The ambush appears to have been carried out in an attempt to pressure the UnitedStates into releasing Shaykh Rahman, who is serving a life sentence in federal prison for his part in planning attacks against the president of Egypt and several sites in New York City.

Since his imprisonment in 1995, followers of the Shaykh have issued several threats warning of violence in retaliation for his continued imprisonment. The FBI continues to monitor these threats very closely.

Terrorism is perpetrated by individuals with a strong commitment to the causes in which they believe. An action in one location often brings reaction in another, although not necessarily a coordinated one. The web-like nature of terrorism underscores the need for vigilance in counteracting terrorist groups. Unfortunately, American successes can spur reprisals. As the United States develops a stronger investigative and prosecutorial response to terrorism, we may witness more attempts at reprisals both here and abroad.

Presence of Foreign Terrorist Groups in the United States

Today, due to the foresight of the Congress and Executive Branch in the aftermath of the World Trade Center and Oklahoma City bombings, the FBI has an enhanced capability to track the activities of foreign terrorist organizations maintaining a presence in the United States.

There are obvious operational considerations that limit what we can discuss in an open forum about the presence of terrorist groups in the United States. I can tell you that the FBI has identified a significant and growing organizational presence here.

Palestinian Hamas, Iranian-backed Hizballah, and Egyptian-based al-Gama' at al Islamiyya each has established an active presence in the United States. The activities of the

American wings of these organizations generally revolve around fund-raising and low-level intelligence gathering.

In addition, there are still significant numbers of Iranian students attending US universities and technical institutions. In 1997, 419 student visas were issued to new and returning Iranian students. A significant number of these individuals are hardcore members of the pro-Iranian student organization known as the Anjoman Islamie, which is comprised almost exclusively of fanatical, anti-American, Iranian Shiite Muslims. The Iranian government relies heavily on these students studying in the United States for low-level intelligence and technical expertise. However, the Anjoman Islamie also provides a significant resource base which allows the government of Iran to maintain the capability to mount operations against the United States, if it so decided.

Response to Terrorism

In the face of these potential threats, the US government has significantly enhanced its response to international terrorism in the five years since the World Trade Center bombing. There are five traditional offensive ways through which the government fights terrorism: diplomacy, sanctions, covert operations, military options, and law enforcement action. Some of the measures in place span more than one of these areas. For example, the Antiterrorism and Effective Death Penalty Act (AEDPA) of 1996 includes both diplomatic and law enforcement provisions.

Enactment of the AEDPA has enhanced the ability of the US government to respond to terrorist threats. As I mentioned, this act includes a wide range of counterterrorism provisions. For example, section 302 of the Act authorizes the Secretary of State, in conjunction with the Attorney

General and Secretary of the Treasury, to designate as foreign terrorist organizations (FTOS) groups that meet certain specified criteria. This designation means that funds raised in the United States by FTOS can be blocked by US financial institutions.

The Act provides law enforcement with a potentially powerful tool. Among other things, it gives us a means to disrupt the ability of terrorist organizations to fund their destructive activities.

However, it would be overly optimistic to consider this act a panacea to the problem of international terrorism. Financial investigations are by their nature personnel-intensive and time-consuming. Investigations into the financial operations of clandestine organizations on the shadowy fringes of transnational politics can be particularly complex.

It will take time for the AEDPA to have significant impact on the 30 groups designated as foreign terrorist organizations.

I encourage the Congress to give the AEDPA time to work. As with many measures of this type, its most powerful impact may stem from its deterrent effect. As investigators build successful cases and prosecutors develop sound prosecutorial strategies to enforce the provisions of the AEDPA, targeted groups may decide that fund-raising activities in the United States are not worth the risks.

As you are aware, recent congressional appropriations have helped strengthen and expand the FBI's counterterrorism capabilities. To enhance its mission, the FBI centralized many specialized operational and analytical functions in the Domestic Counterterrorism Center.

Established in 1996, the FBI Counterterrorism Center

combats terrorism on three fronts: international terrorism operations both within the United States and in support of extraterritorial investigations, domestic terrorism operations, and countermeasures relating to both international and domestic terrorism.

The FBI Counterterrorism Center represents a new direction in the FBI's response to terrorism. Eighteen federal agencies maintain a regular presence in the center and participate in its daily operations. These agencies include the Central Intelligence Agency, the Defense Intelligence Agency, and the United States Secret Service, among others. This multiagency arrangement provides an unprecedented opportunity for information-sharing and real-time intelligence analysis.

This sense of cooperation also has led to other important changes. During the past several years, the FBI and CIA have developed a closer working relationship. This has strengthened the ability of each agency to respond to terrorist threats, and has improved the ability of the US Government to respond to terrorist attacks that do occur. Because warning is critical to the prevention of terrorist acts, the FBI also is in the process of expanding the terrorist threat warning system first implemented in 1989. The system reaches all aspects of the law enforcement and intelligence communities. Currently, more than 35 federal agencies involved in the US Government's counterterrorism effort receive information via secure teletype through this system. The messages also are transmitted to all 56 FBI field offices and 33 foreign liaison posts.

If threat information requires nationwide unclassified dissemination to all federal, state, and local law enforcement agencies, the FBI transmits messages via the National Law Enforcement Telecommunications System. In addition, the terrorist threat warning system allows for the dissemination of unclassified terrorism warnings to the US corporate community as well as the public at large, via the Internet, press releases, and press conferences.

The FBI's counterterrorism capabilities also have been enhanced by the expansion of our Legal Attache—or Legat offices—around the world. These small offices can have a significant impact on the FBI's ability to track terrorist threats and bring investigative resources to bear on cases where quick response is critical. As I've mentioned, the FBI currently has 33 Legat offices. Many of these have opened within the past 5 years in areas of the world where identifiable threats to our national interests exist. We cannot escape the disquieting reality—as evidenced by the World Trade Center bombing—that in the late 20th century, crime and terrorism are carried out on an international scale. The law enforcement response must match the threat. By expanding our first line of defense, we improve the ability of the United States to prevent attacks and respond quickly to those that do occur. Given the nature of the evolving terrorist threat and the destructive capabilities now available to terrorists, the American people deserve nothing less.

Terrorism is increasingly an indiscriminate crime. The World Trade Center bombers exhibited little concern about who their victims would be. Their primary interest seemed simply to ensure a high number of casualties. Likewise, though Shaykh Omar Abdel Rahman and his plotters targeted specific facilities, such as the UN Headquarters and a federal building housing the FBI's New York City field office—in addition to other sites throughout the city—they evidently gave little thought to their potential victims. Again, the nature of the planned attacks indicate that the primary goal was to cause as much destruction and as many casualties as possible.

How a free society responds to such threats is a question that the Congress has addressed in years past and undoubtedly will continue to confront for years to come. During the past five years, the United States has made great strides in strengthening its counterterrorism capabilities. But, there is more to be done.

Future needs I would like to close by talking briefly about steps we can take to further strengthen our abilities to prevent and investigate terrorist activity.

One of the most important of these steps involves the adoption of a balanced public policy on encryption. Court authorized electronic surveillance (wiretaps) and the execution of lawful search and seizure warrants are two of the most critically important law enforcement investigative techniques used to fight crime and prevent terrorism. Law enforcement remains in unanimous agreement that the continued widespread availability and ever increasing use of strong, non-recoverable encryption products will soon nullify our effective use of these important investigative techniques and will ultimately devastate our ability to effectively fight crime, prevent acts of terrorism and protect the public safety and national security of the united states.

Most encryption products manufactured today for use by the general public are non-recoverable. This means that they do not include features that provide for timely law enforcement access to the plain text of encrypted criminally-related and lawfully seized communications and computer files. Other than some form of a key-recovery system or feature, there is no viable technical solution to this problem for law enforcement. Non-recoverable or uncrackable encryption is now and with ever increasing regularity, allowing violent criminals and terrorists to communicate about their criminal intentions with impunity and to store evidence of their crimes on computer, impervious to lawful search and seizure.

In many of our important investigations today, effective law enforcement is being frustrated by criminals and terrorists using commercially available, non-recoverable encryption products. Examples include the Aldrich Ames spy case; the Ramzi Yousef international terrorist case, which involved a plot to blow up 11 US commercial aircraft in the Far East; and numerous international drug trafficking investigations, to include those along the southwest border of the United States.

It is for this reason that law enforcement is urgently calling for our nation's policy makers to adopt a balanced public policy on encryption. Several bills have been introduced in Congress that address certain aspects of the encryption issue. Unfortunately, most of these legislative proposals, with the exception of a proposal adopted by the House Permanent Select Committee on Intelligence, fail to adequately address law enforcement's needs in this area and would promote the widespread availability and use of non-recoverable encryption products regardless of the adverse impact on public safety, effective law enforcement, and national security.

Law enforcement believes that we are now at a historical crossroad on this issue. If public policy makers act wisely, the safety of all Americans will be enhanced for decades to come. But if narrow interests prevail, law enforcement will soon be unable to provide the level of protection that the American people properly expect and deserve. We do not think it is too late to deal effectively with this issue and I would encourage the subcommittee to look closely at the action taken by the House Permanent Select Committee on Intelligence in their efforts to adopt a balanced encryption policy.

Another area of vital interest to the FBI is the proliferation of chemical, biological, and nuclear materials within the criminal and terrorist communities. These weapons of mass destruction represent perhaps the most serious potential threat facing the United States today. In response to this threat, the FBI has significantly expanded its investigative capabilities in this area.

Prior to the World Trade Center and Oklahoma City bombings, the FBI had dedicated a very small staff to weapons of mass destruction (WMD) investigations. Those two investigations, which required thousands of FBI Agent and support personnel, prompted the Attorney General to request an increase of 175 field agents to the WMD program, which the Congress subsequently supported. To coordinate the activities of these personnel, the FBI has created two WMD units at FBI Headquarters: one to address operations, cases, and threats, which tripled in 1997 over 1996 figures, and another to implement our countermeasures program, which coordinates exercises, deployments, and the first responder training initiative.

A successful WMD terrorist attack could prove catastrophic and would require a unified response from various agencies at the federal, state, and local levels. To improve response capabilities on a national scale, the FBI is working closely with five other federal agencies—the Department of Defense, the Department of Energy, the Public Health Service, the Environmental Protection Agency, and the Federal Emergency Management Agency—that make up the nucleus of the response to WMD incidents. The FBI also maintains extensive liaison with members of the intelligence community, including the CIA, the National Security Agency, and others involved in WMD and counterproliferation matters.

As the 1995 sarin attack on the Tokyo subways demonstrated, unconventional weapons are no longer purely the domains of military arsenals. In the hands of terrorists, they can pose a grave risk to our citizens and our nation's interests. Again, Congress and the Executive Branch should be commended for their foresight in responding to this threat. Given the potentially grave consequences of inaction, I encourage continued support of the FBI's initiative to confront the WMD threat through proactive investigations and cross-agency training.

Cooperation among law enforcement and intelligence agencies at all levels represents an important component of a comprehensive response to terrorism. This cooperation assumes its most tangible operational form in the joint terrorism task forces that exist in 16 cities across the nation. These task forces are particularly well-suited to responding to internationalterrorism because they combine the international investigative resources of the FBI and other federal agencies with the street-level expertise of local law enforcement agencies. This cop-to-cop cooperation has proven highly successful in preventing several potential terrorist attacks.

Perhaps the most notable cases have come from New York City, where the city's Joint Terrorism Task Force has been instrumental in thwarting two high-profile international terrorism plots--the series of bombings planned by Shaykh Rahman in 1993, and the July 1997 attempted bombing of the New York City subway.

These plots were prevented. Today, the conspirators who planned them either sit in federal prisons, or are awaiting trial thanks, in large part, to the comprehensive investigative work performed by the Joint Terrorism Task Force.

Given the success of the Joint Terrorism Task Force concept, the FBI plans to develop additional task forces in cities around the country. By integrating the investigative abilities of the FBI and local law enforcement agencies these task forces represent an effective response to the threats posed to individual American communities by international terrorists.

Conclusion

The bombing of the World Trade Center was a watershed event. It taught us in a painful but unmistakable way that international terrorism can and does occur in the United States. This case also demonstrated the ability of American intelligence and law enforcement agencies to track and apprehend the perpetrators of such atrocities. Today, Ramzi Yousef and most of his co-plotters are sitting in federal prison, deprived of the freedom they so recklessly exploited. The World Trade Center bombing heralded a new era—but not one of increased numbers of foreign-directed terrorist acts in the United States. Rather, it has led to a renewed and enhanced focus on responding to the international terrorist threat confronting the American people.

To adequately understand the international terrorist threat currently facing the United States, we must appreciate the unique position America occupies in the world today. As the sole super power, the policies of the United States are viewed with intense interest by nations around the world. To individuals and groups who feel powerless to effect their own destinies through legal means, the breadth of influence and power wielded by the United States represents a stunning contrast—and an attractive target for their frustrations.

The FBI has developed a broad-based response to the many external threats that confront the United States today. Due to the measures I've discussed and several other initiatives, we are much better prepared to address the international terrorist threat than we were five years ago. With the continued support of Congress and the Executive Branch, and in cooperation with the intelligence and law enforcement communities, we will continue to enhance our ability to protect the American people from the threat of international terrorism.

APPENDIX D

Cockpit Voice Recorders (CVR) and
Flight Data Recorders (FDR)

Large commercial aircraft and some smaller commercial, corporate, and private aircraft are required by the FAA to be equipped with two 'black boxes' that record information about a flight. Both recorders are installed to help reconstruct the events leading to an aircraft accident. One of these, the Cockpit Voice Recorder (CVR), records radio transmissions and sounds in the cockpit, such as the pilot's voices and engine noises. The other, the Flight Data Recorder (FDR), monitors parameters such as altitude, airspeed and heading. The older analog units use one-quarter inch magnetic tape as a storage medium and the newer ones use digital technology and memory chips. Both recorders are installed in the most crash survivable part of the aircraft, usually the tail section.

Each recorder is equipped with an Underwater Locator Beacon (ULB) to assist in locating in the event of an overwater accident. The device called a 'pinger,' is activated when the recorder is immersed in water. It transmits an acoustical signal on 37.5 KHz that can be detected with a special receiver. The beacon can transmit from depths down to 14,000 feet.

Following an accident, both recorders are immediately removed from the accident site and transported to NTSB headquarters in Washington DC for processing. Using sophisticated computer and audio equipment, the information stored on the recorders is extracted and translated into an understandable format. The Investigator-in-Charge uses this information as one of many tools to help the Safety Board determine the Probable Cause of the accident.

The Cockpit Voice Recorder

The CVR records the flight crew's voices, as well as other sounds inside the cockpit. The recorder's 'Cockpit Area Microphone' (CAM) is usually located on the overhead instrument panel between the two pilots. Sounds of interest to an investigator could be engine noise, stall warnings, landing gear extension and retraction, and other clicks and pops. From these sounds, parameters such as engine rpm, system failures, speed, and the time at which certain events occur can often be determined. Communications with Air Traffic Control, automated radio weather briefings, and conversation between the pilots and ground or cabin crew are also recorded.

A CVR committee usually consisting of members from the NTSB, FAA, operator of the aircraft, manufacturer of the airplane, manufacturer of the engines, and the pilots union, is formed to listen to the recording. This committee creates a written transcript of the tape to be used during the investigation. FAA air traffic control tapes with their associated time codes are used to help determine the local standard time of one or more events during the accident sequence. These times are applied to the transcript using a computer process which provides a local time for every event on the transcript. More precise timing for critical events can be obtained using a digital spectrum analyzer. This transcript contains all pertinent portions of the recording and can be released to the public at the time of the Safety Board's public hearing.

The CVR recordings are treated differently than the other factual information obtained in an accident investigation. Due to the highly sensitive nature of the verbal communications inside the cockpit, Congress has required that the Safety Board not release any part of a CVR tape recording. Because of this sensitivity, a high degree of security is provided for the CVR tape and its transcript. The content and timing of release of the written transcript are strictly regulated. In the case of TWA 800, the CVR transcipt has been released (subsequent to the majority of the report (Appendix B) and is presented as Exhibit 12A of the NTSB report.

The Flight Data Recorder

The FDR onboard the aircraft records many different operating conditions of the flight. By regulation, newly manufactured aircraft must monitor at least twenty-eight important parameters such as time, altitude, airspeed, heading, and aircraft attitude. In addition, some FDRs can record the status of more than 300 other in-flight characteristics that can aid in the investigation. The items monitored can be anything from flap position to auto-pilot mode or even smoke alarms.

With the data retrieved from the FDR, the Safety Board can generate a computer animated video reconstruction of the flight among other important tools necessary for the accident reconstruction. The investigator can then visualize the airplane's attitude, instrument readings, power settings and other characteristics of the flight. This animation enables the investigating team to visualize the last moments of the flight before the accident.

Both the Flight Data Recorder and the Cockpit Voice Recorder have proven to be valuable tools in the accident investigation process. They can provide information that may be difficult or impossible to obtain by other means. When used in conjunction with other information gained in the investigation, the recorders are playing an ever increasing role in determining the probable cause of an aircraft accident.

Specifications

Flight Data Recorder
Time recorded
 25 hour continuous
Number of parameters
 5 - 300+
Impact tolerance
 3400Gs /6.5ms
Fire resistance
 1100 degC/30 min
Water pressure resistance
 submerged 20,000 ft
Underwater locator beacon
 37.5 KHz
Battery: 6yr shelf life
30 day operation

Cockpit Voice Recorder
Time recorded
 30 min continuous,
 2 hours for solid state
 digital units
Number of channels
 4
Impact tolerance
 3400 Gs /6.5ms
Fire resistance
 1100 deg C /30 min
Water pressure resistance
 submerged 20,000 ft
Underwater locator beacon
 37.5 KHz
Battery: 6yr shelf life
30 day operation

COCKPIT VOICE RECORDER & FLIGHT DATA RECORDER EXTRACTS

NATIONAL TRANSPORTATION SAFETY BOARD
December 12, 1997 REPORT

[Authors' Note: The following specific extracts were taken from Exhibit 12A & 10A of the NTSB report presented in Appendix B. The table below was reproduced from pages 54 and 55 of Exhibit 10A of the NTSB report. This extract contains the final minute of recordings on the Cockpit Voice Recorder. There are several items of curious and potential significant interest.

Why was Flight Engineer trainee Oliver Krick so distracted to miss the Captain's command for climb thrust?

What was the mechanical sound at 2030:42? Could that have been one of the first detectable events?]

INTRA- COCKPIT COMMUNICATION		AIR- GROUND COMMUNICATION	
TIME and SOURCE	CONTENT	TIME and SOURCE	CONTENT
		2030: 19.2 RDO- 2	TWA's eight hundred heavy climb and maintain one five thousand leaving one three thousand
2030: 24 CAM- 1	Ollie.		
2030: 24 CAM- 3	huh.		
2030: 25 CAM- 1	climb thrust.		
2030: 28			

CAM- 1	climb to one five thousand.
2030: 35	
CAM- 3	power's set.
2030: 42	
CAM	((sound similar to a mechanical movement in cockpit))
2031: 03	
CAM	(unintelligible)
2031: 05	
CAM	((sounds similar to recording tape damage noise)).
2031: 12	
	end of recording.

FLIGHT DATA RECORDER TRACES

The traces below were extracted from Plot 8, page 52, Exhibit 12A, of the NTSB report and cover the time period from 2030:40 to 2031:20. No attempt has been made to identify specific trace lines; actual notation is provided in the NTSB report. References and calculations throughout the NTSB report refer to the FDR loss of power at 2031:12 as being the primary moment in the break-up sequence.

What is significant is the major spikes in nearly all parameters at 2031:12. Please note the trace using +'s to show the pitch trim stabilizer position; it is the only parameter that continues without a spike at 2031:12, although it does flatline which would probably indicate inputs to the drive motor were severed, but the position resolver continued to indicate the position of the stablizer. However, the most interesting indication in these traces is that some parameters stop, while other parameters continue for at least another 8 seconds, with some flatlining at the last value and others continuing to indicate a valid input signal, thus not being a total loss of power. The spike lasts approximately 1.2 seconds, then the only remnants of the event are the missing parameters, the shift in values and the almost unaffected parameters.

As noted earlier in the radar data, there was a pronounced flattening of the radar flight track at 2030:42 which exactly coincides with the 'mechanical sound' on the CVR recording and the disappearance of the 'mystery blip' on the FAA radar tapes. The FDR data appears to show that whatever happened at 2030:42, other than affecting the flight path, did not alter engine performance or other flight parameters

None of these anomalies can be considered definitive without other corroborating data. The principal reason for drawing the attention of the reader to these anomalies is the lack of any discussion regarding these unusual elements.

In some aspects, there is no discussion of what might have occured prior to 2031:12, and yet other aspects of the analysis stop at that time. Something quite obviously happened at 2031:12. Some of the story of what happened to TWA 800 lies in each of those parameters before and after the primary time.

Data to the right of the END OF TWA 800 DATA notation, between 2031:12 and 2031:20, may be overwritten data from 30 minutes prior; it is impossible to tell from the data traces provided. Either the chart time notation was in error, or there was more recording after the primary event. If it is the latter, there is considerable significance to this information that has not been analyzed.

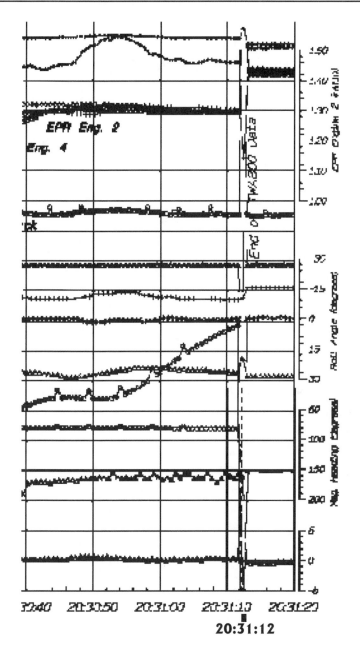

20:31:12

APPENDIX E

BACKGROUND ON THE POLITICAL AND RELIGIOUS SITUATION IN IRAN

Since its founding in 1979, the Islamic Republic of Iran has shown itself willing to use many forms of violence to further its cause, both at home and in foreign countries. This propensity for violence, assassination, bombings and covert activities in foreign jurisdictions has led the United States to an increasing level of confrontation on both a military and economic front. It has also led to situations such as that in Germany where the Federal Prosecutor in Berlin has recently named several senior Iranian officials in a murder indictment involving the death of a prominent Kurdish leader in Berlin. The very curious '*fatwa*' or death sentence levied on author Salman Rushdie is also evidence of Iran's unique perspective on foreign assassinations.

While the theory asserted in this book, that Iran sent one of its submarines on a long mission into American waters to down an American airliner in retribution for a similar downing of an Iranian plane by American naval units, would seem ludicrous if said of most other nations. It is not at all ludicrous when the unique political and religious situation of the Islamic Republic of Iran is understood, and this past history is reckoned with.

To this end, we have included the following information prepared for the Canadian Security Intelligence

Service (CSIS) by its strategic analyst on the Middle East, Dr. William Millward. This material, called a 'Commentary' by the CSIS is an analysis of the situation of Iran in international politics and also includes two Commentaries on the unique internal political and religious situation in Iran.

The following material is reprinted with permission of the Canadian Security Intelligence Service and its author, Dr. William Millward. Inclusion of this material in this book does not imply CSIS authentication of the information in these excerpts nor in this book and does not imply CSIS endorsement of the authors' views.

COMMENTARY No. 63
a CANADIAN SECURITY INTELLIGENCE
SERVICE publication

CONTAINING IRAN

November 1995 Unclassified

[CSIS] Editors Note: *The principal reasons for Iran's isolation from the mainstream international community are, at least on the surface, relatively easy to list: the absence of formal diplomatic relations with the USA since the hostage-taking incident in 1979; Iran's alleged nuclear ambitions; its opposition to the Middle East peace process; its support for terrorists in the region; its internal human rights abuses; assassinations of those opposed to the régime abroad; the "eternal* **fatwa***" calling for the death of author Salman Rushdie; and in May 1993, the American government's announcement of its "dual containment policy" aimed at Iraq and Iran. Most recently (April 1995), the American Administration imposed a total trade embargo on Iran and* *has subsequently sought the support of its allies in Europe, the Middle East and Asia. Clearly the noose has tightened, and the rhetoric has heightened.*

Below the surface, what is behind this hardening of attitudes? How has Iran, and the rest of the international community, reacted?

After a period of relative quiescence, when the United States and its coalition allies were preoccupied with the lingering threat of Iraq under Saddam Hussein, the American government and some congressional leaders have gradually upgraded their anti-Iran rhetoric. Not content with demonizing the Islamic Republic as a rogue state and pariah in the international community, American officials have recently followed up with concrete actions designed to punish Iran for what they consider objectionable behaviour. This apparent hardening of attitudes, and escalation of anti-Iran rhetoric and actions, come at a time when Iran has been absorbed with its own economic and social problems and has been comparatively quiet on the regional and international scenes. These developments puzzle many of Washington's friends and allies, who wonder what may be motivating this shift of emphasis at this time.

USA - Iran Relations

Relations between Iran and the United States have become an important barometer of current foreign policy positions and trends in both countries. To an extent, their mutual relations have in fact become hostage to these trends. The long absence of formal diplomatic relations between the two governments since the seizure of the US Embassy and hostage-taking incident of 1979 runs contrary to the historic internationalist and cosmopolitan traditions of both states. Despite the great difference in age between the two societies, neither state has been allowed the luxury of serious or prolonged isolationism for a variety of historical and geostrategic reasons. The predominant internationalist impulse of both countries, though situated on opposite sides of the globe, would normally be expected to bring them into a degree of constructive engagement and advantageous commercial exchange, despite their traumatic disagreement 16 years ago.

But both societies have a strong sense of national identity and a propensity for the imperial mission, either in the classic tradition of the eastern regional empire, [we are reminded that Iran was one of the ancient world's earliest superpowers], or in the neo-imperialist mould of a modern superpower, able and willing to project its power regionally and globally when its national and international interests are deemed to be threatened. These two imperial traditions are at loggerheads in the Persian Gulf and the Middle East region generally; and on the issue of terrorism, they clash on an international front. Recent American decisions suggest that greater effort will be made to impose a measure of containment and isolation on Iran which is incompatible with that country's historic reflexes and self-image. The question that engages the attention of foreign policy analysts in both states is whether such efforts can have any serious expectations of success.

In the aftermath of Desert Storm and the application of sanctions on Iraq by the international community, the American government unveiled its own policy of dual containment [DCP] in May 1993. The DCP was brought forward initially by Martin Indyk, now American Ambassador to Israel. A former American Israel Public Affairs Committee [AIPAC] staff member, Indyk became a Clinton White House adviser on Middle East policy as a member of the National Security Council. The DCP was designed to neutralize the threat of Iraq under Saddam Hussein's leadership, and limit the capacity of the Islamic régime in Iran to create mischief in the region. The objectives of the policy were to effect a change of government in Iraq, but not in Iran. For the Islamic Republic of Iran the intent was to apply sufficient pressure to induce change in the régime's behaviour, considered unacceptable in several respects, including its quest for nuclear weapons, domestic human rights abuses, support for terrorist activities in the region and assassination of alleged régime opponents abroad, and its shrill opposition to the Middle East peace process. The DCP soon came to be known as the Iran Containment Policy, and skeptics quickly discounted the notion that there was no intention to encourage a change of régime in Tehran, as in Baghdad.

The DCP was widely criticized by domestic and foreign observers, chiefly because of its assumption that the United States would receive the support and assistance of its allies needed to make the policy hurt Iran badly enough to bring about behavioural change. The hoped-for support was not forthcoming for the reason that European and Japanese investments in the Islamic Republic would be put at risk by applying economic pressure on the Iranian government. Only Israel among American allies signed on to the policy unequivocally. By summer 1994 the Israeli Foreign Ministry had set up a special unit to appeal to the industrialized countries to limit their economic ties with Iran and refrain from selling advanced technology to the Islamic Republic because its support for terrorist activity in the region and outside, and its desire to acquire a nuclear program, made it a paramount threat.

Fine-tuning the DCP

By November 1994, both domestic and foreign critics charged that the DCP was being applied inconsistently and was showing few results. The American administration thereupon conducted an Iran policy review at which Secretary of State Christopher is said to have recommended a full trade embargo. This suggestion was opposed by the Departments of Commerce, Defense, Energy and the Treasury, all of whom argued that it would have little effect on Iran's behaviour and only hurt American companies. The Administration found itself facing an even more aggressive competitor in foreign policy from the newly installed Republican Congress.

On 6 March 1995, Conoco, Inc. announced that its Dutch-based subsidiary, Conoco Iran SV, had signed a $1 billion contract to develop Iran's offshore oil resources, the first energy agreement between the USA and Iran since 1980. Senator Alphonse D'Amato (Rep-NY) seized the initiative and promised to hold congressional hearings aimed at tightening the economic embargo on Iran. This move led the Administration to counter with an Executive Order under the authority of the *International Emergency Economic Powers Act*, aimed at preventing American companies from developing Iranian oil and gas reserves, effectively precluding the Conoco deal.

Iranian officials reacted to the cancellation of the Conoco deal by insisting that it would have no significant impact on Iran's oil production plans, and that Iran would quickly find other partners for oil development. While official

Iranian reaction was predictably defensive, other Iran-based critics emphasized the short-sightedness of the decision which would deprive the USA of an opportunity to strengthen economic ties and improve its relations generally with Iran. By July 1995 the National Iranian Oil Company [NIOC] was able to sign a $600 million contract with the French oil company Total SA to develop oil fields in the Persian Gulf.

Meanwhile, Iran and South Africa signed an agreement for the lease of two underground oil storage tanks at Saldanha Bay on the Atlantic coast of South Africa. This permits Iran to store 15-20 million barrels of Iranian crude for sale in Europe and elsewhere on a joint-venture basis, thus enhancing its international marketing position. While in each of these transactions the USA appealed to the government concerned not to promote trade and development contracts with Iran, there has been no positive response to date.

Item six in the Republican Congressional Caucus's 'Contract With America' calls for a strong national defense, including, among other elements, "...a missile defense system against rogue dictatorships." Whether the authors had Iran specifically in mind we cannot be sure, but it seems safe to assume. Following their sweep of American elections last November, it was only a matter of time before competition with the Administration to confront and deal with rogue behaviour among world states would fire up the anti-Iran sentiment in political circles and precipitate action.

On 30 April 1995 President Clinton announced a total trade embargo on Iran, pre-empting prospective legislation in Congress to implement a secondary boycott on trade with foreign companies doing business with Iran. The fact that he made this announcement at a dinner in New York sponsored by the World Jewish Congress only lent added fuel to Iranian critics who claimed it was further proof that his policies were driven by Zionist interests. The Clinton *fatwa*, as one Washington newspaper described it, prohibited all American companies, and foreign branches under their control, but not separate foreign subsidiaries, from trading with and investing in Iran. The rationale for this measure was that it would curtail Iran's drive for nuclear weapons and its support for terrorism.

The thirty-sixth annual AIPAC conference held in Washington, DC 7-9 May, 1995 illustrated the rising concern about Iran in the American capital. At the opening plenary, AIPAC's executive director, Neil Sher, told the audience that "containing Iran" was number one on the list of the lobby's priorities, ahead of the more traditional aims of supporting continued aid to Israel and securing the status of Jerusalem as Israel's capital. The same conference featured three panels that dealt primarily with Iran. One report of the conference's proceedings claims that the Islamic Republic was described as, among other things, the source for the export of "radical Islamic fundamentalism," a nation on the "brink of nuclear capability" and an alleged financier of terrorism around the world. A clear perception was presented that Iran represented the greatest threat not only to Israel today, but also to peace and stability in the region and the world. Every prominent American and Israeli official who attended the conference, including President Clinton and then Prime Minister Rabin, spoke of the Iranian threat. The same theme has been articulated by other American and Israeli leaders for the past year and more. These pronouncements demonstrate a remarkable congruence of viewpoint on Iran and its alleged global threat on the part of the two governments. Clearly, the Islamic Republic is currently their number-one demon.

Reaction to the American Embargo

Reaction to this move was more or less predictable. Despite appeals to America's allies to join the embargo, the Europeans and Japanese declined. A consensus on the denial of dual-use nuclear technology was one thing, but a total trade boycott was more than any of the allies had bargained for. The Europeans preferred to continue their policy of "constructive engagement" rather than resort to punitive sanctions. Using the analogy of relations with the former Soviet Union, where dialogue was maintained even on contentious issues such as human rights, with ultimately positive results, the Europeans have preferred to keep their trade options and communications channels open, in the belief that this gives them an avenue of influence, and that Iran is not, under its present leadership, irredeemable or impervious to reform.

China and North Korea both condemned the embargo as meddling in the internal affairs of developing nations and promised to make efforts to increase their trade with Iran as a partial counterweight. Even Jordan, a nominal ally of the USA in the Middle East, and dependent on debt relief for help in overcoming the economic morass caused by the embargo on Iraq, declined to join the new embargo. Further, Jordan indicated its desire to upgrade trade ties with Tehran and open an Iranian trade fair in the kingdom.

Reaction in Russia was muted; Moscow's policy towards Iran is ambivalent. On the one hand it is heavily engaged with sophisticated arms sales, including submarines and the provision of nuclear assistance in the completion of the Bushehr reactors left unfinished by the Germans. It also provides training programs for Iranian specialists. Despite American objections to these moves, the programs are going ahead. The dominant motive in Russia-Iran relations currently appears to be economic. The relationship is being nurtured by high-level visits by officials on both sides. A recent visitor in Moscow was the Iranian Minister of Intelligence and Security, Ali Fellahiyan, hosted by his Russian counterpart, Yevgeny Primakov.

On the other hand Moscow has concerns about the real and potential influence of Iran in the former Soviet republics such as Azerbayjan, Tajikistan and Turkmenistan. It has a natural interest in preserving its own influence in these lands as a bulwark against the possible spread of Islamist sentiment there in favour of Iran. To an extent the American position is helpful to Russian policies in raising objections to energy pipelines running through Iran and limiting Iran's access to international financing.

A wide variety of motives and factors are at play here. For Moscow, there are the factors of traditional geostrategic interest, competition with the West for influence in the Middle East generally, the cultivation of sources of hard currency, and the desire to show potential buyers that Russia is a reliable supplier of modern technology. For Tehran, Russia provides a valuable means of demonstrating it cannot be isolated, and serves as a counterweight to Western pressure. Despite its condemnation of Russian goals and actions in Chechenya, Tehran pays for continued Russian support by muting its criticisms of Moscow.

Reaction in the Islamic Republic of Iran [IRI]

The reaction in Iran to the announcement of the American embargo was defiant. Officials insisted the embargo would have little or no effect on the Iranian economy. Other partners would soon be found to purchase the 500,000 b/d of Iranian crude previously lifted by American companies, and the drilling equipment and spare parts purchased from American firms would either be made up locally or in joint venture industries by agreement with the Russians. Other suppliers of oil field technology and equipment, especially those desperate for dollars, would rush to fill any vacancy in an Iranian market vacated by the USA.

What the IRI authorities could not prevent was a drastic decline in public confidence in the domestic economy and currency. The ban caused panic among ordinary Iranians, businessmen, importers and others, who feared the move could help push the already troubled economy deeper into recession. In the two weeks following the embargo's announcement, the Iranian rial fell to its lowest level against the dollar since the revolution. This retreat was in addition to the 30% loss of value experienced by the rial in a three-week period in January. At that time there was a rush to buy American dollars which reduced the rial to 7,000 to the dollar. The government followed up by banning free currency exchange and set a fixed rate for the rial of 3,000 to the dollar. In late January 1995, authorities arrested 330 currency dealers and seized $2.5 million in a crackdown on unauthorized currency transactions.

The short-term prospects for Iran as a result of the embargo are difficult to estimate. The prohibition on American companies lifting Iranian crude could threaten

Iran's oil market share until new customers can be found. NIOC officials will be watching closely to see that other OPEC producers do not increase their output at Iran's expense. This suggests that Iran could also seek a higher OPEC quota for 1996 if the producers' group decides on a higher output ceiling at its year-end meeting. These same officials are perhaps overly optimistic; the embargo has to be renewed each year, but if it has solid bipartisan congressional support, as it would appear, this will not be a problem unless and until future elections bring a change of leadership and, perhaps, new policies. In the meantime American firms are hostage to current regulations.

Another short-term disadvantage for Iran may be that the government's mishandling of the currency crisis, coupled with slightly lower oil revenues, will leave it an estimated $4.5 billion to $6 billion short for debt-servicing purposes next year. If other producers, such as Saudi Arabia, increase their overall output, and traditional customers like Japan cannot be persuaded to buy more Iranian crude, Iran may have to lower its prices to compete in finding new customers. Whether this shortfall will mean fundamental damage to the Iranian economy will depend to a large extent on how long it lasts.

By and large the Islamic Republic has managed to defend itself and its economic interests tolerably well since the American embargo came into force in June 1995. On 1 October 1995, President Rafsanjani presided at the opening of the 21st Annual International Trade Fair in Tehran and declared that it represented a clear response to the desire of the US Administration to isolate Iran. Although it had attended this event in 1993 and 1994, in 1995 the United

States was noted for its absence. Fifty-three countries, including Canada, and 800 commercial enterprises participated. First-time attendees this year included Iraq, Mexico and South Africa.

Disapproval of Iran's behaviour, reinforced by a constant stream of anti-American rhetoric, appears to have broad bipartisan support in American political and policy-formulation circles. The objections are usually laid out with reference to its 1) nuclear weapons ambitions, 2) support for terrorism, including the assassination of régime foes abroad, 3) attempts to destabilize neighbouring régimes, 4) opposition to the Middle East peace process, 5) domestic human rights abuses, and the *fatwa* against Salman Rushdie.

Is Iran nuclearly ambitious?

Perhaps the most controversial aspect of Iranian behaviour in its international implications is the alleged ambition of the country's ruling élite to acquire a nuclear weapons capability, despite regular official denials of any such intention. The country has had a nuclear program since the 1960s. It signed the Nuclear Non-proliferation Treaty [NPT] in 1970 and this year supported the move to have the treaty made permanent. Régime spokespersons justify their claim for the peaceful nature of Iran's nuclear program by alluding to the fact that the Vienna-based International Atomic Energy Agency [IAEA] has regularly inspected Iran's facilities and never found any indication of the diversion of nuclear materials to a military program.

There are currently two causes for concern in this regard. The first is a perception of Iran's wide-ranging procurement activities in Europe and elsewhere stretching back over several years, which suggest military intentions.

This program includes the search for nuclear materials and equipment, technical know-how and trained experts. The second is the January agreement between Russia and Iran for the former to complete the construction of an unfinished power plant in Bushehr. A collateral secret protocol signed by the heads of the two countries' atomic energy organizations committed them to negotiate further scientific cooperation, including the building of a gas centrifuge plant in Iran for enriching uranium.

At the USA-Russia summit in Moscow on 10 May 1995, President Yeltsin, on American urging, agreed not to supply the centrifuge plant because of its potential for creating weapons-grade fuel. Aside from this concession, the rest of the agreement remains intact and raises further concern that it will boost Iran's potential for ultimately acquiring nuclear weapons. The United States and Israel are the driving force behind the campaign to prevent Iran from acquiring the equipment and know-how to go nuclear. Both governments agreed at a joint press conference in January that at its present pace it could take Iran 7-15 years to develop nuclear weapons. That time could be shortened if Iran succeeded in obtaining fissile materials from abroad. But current agreements in place with Russia and China, it is feared, "...could bring Iran significantly closer to a nuclear weapons capability and provide a cover for secret, illegal procurement activities in supplier countries."

Despite the fact that there are serious technical and financial problems in the implementation of these agreements, and that any facilities they might provide would be subject to IAEA inspection, there is still broad concern in supplier countries sufficient to lead many of these states to join an informal agreement not to provide sensitive technology and equipment to Iran. The USA claimed in June that 23 countries had signified their adherence to this agreement. Iranian authorities have frequently voiced their support for the concept of the Middle East as a nuclear weapons-free zone, but have insisted on their right to pursue peaceful nuclear energy programs as permitted by the NPT. In the meantime Israeli spokespersons regularly assert that they will do their best to prevent Iran from reaching a nuclear option. On May 11, then Foreign Minister Shimon Peres told Israeli radio, "Iran is trying to acquire a nuclear option, but Israel has no intention of permitting it to attain this objective."

In the final analysis there may be no need for Israel to take any steps in this regard. The United States has formally added Iran to its nuclear war plan, the Single Integrated Operational Plan [SIOP]. According to a report by William M. Arkin in the July-August issue of *The Bulletin of the Atomic Scientists*, "far more effort has gone into fighting Iran than into forestalling conflict." He points out that although Iran does not have nuclear weapons at present, and may not be able to produce any in the near future, the United States Strategic Command (STRATCOM) has made that country its first "counter proliferation" target, adding sites there to what Arkin calls its "generic template for small-scale [nuclear] attack." Iran is the first priority ["in the bull's eye"] in a new emphasis on targeting the Third World. With this kind of advance preparation it appears unlikely the American military would want to hand off the initiative to, or allow itself to be pre-empted by, Israel.

A collateral concern is with Iranian interest in the acquisition of ballistic missiles, stemming from its eight-year war with Iraq [1980-88]. Iran turned to China and North Korea for aid in the transfer of missiles, or the technology to produce them. Recent Western concerns have focused on Iran's attempted acquisition of North Korea's 1,300 km range Nodong-1 missile, which would bring most of Israel within range. Despite a firm order of 150 of these missiles by Iran, and offers to collaborate in the local production and test-firing of them there, Japanese objections to the project appear to have stalled it, at least temporarily. In the meantime reports of Chinese delivery of ballistic missile components, propellant ingredients and guidance systems to Iran have further aggravated USA-China relations.

Iranian opposition to the peace process

Since its inception, the Islamic Republic has been opposed to the policy of peace negotiations between Israel and its Arab and Palestinian neighbours. This position is based on the ideological objection of Ayatollah Khomeini to the concept of a Jewish state in predominantly Muslim lands, including the Islamic holy sites in Jerusalem. It is no small irony that the example of comparatively smaller numbers of Jews successfully establishing a state in the Middle East based on the ideological premise of membership in a particular faith could have served as a source of inspiration and rationale for the creation of an Islamic Republic.

Opposition to the peace process on ideological grounds is one thing, and direct action to obstruct or sabotage the negotiations another. Official spokesmen regularly repeat the dictum that the Islamic Republic will not take any steps to derail the process, although they believe it is unfair and stacked against the Palestinians. A variant of this position is the claim that if Israel and Syria are able to negotiate an end to their differences, the Islamic Republic will be content. In his 2 July interview with CNN, President Rafsanjani put the IRI view succinctly: "We have said that our view of the peace is that the people of Palestine have been oppressed, and this is not a question of peace. This is a fire on the ashes. [But] we have not taken any practical measures in this regard."

Moral and some financial support for Hamas, Palestine Islamic Jihad and Hizbollah, which began long before the Oslo accords were conceived, are apparently not to be considered practical steps. The financial aid is allegedly given under the heading of humanitarian assistance and not for military purposes, and once given the Iranian authorities have no way of controlling how the funds are actually used. The amounts involved are speculative because of the difficulty of monitoring the transfer of funds.

The Islamic Republic is unlikely to take any further concrete measures to oppose the peace process between Israel and the PLO, but it will almost certainly continue to lend moral and some financial assistance to Islamic groups opposed to this process. However, recent reports have suggested that the IRI has in fact reduced the amount of financial support it provides Hizbollah. Iranian spokespersons regularly insist that support for Hizbollah in South Lebanon is justified because it is resisting Israeli occupation of Arab/Muslim land. When the Israeli occupation ends, so will Iran's assistance to Hizbollah.

The Iranian government will also continue to express its disapproval of increasing ties between Israel and the Muslim states, particularly in Central Asia. The Islamic Republic News Agency [IRNA] recently quoted Iran's Foreign Minister, Ali Akbar Velayati, as having told the Azerbayjani

President, Haydar Aliev, that "the Zionist régime (Israel) is a sworn enemy of the Moslem Ummah (nation)..." and therefore "...any kind of rapprochement between a Moslem state and Tel Aviv would also be harmful to regional peace and security."

The issue of IRI positions toward the peace process has been fraught for some time with the added burden of polarizing statements and attitudes from both Israeli and IRI sources. If some IRI officials believe Israel to be a "sworn enemy" of the Muslim Ummah, the feeling is reciprocated in official circles in Israel, at least as far as the IRI is concerned. Recent reports in the Israeli newspapers *Maariv* and *Yediot Aharonot*, citing military sources, allege that the Iranian secret services had recruited an Israeli citizen in Turkey to undertake the assassination of the late - Prime Minister Yitzhak Rabin, and to use other Israelis to conduct espionage at the Israeli nuclear site of Dimona. According to *Maariv*, Herzl Rad has been accused of spying for and "lending assistance to the enemy." The indictment against him includes the charge that he gathered information from Israeli military sources "in order to assist Iran in its war against Israel and with the objectives of undermining the security of the state."

In conditions of "cold war" between the two states it can be assumed that the IRI's ideological opposition to the peace process will continue unabated, even if it is not a core national security issue for Iran. No form or degree of international pressure is likely to bring any significant change in this position because the régime has invested too much of its claim to religious legitimacy and defence of Muslim interests in this one cause. It cannot retreat further now without dangerous erosion of its domestic credibility already under siege.

The Islamic Republic and terrorism

The charge of terrorism against the Islamic Republic encompasses a variety of activities: support for resistance movements in regional states seeking to overthrow their régimes (Bahrain, Egypt, Algeria); moral and perhaps logistical support for groups like Hamas and Palestine Islamic Jihad seeking to undermine the Middle East peace process or to revenge Israeli attacks on Hizbollah targets in South Lebanon; support for surrogate hostage-taking; collaboration with Sudan in the training of Islamic extremists who conduct operations on an international front; and direct responsibility for the elimination of former régime politicians and dissidents on foreign soil.

The United States has rated Iran as the principal state sponsor of international terrorism. On May 11, American intelligence officials claimed Iran was providing $100 million annually to groups like Hizbollah and Hamas. President Rafsanjani has denied categorically that Iran gives any financial aid to Hamas, claiming it gets adequate funding from Arab sources. In addition to sponsorship, Iran is also accused of engaging in terrorist activities itself, primarily under the heading of eliminating its opponents abroad. In many of the cases under this heading there is insufficient evidence to inculpate the Iranian government directly, but the suspicion is strong. On 6 December 1994 a French court convicted Ali Vakili Rad of having murdered Shapour Bakhtiar, the Shah's last Prime Minister, in Paris in 1991. He was sentenced to life in prison. A former bureau chief of the Iranian broadcasting network, Mas'ud Hendi, was also found guilty of helping Rad to enter the country and received a ten-year sentence. State prosecutors claimed that the Iranian government had ordered the killing.

A more conclusive result was obtained on 16 June 1995 when a special anti-terrorist court in Paris sentenced another six Iranians *in absentia* to life imprisonment for Bakhtiar's murder. Of these six, one was an Iranian civil servant, the first Iranian directly linked to the government of the Islamic Republic to be convicted. The régime's obsessive concern with the imagined threat of former régime representatives and dissident activists in Europe is said to have been the motive for the fatal attacks on Kazem Rajavi, Abdelrahman Boroumand, and Kurdish leaders Abdul Rahman Qassemlou and Bahman Javadi. The campaign against MEK activists is more understandable, but not acceptable by normal diplomatic standards.

The eternal, unrescindable, irrevocable and "unliftable" *Fatwa*

Ayatollah Khomeini's 1989 death warrant on Salman Rushdie for his assault on Islamic sensibilities in *The Satanic Verses* remains the chief bone of contention between the Islamic Republic and many other members of the international community. The initial reaction of most Western governments to the Ayatollah's ruling—apart from revulsion—was that it should be cancelled, rescinded, reversed. From the beginning IRI spokespersons have provided repeated explanations to the effect that the ruling was issued by Ayatollah Khomeini in his capacity as a *faqih* [religious jurist], and that therefore no one could cancel or revoke it during his lifetime or even after his demise. It had a permanent if not eternal validity.

In the case of Salman Rushdie, the late Ayatollah's ruling did not designate any specific individual, government or law enforcement authority to be responsible for its execution. It was apparently a blanket authorization, legally empowering any believer who feels strongly enough about the necessity for action to execute it. The fact that such a ruling from such a source would be considered *ultra vires* in many other legal jurisdictions around the world has not deterred many members of the current régime in Iran from endorsing its message. In an attempt to counter the effect of this ruling, on 15 March 1995 Rushdie won unanimous support from the 34-member Council of Europe, including all the parliamentary democracies, which voted to reject closer political and trade ties with Iran until Tehran "lifted" the *fatwa*.

While Rushdie welcomed this moral support, he observed that what was needed was "action, not words." The German parliament had passed a resolution in 1993 proposing that Iran be held legally responsible for any attempt on Rushdie's life. But Germany-Iran trade, including sensitive technology, continued to flourish. While some Europeans were willing to support Salman Rushdie in his "battle between freedom of speech and terrorist fanaticism," they hesitated to follow up with concrete actions in support of principle, if this meant sacrificing profitable trade. This would mean taking on their own industrial and business communities. Norway, however, is one country that has so far had the courage of its convictions. In July, Oslo downgraded diplomatic relations with Iran, declined opportunities to expand trade, and opposed Iran's bid to join the Asian Development Bank.

Sooner or later, most likely the former, some zealot who feels the burden of this ruling will find the opportunity and seek to execute it. As Rushdie himself speaks out more frequently, and increasingly emerges from seclusion to draw attention to his plight and campaign for international pressure on Iran, he becomes more clearly at risk. If an assassin finally succeeds in reaching Salman Rushdie, foreign governments will then have to decide, if they haven't done so already, to what extent IRI authorities should be held responsible, and what their future dealings with the Iranian régime should be.

Although régime officials insist that Ayatollah Khomeini issued the ruling in his private capacity as a *faqih*, it can scarcely be denied that he was at the same time also head of state and founder of the new system that is still in place. His successor has frequently stated publicly that the *fatwa* is still valid and will be carried out, that Rushdie should be shown no mercy and deserves to die. The clerical head of one of Iran's semi-public foundations continues to renew the reward offered to any Muslim who fulfils the ruling's intent. With this kind of encouragement, what officials say and do to try to appease Western reaction is likely to have little effect.

At the time of the diplomatic negotiations on this issue earlier this year, the radical Tehran daily *Kayhan* gave its view: "We don't know what is happening in our embassies in Europe....But we do know for a fact that Rushdie and his accomplices will not escape death....The Europeans must realize that it will not be our diplomats who chop off Rushdie's head but our *mujahideen* and revolutionaries." If this happens, it would then become moot whether other governments were willing to curtail further commercial and financial exchange with Iran, and perhaps even suspend diplomatic relations.

The Rushdie imbroglio represents a clash of cultural values central to the Western and Islamic social systems. Freedom of expression is an individual right protected by the existing legal system and ardently defended by civil libertarians in most parts of the Western world. In the corresponding Islamic structure social value inheres in the safety and security of the group, the Islamic Ummah as a whole. Anything which menaces this security, or the sensibility on which it is structured, including the honour and integrity of the Prophet Muhammad, is a threat that must be removed. The rights of the group to feel secure and free from ridicule, harassment, incitement or ethnic and religious hatred outweigh the individual's right to say or write whatever he or she may think or feel.

On 30 October 1995, speaking on the occasion of an official visit to Austria, the speaker of the Iranian parliament, Ali Akbar Nateq-Nouri, declared that Iran would not send assassins to carry out the death warrant against Rushdie but declined to put the pledge in writing because "we want to protect our dignity and honour." On the same day, in response to a question in the commons, the British government, through a Foreign Office spokesman, declared that the government of Iran had not yet given "satisfactory assurances" of Mr. Rushdie's safety, and urged it to do so.

It is apparent that both Iranian and European officials want to find a resolution to the issue. In the absence of a more formal understanding, it lingers on and haunts both sides; both would like to see it go away, just disappear, but know full well it will not. Meanwhile the world watches and waits, like a helpless bystander anticipating a shoot-out at the "clash of civilizations" corral, a mechanical duel of competing value systems. It is an urgent necessity that some form of change to the original script of this drama be introduced.

The G-7 (plus Russia) Summit

The most positive sign to date of an emerging consensus on Iran and what to do about its anti-social behaviour was the G-7 meeting in Halifax in June 1995. In a closing statement the participants declared their intention not to help Iran acquire nuclear weapons and called on Tehran to reject "terrorism." "We call on all states to avoid any collaboration with Iran which might contribute to the acquisition of a nuclear weapons capability. We call upon the government of Iran to participate constructively in regional and world affairs, and to desist from supporting radical groups that seek to destroy the Middle East Peace Process and destabilize the region. We call upon all States that assist terrorists to renounce terrorism and to deny financial support, the use of their territory or any other means of support to terrorist organizations," the statement said.

On the surface this summit would seem to be an endorsement of at least some of the objectives of the Dual Containment Policy. The communiqué took aim at four of the usual five points of objection to IRI behaviour. According to one account, deputy National Security Adviser Samuel Berger told reporters afterwards: "We have obtained the strongest language that the leaders have ever used with respect to condemning the behaviour, the conduct, the pattern of action of the Iranian government—its support for terrorism (and) its subversion of the peace process." In order to counter the threat of terrorism, the summit leaders commissioned an experts group to investigate and report back to them before the next meeting of the industrial countries in Lyon, France in 1996.

Since the G-7 Summit in June an informal coalition

of 28 states has emerged from a meeting at the Hague with the common purpose of not selling weapons or high technology goods to Iran and three other "pariah" states: Iraq, Libya and North Korea. This new posse, which goes under the label of The New Forum, and replaces a cold war body, the Co-ordinating Committee on Multilateral Export Controls, aimed at the former Soviet bloc, includes all the members of NATO, all of West Europe's neutrals, Russia and four other members of the old Soviet bloc, and three states from South Asia. The fact that 28 countries were willing to label Iran publicly as a pariah suggests that doubts about the régime's intentions and attempts to isolate it further are taking increasing effect. But enforcement in The New Forum is voluntary, at the discretion of the members. To have more teeth this coalition will need many more member states and a rigorous enforcement mechanism.

A systems threat?

A source of concern for many observers of Iran's role in the international arena is the alleged threat it represents as a competitor and ideological alternative to the prevailing world system. In this frame of reference Iran is thought to be one of the few régimes since the collapse of the former Soviet Union that has the ideological resources to challenge the Western approach to the world, characterized by our own brands of capitalism, human rights and democracy. In a world beset by seemingly insoluble problems which render even the near future doubtful and uncertain, there is a substantial appeal for some in a comprehensive Islamic fundamentalist approach to life where authority is concentrated and where no division of powers exists between the sacred and the secular realms, and a divine text is thought to contain the solutions to all those problems.

A short answer to this concern is that the challenge to the dominant political, economic and social values in the current world system, from exclusivist ideologies that ban pluralism and promote moral absolutism, should not be ignored, but needs to be weighted and discounted in practical terms. Systems that handle the problem of diversity, doubt and uncertainty by totalitarian fiat and the authority of terrorist violence may be comforting to some but are broadly repudiated by majorities in most nation states. The essential problem in the meantime is how to regulate and control the competition between rival ideologies and value systems to reduce friction between states and ultimately enable majority populations to make their own free choice as to which system they prefer. At the present stage of developments in the evolution of the world system, that choice is not likely to be offered soon in many parts of the world.

Outlook

With increased pressure from Israeli officials and the domestic AIPAC lobby, and stepped-up competition from a combative Republican-controlled Congress, the United States government has recently found encouragement and reinforcement for its own intuitive judgement about Iran and elevated that country to the status of the world's number-one villain. But is the intention of America's punitive actions still seriously to change the behaviour of the régime in Tehran, or has the aim itself changed and the intention is now to unseat that régime?

Whichever the ultimate aim, the policy makers have no doubt accepted the need for patience. Unilateral or even multilateral trade and investment sanctions have little chance of bringing about a change of behaviour in the near term.

Without pressure on the allies to fall in line and join the sanctions effort, which would only create other kinds of problems, the American embargo on Iran will not bring the desired results any time soon. The history of sanctions as a foreign policy tool is not encouraging, especially for those who crave quick results. The posse approach to international relations may serve useful purposes when dealing with a clear-cut international outlaw like Saddam Hussein. As coalitions of the willing and able, posses certainly need a strong sheriff to be effective. But posses were successfully enrolled in the old west only in the absence of adequate police powers and only when there was no doubt that a capital crime had been committed.

The history of Iran also demonstrates that pressures applied from without only serve to unite the population behind their government. That government's posture on the issues in question will then most likely become more severe. If President Rafsanjani's "economic adjustment" policy is not already dead, this approach will give it the *coup de grace*. As the President's final term of office winds down, and the country prepares to elect a new political head of government in 1997, the impact of continuing economic and diplomatic pressure from the United States and others will play into the hands of régime conservatives, who will almost certainly be inclined to steer Iran, under a new government, toward a more ideological, hardline foreign policy.

Alternatively, if the real aim of the DCP is to bring down the régime, the prospects are even less promising and fraught with dangerous possibilities. During 16 years of Islamic revolution the authorities have succeeded in excluding or eliminating all other organized secular and civilian-led alternatives. At the same time the forces of civil society have been at work building buffers that attenuate the most irritating frictions between the population and the government. Despite its fanciful claims, the People's Mujahideen of Iran do not represent a viable alternative primarily because they are thoroughly discredited both inside and outside Iran for their alliance with Baghdad. The Council for the Preparation of a Transition Government in Iran, formed in Germany in 1992 and headed by Hassan Nazih, may have more credibility among opposition Iranians at home and abroad, but it lacks the practical mechanism needed for accession to power. The military is the only potentially independent alternative center of power to the revolutionary clerical régime.

There will no doubt continue to be popular discontent with some régime policies and their consequences, especially economic. The régime clergy still face substantial opposition from the traditional clerical establishment in Qom and other religious centers, but not as rivals for the reins of political power. The unresolved contradictions of the Islamic republican system and its consequent policy paralysis mean that the Islamic Republic is facing an existential crisis. In this sense the régime is its own worst enemy because it cannot make good on its promises of a better life for the mass of Iranians, nor provide the leadership it claims, especially the material and monetary support, for the Islamist international. Some senior military officers have voiced discontent with and criticism of the régime's performance, but to date there is no clear evidence that the military is preparing to withdraw its support or is poised to challenge the authorities for the prize of supreme power. In these circumstances it will be difficult for the DCP to achieve its aims in the near future.

APPENDIX F

The following material is reprinted with permission of the Canadian Security Intelligence Service and its author, Dr. William Millward. Inclusion of this material in this book does not imply CSIS authentication of the information in these excerpts nor in this book and does not imply CSIS endorsement of the authors' views. See Appendix E for an explanation of these materials

COMMENTARY No. 39
a CANADIAN SECURITY INTELLIGENCE SERVICE publication

LEADERSHIP IN THE ISLAMIC REPUBLIC AND THE HIERARCHY OF SHI'A ISLAM
January 1994 Unclassified
[CSIS] Editors Note:

Since the author first dealt with the leadership structures in Iran, a number of forces, and a number of deaths among the senior ranks, prompt a closer look at the hierarchy of power in Iran. The departure of the old guard raises central questions not only of succession, but of who decides.

All political systems are subject to a degree of internal tension and stress. At one end of the political spectrum the level of tension under individual or single-party dictatorships is relatively high and dissent is minimal or non-existent. At the other end the competition between parties and factions generates a lower level of stress intermittently at general elections or during debate on contentious legislative initiatives. In most democratic systems the principle of opposing or alternative viewpoints on public policy is built into constitutions or mandated by custom and tradition. Whatever the system, leadership plays an important role in defusing tension and promoting the efficient operation of the governing mechanism. Traditions of leadership in Iran, both in government and in the clerical institution, have recently sustained pressures and changes imposed by the exigencies of practical power, and a number of key deaths in the senior clerical ranks.

In the political history of Iran, the secular rulers of various dynasties have been especially intolerant of dissenting opinion, even from trusted lieutenants or first ministers, as challenges to their absolute authority and sovereignty. Ideally political leadership came from the individual who could concentrate a maximum of power and authority in a single persona. The imperial political tradition of past millenniums had established the principle of the monopolization of power in the person of the shah as the ideal of leadership. Division of the imperial ruler's authority into rival centres of power could only be sanctioned by an elaborate system of investiture and swearing allegiance to the shah of shahs. Any alternative would leave the polity vulnerable to attack from within and threaten its survival.

Authority and Leadership in Twelver Shi'ism

In the religious sphere, the ideal of leadership, as it evolved among the learned men [*ulama*] of Shi'a Islam in Iran and Iraq from the middle of the eighteenth century, was embodied in the most learned practitioners of the sacred law [*shari'a*] and its ancillary sciences. Recognition in this domain was only obtained after long years of study, teaching and writing in one or another of the seminaries in the principal shrine centres of the Shi'a world. A rough hierarchy of rank gradually emerged among the more learned of the jurisprudents and their students, culminating in the office of "source of emulation" [*marja' al-taqlid*]. Having succeeded as students, mullahs would then, depending on talent and intellectual capacities, pass through the ranks of Hojjatoleslam, Ayatollah, and eventually, a few would attain the rank of Grand Ayatollah [*ayatollah al-'ozma*]. Only the leading and older ayatollahs, and grand ayatollahs, would normally achieve the status of "marja." This would depend on their producing a canon law guide [*risala 'amaliyya*] in their own name, and building up a reputation for learning and piety reflected in a body of published scholarship, and a large number of students and personal followers [*muqallidun*] who would take their guidance from the "source" and pay their religious dues to him or his representative.

Because the centres of religious training and scholarly activity were normally associated with the Shi'a shrine centres, of which there were several, leadership in the clerical hierarchy was normally diffuse and pluralist. Occasionally, within the community of Shi'a Islam in Iran and Iraq, during the nineteenth and twentieth centuries, one or another of the great scholars and jurists among these "sources" would win recognition and gradually 'emerge' as pre-eminent, the *primus inter pares* of the Shi'a religious hierarchy. But this individual's authority could not be considered exclusive or monopolistic, as with his counterpart in the secular sphere, or with a Pope. The life-blood of the system has been the freedom of the practising Shi'i Muslim to choose which of the accessible "sources" he or she prefers as a guide for religiously correct behaviour.

Theocracy Replaces Monarchy - The Turban for the Crown

An alleged theocratic system of government was put in place in the Islamic Republic of Iran in 1979 to accommodate the charisma and prestige of its founder, Grand Ayatollah Ruhollah Khomeini, a leading figure in the hierarchy of the Shi'ite Muslim clergy [*rowhaniyat*]. The Shi'a clergy in Iran had functioned in effect as a separate and independent social institution with its own structure of authority, its own resources and revenues and its own influence with the public. To the ayatollah's standing as a prominent member of this institution there was suddenly added the authority normally associated with the political system of royal government under the shah.

The new political structure of the Islamic Republic had to provide for the concentration of the combined power and authority of these two institutions. The results of this combination were embodied in an Islamic constitution ratified on December 3, 1979, in which the dominant and final authority of the new system was enshrined in the office of Spiritual Leader or Vali Faqih, according to the principle of "the governance/trusteeship of the jurisprudent" [*velayat-e faqih*]. (See articles 107-112).

Under this new system and its constitution, the day to day business of government and the administration of public affairs were carried out by the ayatollah's followers, many of them members of the clergy themselves, but of much lower rank than the Spiritual Leader. The most trusted among the ayatollah's followers were those who had supported him during his long campaign of opposition to the Shah's government from 1962 onwards, especially those who had spent time in prison for their opposition stance. During the first decade of the Islamic Republic, the internal competition and rivalry in the new system was expressed sometimes through ideological factions, and sometimes through key personalities. The radical, left-leaning clergymen and their lay supporters in government in the mid-80s favoured policies which promoted self-reliance and government control over foreign trade, and prevented the concentration of capital or land holding in private hands. Their champions were figures like the former deputy-Speaker of the Majlis, Mehdi Karubi, the former Solicitor-General, Muhammad Khoeniha, and the former Prime Minister, Mir Hussein Mousavi.

In the opposite camp were those clergy and their lay counterparts, the so-called moderates, who endorsed a limited degree of foreign borrowing and investment, less state control over foreign trade, more active distribution and return of property to private ownership, and a more constructive approach to regional co-operation and foreign relations. The individual who gradually emerged as the leader of this faction was the then speaker of the Majlis, Hojjatoleslam Ali Akbar Hashemi-Rafsanjani. Whenever a legislative or administrative impasse arose between these factions, the issue would be referred to the ayatollah for final decision. While he lived the record shows he exercised a marvellous penchant for impartiality, sometimes favouring one side, sometimes the other.

When the founder of the Islamic Republic and its political system died in June 1989, changes were called for to adapt the workings of the system to new realities. He was succeeded at the top of the Islamic power structure by Ali Khamneh'i, a relatively low-level clergyman, but one of his trusted lieutenants who had by then gained a good deal of political experience as the incumbent of the largely ceremonial office of President, as well as a few scars from injuries received in an assassination attempt. The fact that he did not possess all the qualifications specified by the constitution for the top job meant that amendments were needed, and these were duly effected in the summer of 1989. It was no longer necessary for the Spiritual Leader to be a *marja'*; from now on it would be enough that he hold the highest degree of certification in canon law studies [*ijtihad*], have a reputation for piety, and political experience. [*The Constitution of the Islamic Republic of Iran,* (2nd edition - with amendments), Tehran 1410/1990. Art.109].

These same changes also abolished the office of Prime Minister and gave additional powers and authority to the new office of the Presidency. The first incumbent of this new power pole was the former Majlis speaker Ali Akbar Hashemi-Rafsanjani. From 11 June 1993 he embarked on his second, and final, term as President and chief of the Executive Branch of the Islamic Republic. Some observers of the mechanics of power distribution in the Islamic Republican system are inclined to view its internal tensions as a reflex of inherent structural contradictions rather than a manifestation of the normal interplay of competition and rivalry between personalities and programs. The effective blockage of several cabinet appointments or the forced resignation of a minister by the radicals in the Third Majlis were impediments to the practical application of powers prescribed by the constitution as those of the President. Their objections to some of his policy and legislative initiatives proved to be less serious obstacles.

In the aftermath of the elections to the Fourth Majlis, some commentators were predicting a new confrontation between the conservative and nationalist forces aligned with the Spiritual Leader, Ali Khamneh'i, and his allies in the Majlis and the Council of Guardians, and those aligned with the President, Ali Akbar Hashemi-Rafsanjani, and his technocratic ministers and advisers who are hoping to push forward with a broad program of economic reconstruction and liberalisation. Such conflicts are fuelled as much by differing visions of the programs and policies needed to enable the governing system to deliver on its promises of economic progress as from structural contradictions inherent in the system.

Clergy-State Relations in the Islamic Republic

Before the Islamic revolution clerical attitudes toward the state could be characterized under three headings:

1. Full membership in the state apparatus, and dependent on it for their livelihood. Such clergy were normally regarded by their peers with suspicion, and were frequently referred to by a variety of derogatory names, e.g., "court clergy" or "the sultan's preachers."

2. Indifference and aloofness, the position taken by the vast majority of the Shi'a clergy, especially the Grand Ayatollahs.

3. Open opposition from those who struggled against the state as the source of corruption and oppression. These were the group around Ayatollah Khomeini, who are now in power.

When a comparatively small group of younger and middle-level clergymen, supporters of Grand Ayatollah Khomaini, succeeded in capturing the apparatus of the state in the aftermath of the 1978-79 revolution, the relationship between them and their clerical colleagues in the shrine centres and seminaries was transformed. The change began slowly. The hierocracy now running the government was suddenly preoccupied with a brand new set of problems for which they had had precious little preparation. Fending off a variety of rival claims to a share in power, while drafting an Islamic constitution, totally preoccupied the younger clergy around the ayatollah.

But nothing succeeds like success, even in religious circles. While some junior clerics may have adopted a wait-and-see attitude toward the theocratic experiment that Imam Khomaini and his followers had set in motion, others enthusiastically embraced the enterprise, for their own reasons, including the opportunity it afforded for more rapid advancement and a new avenue of activity outside the austere and competitive environment of the seminaries of Qom, Mashhad and Isfahan. Many of those who came over to the new system were of younger years and more junior rank. Others carried on in their old ways and habits as if nothing had changed. A few more senior people without much success behind them in traditional terms were persuaded to join the regime and take positions in various ministries or the new structures of the revolution, such as the Council of Guardians.

A large number of traditional clergy of all ranks and stages remained at their stations following the revolution and carried on with their studies, or their teaching and other routine clerical functions. Their ranks were soon swollen by a deluge of new applicants seeking to join the seminaries and pursue religious studies. Official estimates suggest there are nearly 25,000 full-time students today in the various Qom seminaries alone. [*Kayhan Havai*, March 4, 1992. p. 15]. Such numbers require a substantial administrative structure to manage their affairs and a sizeable teaching cadre to meet their instructional needs. Judging from a critique of the old ways and methods still being used in the seminary system, made by the Spiritual Leader himself on a visit to the Faiziyeh school in Qom on February 20, 1992, there is still substantial resistance to change in the traditional seminary system, and that student problems resulting from excess demand might be preventing that system from fulfilling its basic tasks.

The Leadership Role

The uneasy and somewhat ambivalent relationship between the clerical and governmental institutions in the early years of the Islamic Republic was at least in part a function of Grand Ayatollah Khomaini's leadership. He treated his peers among the grand ayatollahs with diffidence and contempt at best, and intimidated or placed them under house arrest at worst. Grand Ayatollah Kazem Shari'atmadari, the acknowledged spiritual leader of the Azeri Shi'a Muslims in Iran, was confined to his home in Qom in 1979 when it was feared he might become an alternative pole of political power through his Islamic People's Republican Party. The party was dissolved and twelve of his Tabriz supporters were executed. Two years later, in what was called an "unprecedented move", he was stripped of the rank of *marja'-e taqlid* after accusations that he plotted to overthrow the government. "The clerical populists [around Khomaini] had done what no shah had ever dared to do." [Ervand

Abrahamian, *Radical Islam: The Iranian Mojahedin*, London: I.B. Tauris 1989. p. 58].

For Imam Khomaini, the founder of the new system, the clerical institution was a secondary concern, to be controlled by firm action when necessary, but otherwise ignored for the more pressing business of building an Islamic political system. It may have been the ayatollah's ultimate intention to merge these two social structures into one comprehensive system of political and social control. While he lived, all his attention and energy—and those of his acolytes—were devoted to the immediate tasks of consolidating control of the political domain, and fighting off foreign invaders like Saddam Hussein. Perhaps because he sensed the time was not ripe, he may have preferred the strategy of leaving to his successors the problem of merging the two structures and thereby creating a more perfect theocracy.

The Succession Issue

The starting point for at least some of the tension and friction in Iran between the secular realm and religion [*dunya* and *din*] under the Islamic Republic, between the state and the clerical institution [*dowlat* and *marja'iyat*], has been the question of the succession. Many observers conclude that a key series of events surrounded the person of Husain Ali Montazeri, chosen as heir-apparent to Ayatollah Khomaini by the Imam himself in 1982 and confirmed in that role by the Assembly of Experts in 1985. He served in this capacity for four years, but, by all accounts, very reluctantly. He was removed unceremoniously from his role as heir-presumptive in March of 1989, by order of the ayatollah himself, perhaps under the influence of a campaign led by his son, Ahmad.

Ayatollah Montazeri's case is instructive in several respects. When he was chosen as Khomaini's successor in 1985, he insisted in a radio broadcast that one of the reasons he was reluctant to be considered for the role was "the presence of the great sources," by which he meant the other senior Grand Ayatollahs then present in Qom, most of whom, as contemporaries of Khomaini, were his teachers and much more learned than he. [*FBIS*, Daily Report-South Asia, December 18, 1985]. Nevertheless he himself was elevated to the status of Grand Ayatollah on his confirmation as Leader-designate, chiefly by the regime and its supporters. It is doubtful he was so considered by the opinion-makers in the ranks of the independent clerical establishment.

The chief reason why he would not have been accepted as a Grand Ayatollah by traditional standards at that time was the fact that he had spent so many years in prison, or in internal exile, where it was difficult if not impossible for him to read, think and write, and eventually publish his reflections as a contribution to the store of religious learning, especially in the fields of jurisprudence [*fiqh*] and its principles [*usul*]. And this isolation prevented him from normal teaching activity, another important way in which a senior cleric's knowledge and learning are demonstrated, and prestige acquired. More recently, since retiring to Qom in the early years of the new regime, he has been devoting himself to the normal pattern of activity by remaining there, teaching his classes and tending to the spiritual and practical needs of his many followers. He is also writing and publishing his researches, and depending on how these are received, it seems probable he will soon reach the status of Grand Ayatollah, if he is not so regarded already.

The main question attaching to Ayatollah Montazeri's future is whether he will ever allow himself to be enticed back into political life. It seems unlikely, considering how many of his relatives and supporters have been killed or otherwise damaged by association with him while he was an important player in the political arena. By criticizing the performance of many government officials while heir-apparent, he made opponents and enemies, some of whom are still in government and may be hoping to settle old scores. But his role as a spiritual guide and his potential as a political consultant are frequently confused by his adversaries. When ten Majlismen, including the head of the Majlis budget committee, Morteza Alviri, visited him in Qom in late 1991 in his capacity as a "source," it brought charges of political collusion and threats to the state. Only the timely intervention of the Spiritual Leader, Ali Khamneh'i, prevented Alviri's prosecution by the Special Court of the Clergy.

Supporters of the original concept of the unity of political and religious leadership [*rahbari* and *marja'iyat*] in a single person seized the occasion of the visit to Montazeri as an opportunity to voice their concern that the constitutional review committee had separated these two functions without due consideration for the effect this would have of weakening the Leader in a state which claimed to be both a political and a moral-religious enterprise [*Kayhan Havai*, February 5, 1992. pp. 15-17]. The answer to these concerns was that separating the two positions was in the best interest of both and in any event the state was paramount. The prerogatives of the Islamic ruler [*hakim*], whether he be a *marja'* like Ayatollah Khomaini or not, are unlimited, in keeping with the principle of 'absolute jurisdiction' [*velayat-e motlaqeh*],

and take precedence over the rulings [*fatwas*] of any *Marja'*
or *Mujtahid.*

In purely political terms Ayatollah Montazeri
represents a dilemma for the regime, a thorn in their side
which cannot be extracted or excised. He continues to criticize
the major players for policies and actions he believes
detrimental to the revolution and harmful to the interests of
Islam in general. The government responds by inciting its
supporters to attack his home and teaching centre, occasioning
damage and injury. This provokes a chorus of opposition
from highly regarded sources, such as Grand Ayatollahs Araki
and Golpaygani, and even staunch radical regime supporters,
like Ayatollahs Sane'i and Taheri, condemning the
government's response. Ayatollah Montazeri's continuing
criticisms of regime failures are in line with the time-honoured
tradition of clerical intervention in public affairs when the
interests of Islam and the Muslims are thought to be at risk.
It has led some to conclude that he intends ultimately to return
to the political arena as the champion of true Islam and its
authentic revolutionary program to challenge the pretenders
and deviationists. [Jalal Ganjeh'i, *Showra* (France), 2:6,
March 1993. pp. 51-2]. It may well be that the authorities
would not be able to prevent his return to a political role, but
they could certainly make his life difficult, and in any case,
for personal reasons, the odds are against it.

The Departure of the Old Guard

The leadership debate in Shi'a religious and political
circles in Iran and Iraq was heightened by the death on 8
August 1992 of Grand Ayatollah Abu al-Qasim al-Khu'i in
Kufah in Iraq at the age of 93. A native of the northwestern
Iranian city of Khoy, the ayatollah migrated to Najaf in Iraq

at the age of 13 to pursue his studies in that city's illustrious Islamic seminary. In the intervening 75 years he built himself a reputation as one of Shi'a Islam's great 'sources of emulation' and an outstanding scholarly personality. He is said to have had personal followers around the world. He supervised post-graduate studies in jurisprudence and its principles and groomed students to attain the level of *ijtihad/ Mujtahid* over half a century. Many prominent figures in the Shi'a communities of Iran, Iraq, Pakistan, India, Lebanon, Syria, Bahrain, Kuwait, Saudi Arabia and other Persian Gulf states were among his students.

Apart from his scholarly attainments (he was one of the first religious teachers to record his jurisprudence lectures on audio tape), he set up a worldwide charitable foundation [The Kho'i Foundation] with the object of catering for the needs of the followers of the Ja'fari [Ithna'ashari] school of Islamic thought worldwide. The foundation is headquartered in London and has branches in India, Pakistan, Thailand, Canada and Kuwait. He took the lead in establishing a seminary [*Madinat al-Ulum* - City of Knowledge] in Qom and Mashhad after the Islamic revolution. The foundation supports orphanages, schools, publishing houses, libraries and other social service institutions on a global scale. Among the great sources of emulation of his, and Ayatollah Khomaini's generation, his influence in the spiritual and social spheres, has reached further afield, without the dubious advantage of political involvement.

The key point about Grand Ayatollah Khu'i in the leadership debate was the fact that he never endorsed the principle of the "governance of the jurisprudent" [*velayat-e faqih*]. In his view the clergy did not hold the right to monopolize the governmental apparatus, only to participate in the process. With the death of this religious luminary, the ranks of the top leadership [Grand Ayatollahs] in the world of Shi'a Islam were thinning. Amongst the rough contemporaries of Grand Ayatollah Khu'i, only a handful survive, mostly in Iran. To make matters worse, a prominently mentioned figure amongst the real or potential successors to Khu'i, Abdul A'la Sabzevari, died in Najaf at the age of 86 in August 1993.

The Shift of Power to Iran

When religion and state power were officially joined in Iran in 1979, the center of gravity of Shi'a Islam shifted to that country, away from its traditional sources in the shrine centres of Najaf, Karbala and Kazimayn in Iraq. Because of its larger population base, and its relative economic well-being, there was a sense in which Iran would have assumed even greater weight in Shi'a Islamic affairs even without the revolution. Added to these factors was the fact that the Iraqi government of Saddam Hussein had made it a matter of policy to suppress the role and independent voice of the Shi'a spokesmen in Iraq as representatives of the believing masses. The regime targeted key individuals in the religious hierarchy for execution, prestigious figures like Grand Ayatollah Muhammad Baqir al-Sadr, and members of his family. It is doubtless only the regime's preoccupation with its international political and financial predicament that deters greater attention being given to the repression of the Shi'a establishment. But these concerns have not prevented forceful action against resistance movements among the Shi'a population of southern Iraq since the end of the second Gulf war.

Following the demise of Grand Ayatollah Khu'i a gradual consensus emerged, both in Iran and Iraq, that the clearly pre-eminent *marja'* of the day in the world of Shi'a Islam was Grand Ayatollah Mohammad Reza Golpaygani of Qom, at the time 96 years of age and said to be even then in frail health. His position was strengthened by the official recognition afforded him by the Kho'i Foundation in London. There was little opposition to the recognition of his pre-eminent status from regime clerics. He was one of the founder members of the seminary system in Qom seven decades earlier and contributed significantly to its prestige as the main center of clerical knowledge and training in Iran.

Over the years he built a substantial establishment of his own, including an impressive library, teaching center and social services network, and earned the respect of all those associated with the *howzeh* in its traditional form. Ali Khamneh'i paid tribute to him and his accomplishments on the occasion of his visit to Faiziyeh in February 1992. Although cautious by nature, and highly conservative in most of his rulings relating to social concerns, he was thought to be essentially apolitical because he never publicly accepted or rejected the principle of *velayat-e faqih* in the sense it was given by Ayatollah Khomaini and his followers. A dissenting view is that he in fact compromised himself by flirting with the regime and even for a time contemplated becoming the Imam's successor to preserve religious and political leadership in a single individual. This may have reduced his credibility as a guardian of traditional standards with some influential ulama.

On 6 December 1993 Grand Ayatollah Golpaygani was rushed to hospital in Tehran in critical condition, and died there three days later. His demise reopens the question of leadership in the ranks of the clerical establishment and highlights the issue of who are the main contenders for this leadership in his absence. In the Islamic Republic by definition this whole matter assumes crucial political importance. It is scarcely a secret that some staunch regime supporters, such as Ayatollah Mohammad Yazdi, chief of the judicial branch, would like to see the Spiritual Leader, Ali Khamneh'i, made a Grand Ayatollah and acknowledged as *marja'*. Many others, among them ardent supporters of the revolution, do not accept Ali Khamneh'i as a senior spiritual leader and draw a sharp distinction between his religious and political status. He can be head of state, but not of the clerical hierarchy.

The dilemma for the regime is that if they allow prominent or pre-eminent *marja*'s to be recognized by a process they do not control, and without their approval, such figures could conceivably challenge a political system based on religious legitimacy, and are therefore a potential threat. Such is the case with the widely acknowledged Grand Ayatollah Hasan Tabatabai Qomi, 85, who has continued to oppose the principle of clerical control of government, and criticized its policies on a wide front. As a consequence his movements and activities have been severely limited by government interference. He and other representatives of the traditional clerical establishment fear that if the political authorities are able to determine who among the senior clergy will emerge as *marja'*, then the religious hierarchy becomes subordinate to the state, and would in time be associated with discredited or failed policies. This could lead to popular rejection of the faith identified with such policies, and would represent "a threat to historical Shi'ism." [*Iran Times* (International), December 24, 1993].

Outlook

As long as Saddam Hussein survives as head of state in Iraq, the Shi'a Muslims of that country, leadership and populace, will have to live out their days under virtual siege. The central questions regarding the future of the relationship between the institutions of state and religion in the domains of Shi'a Islam pertain primarily to Iran. Who are the main contenders for the highest office in the traditional hierarchy— the *marja'iyate*—after the passing of Grand Ayatollah Golpaygani, and what will their attitudes be toward the state on the one hand, and the independent institution of the religious orders? Will they accept the politicization of the *marja'iyate*, or will they insist on the continuing role of the 'religious' or 'spiritual' *marja'*, and especially the independent existence of the clerical institution [*rowhaniyat*] and its hierarchy? Will there be one individual who emerges as pre-eminent among them, or will there be several prominent *marja*'s concurrently?

Answers to these questions can only be speculative. The one person who has more actual power to determine them is the Spiritual Leader, Ali Khamneh'i. Despite the concentration of authority in Iran, it seems likely that Najaf and its traditional weight in Shi'a circles will remain a sentimental favourite throughout the world wherever Shi'a Muslims live. It also seems certain that the traditional 'spiritual' *marja'iyate* will be preserved among the students of Grand Ayatollah Khu'i, whether in Iran or Iraq. In Najaf Shaykh Ali Sistani, age 62, is said to be assuming many of the functions and responsibilities of his mentor and gaining the allegiance of many of his followers. He may eventually assume the full mantle of his predecessor, but observers expect the rivalry with other students of the master, who are also contenders, to intensify now that Grand Ayatollah Golpaygani has passed away. [*al-Wasat*, No. 81, 16/8/93, pp. 16-18.].

Among the contenders for the succession to the leadership role of the traditional clerical institution after the passing of the old guard are several prominent *marja*'s currently residing in Iran. A front-runner in the Qom Circle for Religious Studies [*howzeh*] is Mohammad Sadeq Rowhani, with many students and many more personal communicants, and broad support in the traditional commercial sector of the bazaar. Although popular, he suffers from a degree of isolation because he is known to oppose the prevailing situation in Iran (clerical control of the state) and is prevented from leading Friday prayers. Other names frequently mentioned are Husain Vahid Khorasani, whose lectures in Qom draw record crowds, and Javad Tabrizi. In Mashhad the most popular lectures are those of Ali Falsafi.

In theory the power of decision and choice of who will head the clerical institution among Shi'a Muslims is with the mass of believers. By choosing to follow the guidance of one *marja*' rather than another, and by paying their tithes to him or his representative, they show their preference. In practice the power of the state in Iran may be used to pre-empt this freedom to choose. Much depends on what plans the current Leader has for the future of the independent clerical institution. In his address to the assembled dignitaries in Faiziyeh in February 1992, the Leader made it clear he believes the old system in Qom is doomed. The curriculum, he said, needed revision to include more modern subjects; he advocated the "seminar" method of teaching to supplement or replace the traditional lecture; he urged greater use of computers, both for record keeping, and the editing of traditional texts; he chided the audience for not giving more emphasis and practical attention to the urgent business of mission work; he also criticized the standard practice of individual scholarly activity and urged more collective enterprises; he derided the fact that with all the students and stipends paid out in Qom, there was still no Arabic language journal produced there devoted to the problems of Islamic jurisprudence.

In October 1992, following his earlier visit to the Qom Religious Studies Circle in February, the Spiritual Leader, Ali Khamneh'i, is said to have addressed a letter to its teachers and dignitaries calling for wide-scale reforms and warning of the danger of voices urging that a certain distance between the Circle and the Islamic government be maintained. [*Le Monde Diplomatique*, juin 1993. p. 20]. In March 1993 the secretary of the High Council of the Qom Circle, Ayatollah Naser Makarem Shirazi, reported to the Spiritual Leader on the plans and decisions of the Council to give effect to the reform recommendations he had made the year before. [*FBIS*, NES-5 March 1993, p. 63]. These moves have given rise to widespread apprehension that what the Leader has in mind is the ultimate nationalisation of the Religious Studies Circles in Iran, which would transform them into the Shi'a counterparts of the state-controlled religious universities and seminaries in Sunni countries, such as al-Azhar in Egypt. As a reward for his efforts in this enterprise, it is probable that Ayatollah Makarem Shirazi has earned substantial credit for promotion to the rank of Grand Ayatollah.

In the few weeks since the demise of Grand Ayatollah Golpaygani the regime in Tehran has moved vigorously to take control of the succession and ensure the recognition of its own candidate, Grand Ayatollah Mohammad Ali Araki. It appears determined that the choice of the next ranking, or pre-eminent, *marja'* of Iran's Shi'a population should not be the result of the normal process but of a political imperative. What the constitutional review committee put asunder on the death of Ayatollah Khomaini, i.e. the political and religious leaderships, the current authorities now seem anxious to join together again. The reason may well be the perception that without the unity of these two spheres of authority in the hands of a single person they cannot provide effective leadership.

Opposition to Araki is reportedly widespread and vigorous, especially in traditional, pious circles, among other reasons because he has never bothered to issue a canon law guide nor distinguished himself as a teacher. [*Iran Times* (International), 24 December 1993. p. 16]. But he is sympathetic to regime interests, and at or near the century mark in age, is likely to be a transitional figure at best. Some observers see him as a stalking horse to give the regime a little more time to prepare the ground for the eventual appointment of the Spiritual Leader himself as "pre-eminent *marja'*" [*marja'-e a'la*]. This move would restore the unity of political and religious leadership [*rahbari* and *marja'iyat*] in the Islamic Republic. But it would be a risky venture for two reasons: Ali Khamneh'i is not a real *marja'* according to traditional standards, and he lacks the political charisma of his predecessor.

Reports circulated in the London Arabic daily *Ash-Sharq al-Awsat* claim that a letter signed by 76 prominent religious figures who supervise religious training centres in more than twelve Iranian towns and cities, including Tehran, Qom and Mashhad, has been sent to Ali Khamneh'i opposing Ayatollah Araki and pledging support for Ayatollah Mohammad Sadeq Rowhani in Qom or Ayatollah Mohammad Ali Hosaini Sistani in Najaf. Even former Prime Minister Mehdi Bazargan is quoted as saying the public would never accept that the *marja'* should he become "just another government appointment."

And now spokesmen for the regime, in defence of their choice, have turned the question of the next *marja'* into a foreign policy issue as well. The IRNA recently quoted Ayatollah Sane'i referring to "..those who think that with the help of their friends abroad they can take the Qom Circle in hand are grievously mistaken...," thought to be an allusion to Husain Ali Montazeri. "We do not need the BBC to introduce our *marja'* for us; we want a *marja'* like the Imam [Khomaini] who humbled the arrogant with a single *fatwa*."

There are other indications that the Spiritual Leader intends to use the power and authority of his office to turn the independent clerical institution in Iran into a training and service organization for the bureaucratic needs of the Islamic Republic. Although he has treated some members of the traditional hierarchy very delicately, and shown great respect for Grand Ayatollah Golpaygani and his accomplishments, other indicators suggest he may become more aggressive in his efforts to absorb the clerical institution after the latter's passing. In his speech in Qom in 1992 Ali Khamneh'i suggested that the financial system of the *howzeh* needed to be rationalized. He even offered to support the budget required to accomplish this. He and his predecessor have shown little regard for traditional titles of recognition among the Shi'a clergy, demoting some and promoting others without due regard for normative criteria. One of the Leader's supporters recently suggested he be given the title of Imam, as with Ayatollah Khomaini. In one of its mid-summer issues last year the Tehran weekly, *Payam*, published what it claimed were the texts of several *fatwas* of Ali Khamneh'i, describing him with both titles of "Grand Ayatollah" and "Imam." [*Iran Times* (International), 13 August 1993]. Finally, the Special Court of the Clergy has played an important role in controlling and disciplining the men of the cloth from the early years of the revolution and is still used effectively to keep them in line.

If the Islamic regime in Iran decided, sometime in the next few years, to use the absolute authority of its Spiritual Leader [*velayat-e motlaqeh-ye faqih*] to pass a law in the Majlis requiring all citizens of the state to pay their religious dues to him [through a foundation he would establish for this purpose], as the representative of the Hidden Imam [the Mahdi], rather than the *marja'* of their choice, could the clerical institution survive economically as an independent social structure? Would it be able to retain its power to criticize government policy and to intervene strategically in public affairs when it believes the public interest is threatened, as it has done in the past?

Such a move on the part of the state, even a more theocratic one, would doubtless create an uproar and evoke ferocious opposition. It would be resisted strenuously by the more traditional-minded clergy and by many ordinary believers. But the state has its own rationale and monopolizes the levers of coercion. It also has key allies in the traditional clerical ranks, and more and more of its supporters are acquiring positions of influence in the shrine centres and theological seminaries. The power of the purse cannot be overestimated in the relationship between the two institutions. The absorption by the state of a relatively independent social structure like the clerical institution in Iran would be a net loss for all concerned.

APPENDIX G

The following material is reprinted with permission of the Canadian Security Intelligence Service and its author, Dr. William Millward. Inclusion of this material in this book does not imply CSIS authentication of the information in these excerpts nor in this book and does not imply CSIS endorsement of the authors' views. See Appendix E for an explanation of these materials

Authors' Note: Certain time sensitive information in this 1992 article has been edited as it is no longer pertinent, however the bulk of Dr. Millward's comments are still valid regarding Iran today.

COMMENTARY No. 20
a CANADIAN SECURITY INTELLIGENCE
SERVICE publication

RELIGION AND THE DILEMMAS OF POWER IN IRAN

April 1992 Unclassified

[CSIS] Editors Note:

Many countries throughout history have been governed by an élite or priesthood which claims divine authority: Israel after the Exodus; Rome under Caesar; several European countries under the "divine right of kings," to name a few. But whereas most modern countries now live within a relatively comfortable division of church and state, Iran faces a unique dilemma.

In his continuing series on the Middle East, Dr. Millward explores the sources from which the Government of Iran attempts to draw its legitimacy. As he points out, religious authority has increased dramatically over royal authority (the turban over the crown) in Iran since 1978, but the government continues to eye with suspicion the concept of the Iranian populace as a source of legitimate power.

The Islamic Republic of Iran, the symbol of success to which other national or Islamic fundamentalist movements aspire, is nearing the middle of its second decade as the vanguard state of the Islamic movement. Although it came to power through revolutionary upheaval, its example is a source of inspiration for kindred movements in other states with majority Muslim populations, even if the revolutionary model cannot be used to attain power. It is therefore significant that the model state for an Islamic theocracy faces serious problems. The basic issue is the question of leadership and legitimacy. When compounded by severe economic stagnation, this question will assume crisis proportions if the current leadership cannot show rapid improvement by the end of the year.

The legitimacy of the current Iranian régime has been called into question regularly since it took power in 1979, chiefly because it excludes so many Iranians from any participation in government and public affairs. The fact that somewhere in excess of two million Iranians prefer to live in exile than return to live in the Islamic Republic is a *prima facie* compromise on the claims of the régime to represent all Iranians.

Leadership and Legitimacy in Iran

Historically, Iranian tradition recognizes two sources of legitimate authority: religion and royalty, the turban and the crown. In the early stages of the ancient Persian imperial power the two sources coalesced in the institution of sacral kingship. Down through the centuries of Iranian history, pre-Islamic and Islamic, these two poles of authority have continued to act, sometimes together, sometimes separately, as the legitimate sources of political and social control.

By virtue of political and social developments in Iran since the fall of the Safavid dynasty in 1722, the two poles of legitimacy have lived side by side in a largely uneasy, if not overly hostile, relationship, each exercising authority in its own domain. Since the religious institution had its own financial resources—taxes, tithes and land—it could and did function independently of the state.

With the advent of the Islamic revolution in 1978-79, royal authority suffered a substantial degree of de-legitimization. In the process the authority of religion and its custodians has been strengthened and made the primary legitimate bearer of leadership. This principle is enshrined in the new constitution of the Islamic Republic. Some observers believe it is the first authentic example of theocratic government in Iranian history. Others are not so sure.

In modern times, as of old, citizens of Iran were expected to pay their dues to both the spiritual and temporal poles of authority. When one of these poles collapses, as it did in 1979, the question then arises whether the remaining pole can bear the full weight of traditional authority. In relation to Iran's Islamic theocracy, this question is still open. There are serious problems ahead, both theoretical and practical.

A New Source of Legitimacy: The People!

Traditional notions of legitimate authority in Iran have undergone substantial pressures for change since the beginning of the modern era. When the first Iranian constitution (Fundamental Laws) was promulgated in 1906-07, mention was made of the rights of the Persian nation, suggesting that the people of Iran had certain rights before the law and a role to play in the making of new laws. On the basis of a three-fold division of powers, the Iranian populace was acknowledged in law for the first time to have a say in the business of government and the determination of social policies and sanctions. The idea of the people as the source of legitimacy has continued to grow in Iran despite being largely ignored by entrenched élites, both spiritual and temporal.

When Ayatollah Khomeini returned to Iran from 15 years of exile in February 1979, he was greeted by some of the largest crowds ever assembled in the country's history. Many of these same people were among the crowds that had demonstrated their disapproval of the Shah's régime several months earlier. When the Ayatollah issued a decree authorizing Mehdi Bazargan, his newly-appointed Prime Minister of a provisional government, to proceed with a program to establish a constitution and a new framework for elected government, the authority of the popular approval he had received was invoked, along with the Ayatollah's spiritual authority, as a further legitimization of the action prescribed.

In February 1979 very few Iranians knew what an

Islamic Republic was, what shape it would have and how it would operate. Nevertheless, they were urged to participate in a referendum in March 1979 to determine whether they approved of the new system of government to replace the monarchy. The question asked was "Should Iran be an Islamic Republic?" According to official records, 98.2% of the 20,251,000 voters responded in the affirmative. As voter participation was 89%, the result was a clear endorsement. The revolution and Ayatollah Khomeini's concept of an Islamic Republic, insofar as it was understood, was approved and legitimized.

The creation of an Islamic Republic has seemed to many observers, both supporters and opponents, to be an essentially *ad hoc* endeavour, with no detailed blueprints to guide the process. Whenever a structural problem in the new system is encountered, the authorities tinker with the mechanism and improvise a solution. Nevertheless, appeals to popular authority and legitimacy have been constant. At all stages of erecting a new governmental and administrative structure, including the Constituent Assembly to draft a new constitution in June 1979, a referendum to approve the results of its deliberations in December 1979, and in every election since then for the Presidency and the Parliament (*Majlis*), the role of the people as the source of legitimate sanction has been highlighted.

Popular authority has become a virtual shibboleth in the language of all régime politicians and bureaucrats. Everyone claims to be acting in the best interests of the long-suffering, martyr-nurturing, deprived Iranian masses, including those responsible for prolonging their painful involvement in an imposed war with Iraq long after it was reasonable to expect an advantageous settlement.

The deprived masses are still an icon in the political rhetoric of régime supporters, a symbol to be manipulated in the oratory of politicians of all shades and factions. No *Majlis* member, regardless of the current [constituency] he represents, would risk rising to speak on any vital issue without invoking this automatic talisman of his calling at some point in his discourse. In a public session of the *Majlis* on 9 October 1991, the deputy from Nishapur, Muhammad Akbarzadeh, gave a speech in which he presented his own understanding of the role of the masses in the pyramid of authority. "This is because the government of the Islamic Republic is sacred and takes its sanctity from the votes of the Muslim people, who are the real owners of the revolution and the country, from the selected members of their Assembly of Experts, who are chosen by the seminaries, and from the Leader, who is chosen by the Assembly of Experts." [*Resalat*, 10 October 1991, pp. 5, 12, quoted in FBIS-NES-91-226-S, 22 November 1991, p.19]. It is not clear in this formulation which is the primary locus of legitimacy, the people or religious authority, or some combination of the two.

The rights and duties of the Iranian Muslims are spelled out in two sources: the canon law of Islam—the Shari'a—and the Constitution of the Islamic Republic; the former is the bearer of divine will and the repository of sacred sanction in their daily lives; the latter the symbol of popular legitimacy in public affairs. By incorporating the principle of *velayat-e faqih*—the jurisprudent's trust—this constitution is said to have ended the division of secular and religious rule, the former being subsumed by the latter.

Under the new constitution, the government of the

Islamic Republic was given a popular arm through the agency of a 270-member Islamic assembly elected by universal suffrage. The membership of this body has come more and more under the control of the régime; only candidates who meet criteria established by the régime and imposed by the Council of Guardians are allowed to stand for election to it. Having long since excluded all non-religious groups and parties from access to elections for the *Majlis*, the current régime is said to be planning to narrow even further the popular base of legitimacy that this body represents.

The Function of Leadership, Religious and Political

A further contradiction in the enterprise of constructing an Islamic Republic is reflected in the changes made to the requirements for the highest office in the system, the Supreme Guide (*Vali Faqih*), following the death of the founder and first incumbent, Ruhollah Khomeini, in early June 1989. Since the carefully groomed heir-apparent to Khomeini, his long-time confidant and former student, Hossein Ali Montazeri, had been unceremoniously dismissed in March of the same year, and as no other candidates of comparable theological rank and prestige were available, the régime authorities were obliged to lower the constitutional requirements for this office in order to accommodate Ali Khamneh'i, the only ranking régime cleric with broad political experience.

By diluting the standing of this office, the central pillar of the new structure, to this extent, the authorities delivered a self-inflicted but apparently unavoidable blow to the legitimacy and credibility of the whole enterprise. By virtue of his learning and following there was no doubt that Ayatollah Khomeini was one of the half-dozen or so senior figures in the clerical hierarchy in 1970 when he gave his famous lectures on Islamic government in Najaf. By the time he assumed the office of Supreme Guide in 1979 he was the *primus inter pares* of the Grand Ayatollahs in the Shi'ite clerical establishment in Iran in terms of prestige and political stature.

His successor, Ali Khamneh'i, on the other hand, was a mere neophyte in comparison. To disguise his relatively low status in the ranks of clerical learning, he was elevated from Hojatoleslam to Ayatollah by régime supporters. In the same way, he is now sometimes referred to as a Grand Ayatollah, which causes a degree of mirth in traditional clerical circles.

Theocracy, or a Religious Coup D'état?

The basic contradiction of the Islamic Republican system as a viable embodiment of theocracy is the obvious fact that the political and religious institutions are not coterminous or congruent. The one has not been entirely absorbed or subsumed by the other. While the political apparatus of the state continues to dominate and control public life in Tehran and the country at large, the traditional clerical institution and its pillars and supporters carry on with the business of perpetuating the sacred lore of Ja'fari Shi'ism and using it in Qom, Mashad and other centres to provide spiritual and practical guidance to the masses.

The matter of spiritual and temporal leadership in Shi'ite Iran is still evolving. Grand Ayatollah Montazeri represents only a limited threat to the régime because his traditional spiritual credentials and learning are greater than those of the present Leader, Ali Khamneh'i. And yet, ironically, he has long since embraced the theoretical principle of the governance of the jurisprudent (*velayat-e faqih*) as enunciated by his colleague and mentor, Ayatollah Khomeini. So long as he does not repudiate this principle, and offers his allegiance to the present leader as the political head of state, he does not threaten the stability of the régime. But his security is not guaranteed.

The paradox of the present status of the Iranian theocratic experiment is the fact that the majority of the ranking second-tier of Ayatollahs and Marja's in Qom, people like Mohammad Mehdi Shirazi, are nearly all former students of Grand Ayatollah Abol Qasem Khu'i, the acknowledged pre-eminent Shi'i spiritual leader in Najaf, Iraq, and some still subscribe to his negative opinion on the principle of *velayat-e faqih*. In the traditional milieu of Shi'i spirituality, some observers have estimated that as many as 80% of the believing masses acknowledge the spiritual leadership and pre-eminence of Ayatollah Khu'i through his local representative in their area.

As long as there are significant numbers of senior clergymen in the seminaries and teaching centres in Qom and Mashhad who do not subscribe to the concept of the universal or absolute authority of one supreme jurisprudent, who exercises full legal, political and spiritual authority over all the Shi'i believers, it will be impossible to speak of a true theocracy in Iran. The former students of Grand Ayatollah Khu'i, who now have their own followers and teach thousands of their own students, are a guarantee that the religious and political institutions in Iran will never be fully merged. Ayatollah Khamneh'i's political authority and leadership can be, and for the most part is, recognized and accepted without surrendering allegiance to others for guidance on matters of religious law and spiritual ascent. The political edifice is not on the verge of being able to co-opt and subsume the traditional institution of juridical authority and legitimacy in Iran.

A Further Contradiction

In terms of its Islamic legitimacy, one of the Islamic Republic's most costly contradictions is its use of a Special Clerical Court to enforce stifling rigidity and uniformity among even its own devoted followers. The government of the Islamic Republic has recently activated the special clerical court as a tool to intimidate the opposition and any rival clerics who have not lined up squarely behind official policies. Mr. Hashemian, for example, the Deputy Speaker of the Majlis, was allowed to return home after being interrogated, but without a clear announcement of acquittal. Whether some future punishment has been assigned him remains to be seen. A fellow hardliner radical, Hojatoleslam Abolfazl Musavian, the former editor of *Khorasan* newspaper, was not so lucky.

Appointed to the post of editor of *Khorasan* in 1985 Musavian, a 38-year-old cleric, published a rejoinder in the debate over the factional rivalry in régime circles. The article alleged that a moderate faction had claimed to have the support of Ali Khamneh'i, the Spiritual Leader, in its efforts to purge hardliners. In September 1991 he was summoned by the Special Court of Clergy of Tehran, and interrogated in a closed session without the invitation or presence of a jury or the press. These developments pitted the government against one of its own agencies, the Ministry of Islamic Culture and Guidance, which pointed out that they were directly contrary to article 168 of the Constitution, and articles 23-24 of the Press Laws, ratified by the *Majlis*.

On 30 September 1991, the Special Court of Clergy

issued its own communiqué to counter that of the Ministry and advise the Hizbollah nation (the Iranian public) of the basis for its own legitimacy and actions. The court affirmed that it was not restrained by laws governing the judiciary, and its actions were also sanctioned by sacred Islamic religious laws. It promised to deal decisively in the future with violators and deviants at any level, and warned the opposition and the media that lies, slander and distortion were considered crimes according to religions law, which could and would be prosecuted.

The Tehran hardliner newspaper *Salam* led the defence of Musavian and declared that his case was important because it could set a precedent for muzzling the press. But in its issue of 9 November 1991 it carried a special report on the gathering at the mosque of Ferdowsi University two days earlier to say farewell to Hojatoleslam Musavian. His farewell ceremony, before his departure for Qom and three years of internal exile, was attended by hundreds of students, clerics, businessmen and various representatives of the people. It was difficult to disagree in retrospect with the observation made earlier in the ministry's statement that disregard for the constitution and other laws would no doubt occasion social disillusionment and stagnation and militate against the people's professional, social and political security.

The Islamic Republic of Iran today bears scant resemblance to the royal court of James I and Charles I of England in the early 17th Century, but the parallel between the Special Clerical Court and the Star Chamber at the Palace of Westminster is too close to escape notice. The Chamber met in secret, without a jury, wielded arbitrary powers, and dealt severely with opponents of the King who were too powerful for ordinary laws. The message of the Clerical Court was especially chilling in the sense that Musavian was a stalwart upholder of the régime and the principle of the clergy's right to rule. It would be hard to imagine a step the authorities could take which would cause greater unease and insecurity amongst its supporters.

Failure to provide built-in structures for the accommodation of dissenting views and programs, and the insistence of government officials on "unity of thought, word and action" represents a systemic contradiction of the Islamic Republic. Alternative opinions and viewpoints are *ipso facto* sedition. Not even champions of its basic principles are immune from reprisal. In any system based on the authority of God and his law, as interpreted by an all-powerful jurisprudent (Supreme Guide), there is no room left for input from that other source of legitimacy below, the people. And yet it is the source which makes revolutions and overthrows/installs régimes. When the perception finally dawns that the régime which has been calling also on popular approval for its policies cannot guarantee the security of its own staunch supporters, nor deliver practical results which raise the standard of living for the masses, the issue of authority and legitimacy will become moot.

ABOUT THE AUTHORS

KEVIN E. READY

Kevin E. Ready has served as a commissioned officer in both the US Army and Navy. He is a graduate of the University of Maryland with his Juris Doctor from University of Denver. He was an intelligence analyst and Arabic and Russian linguist for military intelligence and was decorated for activities during the 1973 Yom Kippur/Middle East War. He served as an ordnance systems officer onboard a guided missile cruiser off the coast of Iran during the Iranian Hostage crisis and later served as a combat systems officer for a destroyer squadron and as a tactical action officer for a carrier battle group. He also was the command judge advocate for a major military weapons command. Kevin was a major party candidate for US Congress in 1984 and 1994. He is currently a government attorney in California. He is the author of two novels and lives in the Santa Barbara, California area with his wife Olga.

Please visit Kevin's Web site at: http://www.theauthor.com

CAP PARLIER

Cap Parlier is a retired LtCol, USMCR. He is a graduate of the US Naval Academy, Class of 1970. He saw service as a reconnaissance platoon commander in the Western Pacific and Viet Nam theater. After flight school and US Navy Test Pilot School, Cap served as the test pilot project officer for several weapons projects, including the Sidewinder, Zuni and TOW tactical evaluations. Leaving active military duty in 1981, Cap was an experimental test pilot for Hughes and McDonnell Douglas, working on the YAH-64 prototype, Hughes 500MD MMS aircraft, and evaluation of the AIM-9 Sidewinder, Matra Mistral and Stinger missiles for the AH-64 air-to-air capability. He has been an executive with several aerospace companies, and is currently the Chief Operating Officer of Embry-Riddle Aeronautical University in Prescott, Arizona. Cap has written three books and currently lives with his wife, Jeanne, in Prescott.

Please visit Cap's Web site at: http://www.parlier.com